Political Formation

Political Formation

*Being Formed by the Spirit
in Church and World*

Jenny Leith

scm press

© Jenny Leith 2023
Published in 2023 by SCM Press
Editorial office
3rd Floor, Invicta House,
108–114 Golden Lane,
London EC1Y 0TG, UK
www.scmpress.co.uk

SCM Press is an imprint of Hymns Ancient & Modern Ltd
(a registered charity)

Hymns Ancient & Modern® is a registered trademark of
Hymns Ancient & Modern Ltd
13A Hellesdon Park Road, Norwich,
Norfolk NR6 5DR, UK

All rights reserved. No part of this publication may be reproduced,
stored in a retrieval system, or transmitted,
in any form or by any means, electronic, mechanical,
photocopying or otherwise, without the prior permission of
the publisher, SCM Press.

Jenny Leith has asserted her right under the Copyright, Designs and
Patents Act 1988 to be identified as the Author of this Work

British Library Cataloguing in Publication data
A catalogue record for this book is available
from the British Library

ISBN 978-0-334-06303-2

Typeset by Regent Typesetting
Printed and bound in Great Britain by
CPI Group (UK) Ltd

Contents

Acknowledgements	vii
Introduction	1

Part I Locating Christian Formation

1 Ethical Formation in the Church?	17
2 Formation by the Spirit through Doubt and Disruption	44

Part II Ecclesial Formation

3 The Form of Church Polity	73
4 Formation through Conviction of Sin	87
5 Formation through Each Member	115

Part III Formation through Civic Life

6 Radical Democratic Discipleship	141
7 Formation through Civic Participation	161
Conclusion: Forming Common Civic Life	189
Bibliography	222
Index of Names and Subjects	237

Acknowledgements

It is a wonderfully daunting task to have so many people to acknowledge and thank for their contribution to this work.

This book started life as a doctoral thesis, and my first thanks must go to my supervisor Mike Higton, for taking me on as a doctoral student and for the patient, perceptive, encouraging and always humorous way he has accompanied me on this research. I am deeply grateful also to my secondary supervisor Anna Rowlands for her thoughtful reading of my work and her coaching in navigating academic life. I am more thankful than I can say for PhD pals in No. 5 the College and Dun Cow Cottage who made writing a thesis a joyful thing to be shared when things were going well, and something not to be taken too seriously the rest of the time. I would also like to thank my doctoral examiners, Siobhán Garrigan and Frances Clemson, for their close reading and insightful questions and recommendations, which I continue to mull over.

My thinking has been shaped by the wider academic communities where I have shared this research, particularly the universities of Roehampton, King's College London, and Durham, and the annual conferences of the Society for the Study of Theology and the Society for the Study of Christian Ethics. The ecclesial communities and institutions to which I have belonged in Durham and Cambridge – particularly St Giles, St Bene't's, Lyn's House and Westcott House – have also done so much to remind me why theology matters and have kept on gently correcting my tendency to get distracted from the calling to be formed as a Christian by the task of writing about it.

David Shervington and Rachel Geddes at SCM Press have been wonderfully supportive and patient throughout the publishing process, and I am particularly grateful for Elizabeth Hinks' careful copy editing. I would also like to thank the St Matthias Trust, the St Luke's College Foundation and the College of St Hild and St Bede, Durham for their generous financial support.

My family have cheered me on through the process of this research (or, at least, in the case of my nieces and nephew, tried their best to understand what on earth a 'PhD' was and celebrated its completion). My dad has also modelled for me throughout my life what it looks like to undertake academic work with integrity and to engage generously with the work of other scholars. My final thanks go to my husband, Pete, who manages to combine being an all-round delightful human with a wise and insightful theological mind. I cannot express how grateful I am for his kindness and his patient attention to my fumbling attempts to articulate the ideas in this book. Thank you.

Introduction

How do we learn to live well as Christians? And is it the task of the church to teach this way of living to the world? Or does the world have something to teach the church? When I started thinking about these questions, I would have come down firmly on the side of the church teaching the world how to live well. Even when I began to working on the research that has become this book, I intended to write about how the church can form the world for the better. I still think this is something that the church can and does do but, as you will discover, I do not think this is the full picture. I have come to believe that the church also needs to receive from the world in order to become what it is called to be. This shift in thinking came through grappling with two questions that refused to submit to tidy answers.

First, how do we make sense of the ethical purpose of the church in the light of wave after wave of revelations of its moral failings? This is not to say that we live in a moment when the church is especially fallible, but I do think we are perhaps now more aware of the depths of those failings – recently, particularly with respect to white supremacy and sexual abuse. In the face of these revelations of sin, the ecclesial and theological resources offered in response are not always very satisfactory. There is often a tendency to 'round up' the image of the church to still being an *essentially* ethical community, with sin pictured as a kind of add-on – an aberration from the church's usual good enactment of its calling to be hope for the world. In part, I think this 'tidying up' of the ethical status of the church is often driven by a concern to get back to the church's task of shaping the world – perhaps even out of a sense that its ability to do this task successfully will be damaged irreparably if we spend too long talking in public about the ways the church goes wrong.

The second persistent question that shifted my thinking is: what do our day-to-day lives have to do with discipleship? Are we just living out what we receive in the church? Or is there something formative about the contingent situations in which we find ourselves through our work, friendships, family life and so on? Reckoning with this second set of questions grew out of my experience of working in politics, as a parliamentary researcher and then in social policy. During this work I often encountered the rhetoric from Christian advocacy groups that the work of Christians in politics was an act of sacrificial witness to the kingdom of Christ. However, this rhetoric did not really chime with the lived experience of the Christians I knew working in Westminster. Our day-to-day experience was less clear cut and much less dramatic than that evoked by these noble descriptions of sacrifice and witness. The work involves, like any job, many mundane tasks, and many areas where there is no clear 'Christian' course of action, but instead involve a scrappy struggle for integrity amid uncertainty and limited time. It is this kind of ethical tension that dominates, rather than clear moments of choice between a Christian course of action and a course that serves one's own interests. In among this, I became aware, in an inchoate way, that this work was formative. It was not simply a matter of working out in political life an ethical formation that I had already received from the church. Rather, participation in political life was forming me too, in one direction or another.

In response to these questions, this book offers a political theology of Christian formation. It argues that the ethical and political formation of Christians takes place through the work of the Spirit both in the church and in civic life, and that the church too has something to learn from wider political practices and movements. This book is centred, then, on the question of how Christian ethical and political formation takes place: on how Christians are formed by belonging to, and participating in, the polity of the church *and* the wider civic community. I make the claim that Christian ethical and political formation must and *should* take place inside *and* outside the church. Our ecclesial and civic formation cannot be disentangled from one another and, moreover, this is how ethical and political formation *should* happen.

This argument stands in contrast to some of the most visible theological work in this area, which focuses on how formation takes place in the church and flows out into ethical action. Acknowledging the malformation that can take place through the practices of the church tends to come in as an afterthought. In contrast, an account of formation is pursued here that places centre stage a reckoning with the forms of exclusion and marginalization that mar the church, and that can be passed on even in its core practices. This leads me to offer an account of the church as not only ethically formative, but also in constant need of being formed itself. This account of formation also underlines the possibility of being formed as a Christian outside the church: making theological sense of the challenge to the church's life, and to the formation of individual disciples, that can come from wider political practices and movements. This stems from a recognition of the ways of the Spirit, bubbling up in each of our lives in unexpected ways – in both the church and civic life – to lead us deeper into the life of God.

The Church of England is used as an extended case study in which to ground this argument. This situates it in a concrete context, one that has both distinctive problems and resources for thinking theologically about what it is to belong to a political community and to be formed ethically as a Christian through this membership. However, the scope and significance of this work resonates with a wide range of churches and theological traditions.

Contexts and definitions

Contexts

Working in politics

As I have mentioned, this book grew out of my experience of working in politics. This work gave rise to a cluster of questions around how we make sense of our identities as both Christians and political actors and how these can be held together, as well as how these are formed. Working in the Church of England's Mission and Public Affairs Division further developed these questions and broadened my awareness of the continuum of ways in which Church, state and citizenry come into contact and shape one another.[1] These questions also took shape against the political backdrop of discussions of 'British values' and national identity. I found these discussions to be dominated by thin and often zero-sum understandings of civic belonging and led me to seek out richer resources for thinking about what it is to be a citizen. A period spent working for a thinktank led me to explore questions of how one is formed as a citizen, around the locus of counter-extremism policy. This involved thinking about how and where people are formed for public action: how do institutions shape their members? And why are not all members formed in the same ways, when they participate in the same practices? In the light of the church's shifting role in public life, I also had questions about how far its role involved seeking to shape the citizenry to be a particular type of people.[2]

Connected discussions

As my own experience of being brought to think about political formation indicates, the questions that animate this book are ones that are being discussed in the political lives of the church and the nation.

In the field of theological ethics, there is widespread interest in the question of whether, and how, worship is ethically formative. This is a discussion that spans denominations and draws in other disciplines, including psychology and continental philosophy.[3] A broad consensus can be discerned in these discussions: that Christian ethical formation takes place through material practices, which should be understood with reference to the orientation of desire. In particular focus are practices which train the disciple's attention to God. This is grounded in a theological anthropology in which embodiment and relationality are taken to be essential to human, creaturely identity.[4] I engage this scholarship further in Part I.

The question of the ethically formative nature of worship is bound up with questions about how we are to think about the church as a political body. Christian ethical and political formation is often understood as meaning being formed for belonging within the political community of the church. Christian identity is thus understood as a *political* identity, on its own terms. Related to this is a concern with demonstrating that the political nature of the church cannot be contained within the political conceptual categories of other disciplines. Rather, the political character of the church, and of theology, disrupts these categories. I address these themes more closely in Part II.

This interest in ethical and political formation has also aligned with a revival of political and theological interest in civic values and character.[5] Alongside this, there is a large field of scholarship reckoning with the changing position of the Church of England in national political life: asking, what kind of role should the Church play today in seeking to shape citizens and civic life?[6] Past and present archbishops have written on these questions and have sought to articulate what kinds of practices and ways of thinking the Church might be able to offer to national life.[7] I explore this field further in Part III, engaging the ways existing Anglican political theology speaks of the kinds of practices and conversations involved in Christians' civic engagement.

A Church of England approach to formation?

As noted above, the ecclesial context which forms the focus of this project is that of the Church of England. It serves as a central case study in which to ground this exploration in formation – to situate it in particular practices and forms polity and so avoid abstract theorizing about the church. But why choose *this* church as opposed to any other? In part, because it is the denomination to which I belong and am most able to speak about. More substantively, the Church of England, as a historically culturally dominant and constitutionally privileged church, starkly displays many of the characteristic political malformations of minority world Christianity. It has problems that are both distinctive and more widely illuminating of what the church's complicity in systems of oppression can look like. As well as offering a vantage point for recognizing problems, I will also argue that the Church of England's particular social position can offer distinctive resources for thinking constructively about what it is to belong to a national political community and to be formed ethically as a Christian through this membership. This is not, however, an argument solely about the Church of England, and the scope and significance of this work is not limited to this one church.[8]

While I engage with theological work from a wide variety of denominations, it should be said that my central conversation partners – Daniel Hardy, Ben Quash and Rowan Williams – are all white men, ordained in the Anglican churches of the United Kingdom and North America. As such, there is no denying the forms of hegemony of which they are a part. However, these have become my central conversation partners precisely because of the ways their thought can be generative for thinking about ethical and political formation in ways that resist and disrupt the malformations of these hegemonies.[9] This is part of a concern throughout this book with resourcing the cultivation of a self-critical stance in the church. There can be a tendency in Anglican theology towards a certain complacency about the Church of England's cultural position. This is often

INTRODUCTION

bound up with Anglican self-image as essentially bumbling and inoffensive. Yet, this complacency is only possible because of the Church's historical status and influence, which is something that is deeply bound up with the oppression of other ethnic and denominational groups (such as minority dissenting traditions).[10] My recommendation of greater discomfort and self-questioning is, therefore, contingent: it is directed towards a historically dominant church, and to those within it who hold positions of power. In urging greater receptivity towards the contributions of others, I have in mind these power dynamics. This emphasis is not, therefore, intended to present self-questioning and receptivity as stable Christian virtues to be adopted in all situations. It is directed towards those in positions of hegemonic power and privilege, rather than as a tool to demand ever-greater vulnerability from those whose safety is already precarious.

Definitions

Throughout this book I will be talking about both ethical and political formation. So, what is the difference and relationship between these two types of formation? By 'ethical' formation, I mean formation for good action: action both in the church and out in the wider world. By 'political' formation, I mean formation that comes through participation in political relations: relations in which the negotiation of different needs and desires takes place between members of a community. Normatively, political relationships involve recognizing the ways in which the flourishing of each is bound up with the flourishing of all, and so identifying shared goods to be pursued. We can see from these definitions that while these two kinds of formation are distinct, they also significantly overlap one another: ethical formation exceeds (but is inseparable from) the political. In what follows, my focus is initially on ethical formation, with a concern with political formation coming to the fore from Part II onwards.

7

Related to these terms, I talk about formation 'inside' and 'outside' the church. Formation 'inside' the church refers to liturgical practices and 'practical-political' structures and processes (as well as more informal forms of fellowship), through which the visible life of the church is structured and nurtured.[11] These are most fully expressed when church members gather. Of course, members still belong to the church when they are not gathered together, so in speaking of life 'outside' the church I simply mean all the other parts of life which are not directly oriented towards the life of the ecclesial community: for example, working as a teacher in a secular school, or for a trade union. However, as I have already indicated, I am particularly interested in the way formation takes place precisely in the movement between 'inside' and 'outside' the church. So, having set up these broad terms, I will be not be using them as fixed or static locations.

What follows

In exploring Christian ethical and political formation, I begin with the question of how Christian ethical identity is formed. Part I is concerned, therefore, with the location and flow of Christian ethical formation, asking 'where does formation for good action in the world happen for Christians, and how does it happen?'

In Chapter 1 I identify and outline a dominant account of Christian ethical formation, in which formation is understood to happen almost exclusively through participation in the practices of the church (and in certain recognized Christian practices). The chapter begins by unearthing some of the theological and philosophical roots of this way of understanding ethical formation. I then identify some shared tendencies in influential contemporary theological accounts of ethical formation, before moving to consider the role this understanding of formation plays in the life of the church. Obviously, these individuals and institutions are not all operating with an identical

INTRODUCTION

understanding of how ethical formation happens, but there are, nonetheless, identifiable similarities: particularly a tendency to focus on how one is formed ethically through belonging to the church and taking part in its practices. This runs alongside an understanding of the formation offered by the world as antithetical to discipleship. In engaging with the work of Graham Ward and Sam Wells in particular, I identify some limitations with this way of thinking about formation – namely, an overconfidence in the reliability of the ecclesial practices through which ethical formation is understood to take place; and, relatedly, that discipleship is only really accounted for within the church and the Spirit's activity outside the church underemphasized.

In Chapter 2, I set out a fuller account of ethical formation which is better able to reckon with the complexities of participating in the life of the church and in the world. I propose that Christian ethical formation centrally involves cultivating doubt about our desires, and about the ability of any practice to unproblematically form our desires. I also draw out a positive flipside to this, showing that this ongoing unsettling is reflective of the abundant dynamism of God's ways with the world, which continually bring us to new understandings of what it means to live as a Christian. Christian ethical formation therefore requires openness to surprising encounters with the Spirit out in the world. In this way, I end up pushing away from the idea that there is a ready-made, or easily available source of good formation available in the practices of the church. Rather, being formed by the Spirit involves engaging with the world in all its particularity and messiness, expecting to encounter God in new ways and to receive new gifts from unlikely sources – including from the world outside the church.

Part II then asks: if we do not have such a picture of a basically finished church which is capable of providing the formation we need, what do we put in its place? How can we think about the church itself as a body needing to be formed (and to go on being formed), especially at the level of polity? The focus shifts here from the formation of individuals within the body to the ongoing formation of the body itself. In answering these questions, I set out an account of the dynamics and structures that the church needs if it is to be formed in this way. I imagine the church we need, but not in an idealistic way. Instead of looking at the sinfulness and brokenness of the church as an afterthought, or as a topic that comes as a caveat *after* the description of what the church should be, I place it right in the heart of my account.

Chapter 3 sets out some basic parameters of this way of thinking about the calling of the church: the church is (or can be) a *polis* that is also an *oikos* (and vice versa); it is (or can be) marked by humble confidence and confident humility; its life does (or should) take place in gathering and scattering, intensity and extensity. These dynamics give us a picture of a church in which we say that the church is called into being by God, *and* that the church is always learning, and that it is never finished or complete.

Chapter 4 then turns directly to the problem of sin: this confident and humble, gathering and scattering church is, at multiple levels, marked by sin – including in the very ways it works as *oikos* and *polis*. I show that sin is pervasive and deep-rooted, not just in individual believers but in the practices, structures and relationships that constitute the church, including in those elements of its life that are meant to help us identify, confess and turn away from sin. I identify three levels of ecclesial malformation: first, the church's mirroring and compounding of the oppressive systems of the world; second, the church's creation of its own matrices of power; and, third, the church's instigation of wider forms of social oppression. I argue that there is a particular Spirit-led ecclesiology (one which rests on the contribution of each member) that can only emerge when we attend to sin as an ongoing and pervasive presence in the life of the church, not just an occasional blip.

In Chapter 5 I give my fullest description of the polity of the church, precisely as a response to what Chapter 4 has shown. I show that the polity the church needs is precisely a polity capable of going on identifying its own sin and repenting of it.

INTRODUCTION

The church needs to be structured so as to put it in the way of the convicting work of the Spirit, which will mean openness to receiving the distinctive gifts of every member. With this in mind, I consider how the practices of confession, forgiveness and reconciliation can be part of shaping ecclesial polity. The recognition of the body's need to receive the gifts unique to each member also means seeking to foster a polity whose life truly depends on the participation of all members – both in the way liturgy is conducted, and in the way more practical-political matters are managed. An ecclesial polity in which we look to receive from one another the disruptions of grace will also recognize that the movement of the Spirit of Christ is at work in members' 'scattered' lives. This awareness will inform the ways in which the 'sociality' of the church shapes its practices – for example, in intercessions and offerings.

From Parts I and II, we see that the extant resources of the church are not sufficient for ethical and political formation, and that engagement with the world is necessary. So, in Part III, I ask what kind of engagement is that? That is, what position does this put Christians in vis-à-vis the world? And what conversations and exchanges are they engaged in as they are formed?

In Chapter 6, I argue that the possibility of being formed as a Christian through taking part in civic life beyond the church is an important dimension of discipleship, but one that has often been overlooked in recent theological discussions of formation. In response, I draw on the account I have been advancing of extra-ecclesial formation as part of a wider pattern of being formed by the work of the Spirit in the world. Bringing this pneumatology into conversation with radical democratic thought, I outline the practices involved in making ourselves open to encountering the Spirit in civic life, highlighting the need for a posture of attentive openness to receiving the Spirit's gifts from unexpected quarters – including through engagement with strangers. This openness to being surprised also has implications for the ongoing formation of the church.

Chapter 7 continues this exploration, making it more concrete, by looking at engagement with civil society and the state.

POLITICAL FORMATION

I make the argument that Christians are formed (as disciples, as church, as citizens) by their engagement with civil society *and* the democratic state (which has tended to be overlooked in recent theology as an arena for participation), as well as by their ecclesial liturgies and Christian practices: they are formed in the interaction of all these. So, the Christian's ethical and political vocation includes participating in the civic community outside the gathered practices of the church, with the expectation that through this civic participation one will be formed as a Christian. I show that civic life is not only an arena for working out our Christian calling, but is also a site of the Spirit, where we can and should be formed as disciples.

In the concluding chapter, I turn to the question of the difference the picture of formation I have set out could make for the way Christians live in the world – what the world might receive through this formative exchange. Specifically, I explore where all of this leaves us in thinking about how the Church of England could play a part in forming civic identity and belonging in a national polity. I propose that reckoning with the Church of England's failures of political formation can actually offer resources to the formation of common life in the nation.

Notes

1 I will be using 'church' to mean the whole church, and 'Church' when designating the Church of England specifically.

2 I began this research from the starting point that Anglican social and political theology should and does have something to say about the formation of citizens, against the current political and theological backdrop. However, as I began this research, I came to see that behind this lay an unresolved question about how *Christian* ethical and political formation takes place. This has implications for the wider citizenry, for if the practices of the church form its members ethically and politically then these practices therefore also have implications for civic life as a whole. However, the starting point had to be one step back from where I thought I could begin, with the question of how Christian political identity is formed.

INTRODUCTION

3 See, for example, Joanna Collicutt's engagement with this question from a psychological perspective in *The Psychology of Christian Character Formation* (London: SCM Press, 2015) and Joshua Hordern's engagement with philosophical psychology in *Political Affections: Civic Participation and Moral Theology* (Oxford: Oxford University Press, 2013). See also James K. A. Smith's engagement with Maurice Merleau-Ponty's phenomenology of perception in *Imagining the Kingdom: How Worship Works* (Grand Rapids, MI: Baker Academic, 2013).

4 This discussion of Christian identity has as its backdrop concerns over whether the one created as image bearer still bears the divine image, albeit marred, or whether the image has been erased. Understandings of the limits and possibilities of Christian formation derive from where boundary markers are laid in this discussion. Among the set of thinkers engaged in Part I the discussion takes place within a fairly narrow space of consensus that rejects both natural perfectibility *and* the idea that the image of God has been entirely erased by human sin. The question therefore centres on how deeply the image is marred; how far that marring can ever be recognized; and how it can be restored.

5 Including the work of Bernd Wannenwetsch, Charles Mathewes, Eric Gregory and Thomas Bushlack. See also the political theoretical work of Richard Sennett and David Brooks.

6 Including: Sean Oliver-Dee, 'Integration, Assimilation and Fundamental British Values: Invested Citizenship and 21st Century "Belonging"', *Cambridge Papers* 26, no. 3 (September 2017) and Julian Rivers, 'Fundamental British Values and the Virtues of Civic Loyalty', *Ethics in Brief* 21, no. 5 (Summer 2016) (initially drafted for the Church of England's Higher Education Development Group).

7 For example, Rowan Williams, *Faith in the Public Square* (London: Bloomsbury, 2012) and Justin Welby, *Reimagining Britain: Foundations for Hope* (London: Bloomsbury, 2018). These contributions have also coincided with a revival of interest in the loose body of thought that is Anglican social theology, with the publication of Malcolm Brown et al., *Anglican Social Theology: Renewing the Vision Today* (London: Church House Publishing, 2014) and Stephen Spencer, ed., *Theology Reforming Society: Revisiting Anglican Social Theology* (London: SCM Press, 2017).

8 In drawing a circle around one particular church, I do not wish to create the impression that the Church of England can be studied in isolation. The identity of the Church of England does not exist in a vacuum: it only exists in relation to the wider Anglican Communion and other churches in UK. This interrelatedness is a theme that will be discussed particularly in relation to the Church of England's involvement in the British Imperial project and in the relationship with other denominations domestically.

9 In so doing, I have come to see that the categories I work with – particularly that of the 'political' – needed to be expanded to include experiences and activities which have not tended to be accounted for as political. I look forward to going on to spend time thinking more fully about the ways my canons and categories need to be made open to such disruption, and for this to carry through into my choice of conversation partners.

10 Attempting to articulate a non-triumphalist Anglican political theology will, therefore, also involve not mythologizing or romanticizing Anglican pragmatism.

11 Daniel W. Hardy, 'A Magnificent Complexity' in *Essentials of Christian Community*, eds David Ford and Dennis Stamps (Edinburgh: T&T Clark, 1996), pp. 338–9.

PART I

Locating Christian Formation

I

Ethical Formation in the Church?

In exploring Christian ethical and political formation, we begin with the question, 'where does formation for good action in the world happen for Christians, and how does it happen?' By looking at formation in terms of where it is understood to take place, a dominant account of Christian ethical formation is brought into view, in which formation is understood to take place primarily through participation in the life of the church, out of which flows action in the world.

A dominant account and its roots

As noted in the Introduction, I make this exploration in the context of an increasing Anglophone theological concern with Christian formation. In particular, there is a well-established sense that Christian discipleship has ethical and political implications baked into it. This is a wide-ranging discussion, but some shared commitments can be discerned: that Christian ethical formation takes place primarily through participation in the gathered worship of the church – in material liturgical practices – through which one's desires are reshaped by the Holy Spirit. That Christian formation from the church, especially in worship, flows out into ethical action in the world. And, finally, that these ecclesial practices offer a kind of formation for the Christian that is at odds with the formation offered by the world – a counter-formation to the social, cultural, economic and political practices of late modernity.[1]

While we cannot, of course, pinpoint a single moment out of

which this sensibility has grown, movements in Catholic liturgical theology have undoubtedly been influential.[2] Another significant Catholic influence has been that of the philosopher Alasdair MacIntyre, whose work is centrally concerned with the communal practices by which virtuous character can be formed.[3] That ethical formation takes place through worship has become something of a truism in Protestant theology too over the past 30 or so years, which has been deeply marked by a retrieval of Aristotelian virtue ethics. James Gustafson played a significant role here, with his affirmation of the importance of bodily practice for character development informing his exploration of the role of the church in forming persons.[4] The work of Gustafson's student, Stanley Hauerwas, on Christian character has perhaps more than any other contemporary theologian set the agenda for Anglophone theological thought on this theme. Self-confessedly indebted to MacIntyre, Hauerwas understands Christian ethical formation to take place in a localized ecclesial context – in a community that has its own social ethic, shaped by its own stories and traditions.[5]

These influences can be clearly seen in, for example, James K. A. Smith's popular *Cultural Liturgies* series, which seeks to equip readers to exegete the liturgies of their own lives for themselves, through offering an account of humans as 'worshipping creatures' whose character is formed through the 'cultural liturgies' of daily life, as well as through the liturgy of the church.[6] Among other popular iterations, the forms of new monasticism advocated by, for example, Rod Dreher and Shane Claiborne are also centrally animated by seeking Christian formation through the resumption of faithful ecclesial praxis.[7] Within the Church of England, this kind of approach to formation is also evident. It has perhaps had most traction in the context of education – both in the way ministerial training is approached, and in the way education in church schools in envisaged.[8]

So, there is today a dominant picture of Christian ethical formation floating in the air. Yet, in spite of (or perhaps *because* of) the popularity of the term, there is, as Jeremy Worthen

ETHICAL FORMATION IN THE CHURCH?

has noted, a lack of precision over what is meant by Christian formation.[9] This may be in part because, while there is this widespread affirmation of the importance of understanding how formation happens if we are to understand our ecclesial and political surroundings, formation itself is not often approached directly as the primary topic of consideration. We have arrived at this 'soft' account of what is involved in Christian formation through discussions of practices, ecclesiology, citizenship and so forth. Formation-talk has come to be pervasive without it actually having received much theological attention in its own right.

It is therefore necessary to begin my search for an account of how Christian ethical and political formation should take place by unpicking and bringing to light some prevalent foundational understandings of how Christian identity is formed. Through unearthing what is going on in the crowded room of discussion about formation, I argue that, at heart, the dominant account centres on the location and flow of ethical formation: that is to say, where this formation happens, and what follows from it.

I am going to look in more detail at some of the content of this broad approach to understanding Christian ethical formation through spending some time with two sophisticated theological iterations of it – those of Sam Wells and Graham Ward. Fleshing out this dominant account as it finds expression in the thought of Wells and Ward brings into focus both the possibilities and the problems of this approach.[10] In this chapter I spend more time drawing out some of the problems with this approach, and turn in the next chapter to work with the possibilities offered.

Formation as located in the life of the church

We begin with the work of Sam Wells.[11] Wells' insistence on the importance of the church for ethical formation can be seen in his emphasis on the formative relationship between practices, community, tradition and habit. For Wells,

POLITICAL FORMATION

What sustains human life is a pattern of practices – good ways to relate to one another, honed in community and developed by tradition, learned by apprenticeship and embodied in habit. The practices are fundamentally gifts of God. They are the ways his will to companionship is expressed in human life. They not only draw people closer to him but also foster their flourishing.[12]

This account is strongly Hauerwasian, and this shared conceptual framework is also evident in Wells' affirmation that entering into the communal practices of the church also means entering into a story. Hauerwas famously argues that narrative is the form of God's relationship with his people: 'We are "storied people" because the God that sustains us is a "storied God" whom we come to know only by having our character formed in relation to God's character.'[13] This storied relationship unfolds through the particular narratives of the people of God, and through the way Scripture as a whole tells of God's ways with the world.[14] Together these form a story that is enacted, week after week, in the practices of the church (and through which the Christian is incorporated into the story).

It is in this insistence that the formation of character through story requires the existence of a corresponding storied society, that the church's distinctive formative importance comes into focus.[15] For both Wells and Hauerwas, character arises out of narrative yet remains insufficient for understanding Christian identity without community.[16] The church thus emerges as the place where formation of character and narrative meet: 'The community is shaped by the Christian story, and in turn shapes the character of its members by the performance of the story. The story is performed liturgically and through distinctive practices such as peace-making and disciplined forgiving.'[17] So, by this account, the Christian's ethical vocation is not simply to decide moral questions on a different rational basis from that used by the world, but to be formed as part of a different people – to learn to see and enact one's identity as a participant in a different story. Ethical formation is thus understood as the formation of character, by narrative, in community.

We can see Wells' account of Christian formation as taking place through entering into the storied community of the church – of how 'Christians find their character by becoming a character in God's story' – at play in his account of the kind of formation happening in catechesis and baptism.[18] He pinpoints catechesis as one practice through which can be seen the Christian's entry into this story, describing this as 'the process by which the new believer is conformed to Christ in body, mind and spirit and made ready to become a disciple' through discovering 'how the story and practices of the Church enable disciples to worship God, be his friends, and eat with him.'[19] Wells continues:

> The process of catechesis prepares new believers for the event of baptism. Baptism embraces the whole of God's story, from the water of creation to the fire of judgment. It enacts the crossing-over from slavery to freedom, darkness to light, death to life, despair to hope.[20]

Entering into this liberating story marks a strong point of disjuncture between the old and new self: baptism is, for Wells, where a person's 'true identity' is 'discovered', and where the old identity, which was destined for death, is stripped away.[21]

This transformation into conformity with Christ continues through practices of 'study, fasting, reflection, direction, imitation of the saints'.[22] The disciple's integration into the body then continues through beginning to participate in what Wells names as the 'politics' of the church:

> The members of the body deliberate over the goods of their life and the gifts God has given them; through casuistry they establish the practicalities of witness in the particularities of service; through mission they seek to extend the goods of their fellowship into partnerships in all corners of the world, especially the most benighted ones, longing for the kingdom,

looking for the work of the Spirit, and expecting to meet Christ in friend and stranger; through prayer they adore the God they have seen and heard, and implore him to reveal and rescue where witness and service fall short.[23]

All of this happens through *first* entering into the storied community of the church. The Christian receives here an identity that is opposed to the life they lived before – running counter to the old, distorted identity formed by the world. Participation in the gathered practices of the storied community of character that is the church forms, for Wells, people capable of deliberation, witness, fellowship, prayer and so forth. That is, it forms people capable of good action in both the church and the world.

This emphasis on the central formative role of the church's practices is also an important feature of Graham Ward's thought. While Ward perhaps places a greater emphasis than Wells on the counter-formative, or reparative, role of ecclesial practices (as we shall see below), Ward likewise sees the embodied practices of the church as the site for this (re)formation. For Ward, the pre-eminent embodied practice of the church is the Eucharist, and it is around this practice that Ward's account of the formation of Christian desire centres. Christians experience 'the formation of that Christ-likeness which is ours truly insofar as we occupy this place *en Christoi*', and so have their desires reoriented 'to that which exceeds what we think we know about ourselves and the world we live in'.[24] Desires and relationships are thus reconfigured *within* the ecclesial community, in which 'Becoming one flesh is the mark of participation itself.'[25] In eucharistic terms, this communal overflow is, for Ward, the outward-reaching 'logic of the fracture': 'both celebrating the intimacy of oneness and taking that celebration out into the world: "we *break* this bread to *share*"'. So, 'In the breaking, the fracturing, the extension beyond a concern with one's own wholeness, is a sharing that will constitute our own true wholeness.'[26] The Christian desire that is formed through participation in the embodied practice of the Eucharist is, therefore, inherently communally structured.[27] As Ward argues, 'our loving as it participates within God's loving is always reaching beyond and forgetting itself, but, in that very activity, loving itself most truly'.[28] While the Eucharist is practised in the gathered worship of the church, its ethical effects flow outwards, and this sharing will constitute wholeness of Christian identity. The formation of Christian desire therefore leads to the formation of communities of desire (which in turn continue to reorient the desire of their members).

If the Eucharist is where the 'analogical world view' is received (through which we see how the things around us participate in, and receive their meaning from, Christ), then prayer, for Ward, is where this attention both to God and to the world is deepened and refined. In prayer, he argues, we open ourselves 'to the infinity of what is God', with prayer expressing the way that following Christ requires us to 'wait to receive' an understanding of what it is to be a Christian.[29] We are also opened up to the world in prayer: it leads the Christian into a 'deep inhabitation of the world, its flesh and its spirit' as we pay attention to 'The world's events', and they 'pass through us and change us'. At the same time, in prayer we listen to our own yearning for communion with Christ, and, through this desire, we also listen, at least in part, to 'the yearning in the heart of Christ to heal and transform'.[30] Beyond teaching us *how* to attend, prayer also teaches *what we should expect to see*. This is so because, for Ward, prayer's concern is always with ushering in the kingdom of God – seeking to participate in and glimpse the 'eschatological remainder'.[31] So, discipleship for Ward involves attending to the new things that will come into being.

Formed by the church for the world

In both Wells and Ward, then, there is a central emphasis on the formative role of ecclesial life. Of course, for both, we are not formed simply for the sake of the life of this community, but for the sake of ethical action, for the sake of life in the world. As Ward suggests, we are formed in the church, ultimately, in order to transform the world: to bring it into alignment with the community of *caritas* that is pointed to, and made present, through the practices of church.[32] We can also see this logic at work in Wells' emphasis on the formative nature of life in the church as not only storied but also dramatic: a story that is performed.

Wells argues that a dramatic understanding of the community of faith, and so too of formation within this community, is necessary because ethical action involves the narrative text *and* 'its interpretation and systematic construal'. That is, ethical action involves the way it is embodied in, through being performed by, a particular community. Wells describes this dramatic performance of the narrative as 'a dynamic, spiralling process of constant repetition, transfer, and restoration of meaning, of things never being the same again and other things being rediscovered, ever new'.[33] Within the sphere of the dramatic, Wells particularly commends the discipline of improvisation – understood as an imaginative practice that is oriented towards encountering new situations – as best able to capture what is going in Christian ethical action in the world. Wells proposes that Christian ethical formation takes place both *for* and *through* improvisation.[34]

As I will explore in more detail below, we can begin to see in Wells' account of the role of improvisation in ethical formation some resources that take us beyond the dominant picture of formation that I have been outlining thus far. In improvisation, Wells suggests, we have to adopt the posture of being in receipt of gifts, in which 'the Church finds itself more often in the role of receiver [of offers of grace] than of giver'.[35] Rather than simply seeing ethical identity as flowing *from* formation in the church *out into* action in the world, there is the possibility here of a flow in the other direction. Importantly, however, for Wells, being able to improvise involves having one's imagination formed to take the right things for granted – to find them obvious.[36] He is thus concerned with forming habits, as it is through these that Christians learn to take the right things for granted.[37] This depends on being part of a community 'that trusts the practices it has inherited and allows them to shape its unconscious'.[38] So, Wells sees improvisation as depending on a learned deep trust between the members of the church, and in the practices they have received.[39] As he puts it, 'Being obvious means trusting that the practices of discipleship, shaped by the Holy Spirit, are enough' to be equipped for whatever is brought one's way.[40] Consequently, Wells suggests that the formation of Christians that takes place *through* improvisation involves first being formed through re-enacting the story of God in history in the church, and then re-narrating this story that they have received in the context of their lives outside the church: 'The story is told in order that it may be performed when the participants depart in peace.'[41]

Christian formation as counter-formation

Implicit in this notion that we are formed in the church in order to live well in the world is the idea that formation in the church is oriented towards the transformation of and resistance to the ways in which we are formed outside the church. We can see this at play in Wells' suggestion that formation in the church is rooted in learning to be the 'kind of people' who desire and 'can receive' the abundance of God's gifts, gifts that 'derive from carrying out [the] practices [of the church]'.[42] For Wells, this formation stands in opposition to adherence to a false narrative which leads one to fail to recognize the abundant gifts offered by God, and instead causes one to live according to a logic of scarcity. It is from this sense of scarcity, Wells argues, that violence flows: it is the enacted denial of the abundant peace which is the true grain of the universe.[43]

This notion of ecclesial practices as a site of counter-formation can be clearly seen in the work of Ward. Ward conceives of Christian identity as erotic, in the sense that he understands *eros* (parsed as desire) to lie at the heart of human identity.[44] Following from this, Christian ethical formation is principally understood in terms of how desire is ordered or disordered. Desire is oriented by the fundamental grain of creation and, in a similar vein to Wells, the plenitudinous life and grace of God is understood as that which sets the grain for creaturely life.[45] Being caught up in participation in this outward-flowing, self-transcendent divine life means that creaturely being and relationships can and should also display these characteristics of divine desire.[46] Life in this economy of peace and plenitude forms the basic material of Christian ethical identity, and desire that is ordered in line with this foundational metaphysical reality is properly ordered desire.

With this understanding of human identity as it was created to be in mind, Ward attends to the understandings of what it is to be human that are implicit in the modern city. His attention to urban life (which functions in certain ways in Ward's thought as a stand-in for late capitalism) is focused on the modern city's ailments, and the way these reveal underlying commitments about the purpose of human life and society. These ailments are so because of the ways they distort urban dwellers' desires and include: consumption; geographic segregation; atomism and disembodiment; dematerialization and depoliticization; globalization; and secularization.[47]

These social, political and economic trends shaping the modern city are identified as damaging by Ward because of the ways they are, in turn, systematically shaping urban dwellers' desires. As Al Barrett summarizes Ward's diagnosis: 'in the city "certain forms of desire" are both "promoted and patrolled"', with cities '"reorganised as sites for consumption" and "entertainment"' such that 'desire "dismembers" the social, "atomising" us into "monadic consumers"; and the costs of consumption – human, social, environmental – are not just concealed, rather, our "desire to be ignorant" of them is actively cultivated, as "secular desire ... preys on others for its own satisfaction"'.[48]

The chief lever in promoting this socially and ecologically alienating consumption is capitalism, and it is here that we see most clearly what distorted desire looks like for Ward.

He argues that money has become both the instrument and object of modern desire. So, the subject of a capitalist system becomes enveloped in a self-perpetuating economy, with the inner logic of wealth ultimately oriented to self-worship. In this way, the postmodern capitalist city facilitates desire that seeks the 'prolongation of desiring itself', rather than actually seeking consummation.[49] Desire in the postmodern city can ultimately '*never* be satisfied': it 'can never come to an end – or the market would cease'. Rather, 'Desire here operates because we always sense, or are made to sense privation; and we are always attempting to fill that lack or find compensations for unfulfillment.'[50]

This is the way, then, that desire works in Ward's modern city, and it expresses, for Ward, modernity's understanding of the essentially competitive and individually oriented nature of social relationships.[51] Understanding violence and not peace as the grain of the universe, in this way, malforms creatures and their relationships with one another. As members of the postmodern city, Christians are not immune from having their desires distorted in these ways. Against this distorted desire, which is constituted by continually unfulfilled lack (despite reifying 'the object of desire *as object*, as graspable'), Ward is concerned with how Christian desire should be realigned with the fundamental metaphysics of plenitude and harmony.[52] Ward distinguishes this kind of desire from the grasping, consumptive desire formed in the postmodern city, arguing that in the Christian economy 'the object desired is to be enjoyed as gifted; rather than simply used, exploited, consumed.'[53] Christian desire 'is a desire not to consume the other, but to let the other be in the perfection they are called to grow into'.[54]

As we have seen, Ward believes that the site where this re-formation of Christian desire takes place is the church (and, as desire drives formation for Ward, this is also where the Christian life as a whole is reoriented). The church is an 'alternative erotic community' to the postmodern city.[55] As desire is connected to embodiment, to be reformative of desire the ecclesial community must have embodied practices: 'Christian thinking' and principles are insufficient, but rather 'Word and sacrament are means of grace for the alternative formation that is the necessary condition for this community of love to take shape as a colony of the 'heavenly commonwealth; whose Lord is not Caesar but Christ'.[56] Here, as for Wells, the church is identified as an alternative community which is able to supply and correct what is lacking and disordered in the postmodern city.[57] For both Ward and Wells who and what we attend to is central to our formation and, for both, it is primarily the practices of the church that form the Christian's ability to properly attend, reordering their desires and reconfiguring the imagination towards hope.

Some problems with ecclesially-based formation

By looking in more detail at the ways Ward and Wells understand Christian ethical formation to take place, we have put some flesh on the bones of the dominant account of formation identified at the beginning of the chapter. Both Ward and Wells share a concern with the way Christian formation is received through, and inseparable from, ecclesial praxis. For both, the emphasis falls on the ways that being formed ethically as a Christian challenges, opposes and overthrows existing material which has been received from the world around. Both understand late modern society to form its members in a way that is (largely) in opposition to formation by the Spirit in the church. In both, then, there is a sense that ethical discipleship requires a repudiation of the practices by which people's desires are formed outside the church, in the world. The church, by this account, returns the Christian to the eternal way of life for which they were made, aligning the disciple's distorted desires once again with the grain of the universe such that they become capable of ethical action. The flow of social and political transformation that follows comes *from* the church *to* the world.

There is much to commend this approach to thinking about formation. However, there are also some problems which undermine the promise of this account, such that it is not quite adequate for making sense of the complexity of Christian formation – and can, in fact, unhelpfully limit that formation.

Overconfidence in the formative reliability of ecclesial practices

The first problem to reckon with is a misplaced confidence in the reliability of the ecclesial practices through which ethical formation is understood to take place. In identifying this danger, I do not want to suggest that either Ward or Wells deny the ongoing presence of sin in the life of the church. Wells acknowledges that the practices of the church will not mean that sin is no longer part of the life of the disciple; while the church is called to be a community of peace, the church has always confronted – 'or has been forced to confront' – 'the fact that its own practice has sometimes been worse than – or indistinguishable from – that of those forces in society that have taken God's freedom not yet to believe'.[58] Even in the church – the community gathered around the true story – there is no escape from the fallen human propensity to fall for false stories. The church, Wells suggests, is 'mired in sin, complicit in evil, shamed by its silence on injustice, and exposed as a clumsy, flawed, all-too-human failure to embody the gracious Gospel of Christ: in short, an earthen vessel'.[59]

Indeed, Wells argues that recognition and repentance of sin are also part of the pattern of discipleship, and this is reflected in the way these practices are woven into the liturgical rhythms of the church. Confession takes place in a corporate setting, for Wells, so that no one can deceive themselves that they are not implicated in sin. For, self-deception 'is the narrative form sin takes in the mind of the disciple': 'the weaving together of plausible and groundless reasoning and pleading to tell a false story'. So, in confession, the congregation are 'confronted with the falseness of the stories they each tell themselves'.[60] Indeed, Wells argues that 'members [of the church] must positively seek to discover the ways in which they have wronged one another, never being surprised that misunderstanding and hurt occur, but seeing each instance as a prelude to reconciliation, grace, and deeper relationship.' Wells further argues in this vein that making confession together involves explicitly asking 'have I wronged you in any way?' and expecting the answer to be 'yes'.[61] There is an expectation here that sin will persist in the church and will require ongoing recognition, despite it being the primary context for forming Christian character.

In a similar way, Ward acknowledges that the church is not a perfect body, noting that when the church speaks it must be with an awareness that 'its own voice is never pure, never innocent'.[62] Indeed, Ward is concerned with the need to learn to see how the church's own imagination and desires have become distorted. He is particularly troubled by the phenomenon of Christians becoming depoliticized – of failing to understand discipleship to be inherently political. Ward traces Christian depoliticization through secularizing Enlightenment responses to wars of religion, and credits it with playing a role in the rise of capitalism.[63] Western Christians, Ward argues, need to wake up and realize the idolatrous danger of continuing down this path of separating religion and politics.

However, this acknowledgement of the church's flaws does not fundamentally alter the positive account offered of the formative practices of the church. So, after acknowledging the church's inevitable complicity in sin, Ward continues to cast the church's role as 'announcing to the postmodern city its own vision of universal justice, peace and beauty, and … criticis[ing] the structural injustices, violences and uglinesses which resist and hinder the reception of that vision'.[64] The specific injustices discussed in detail end up being 'out there' in the world. There is not much of a sense that the church's complicity in injustice might deeply shape, and in fact compromise, its ability to perceive structural injustice (and so too compromise its ability to form those capable of perceiving and contending with injustice).

There is an expectation here that sin can ultimately be identified through the established practices of the church. While there is an expectation that ecclesial life will involve the ongoing discovery of how we are sinning against one another, it is established ecclesial practices that will reveal this sinfulness. The problem with this account of sin is that it suggests that sin is capable of being remedied by the established practices of the church. There is, in other words, no suggestion that we should expect to be brought to new discoveries of how the sacramental and storied practices of the church are, themselves, shaped by sin. There is a line drawn here between the gifts that have been given by God for our formation and those who receive them. Where there is a problem, it is with Christians' failure to properly receive these gifts – the giftedness of the 'pristine' practices is not seriously in question.[65] As a growing crowd of scholars have highlighted (and as I will explore in more detail in Chapter 4), this fails to account for the ways that ecclesial practices can become flawed such that they not only malform participants' ability to act ethically but also become a source of wider social damage.

Where malformation in the church is acknowledged, then, there is a sense that this has arisen because of a departure from the practices of true Christian tradition. In other words, the implication is that we are reliably able to recognize where practices go wrong and that this recognition (and the repair of damaged practices) is possible on the basis of practices that we already have. Where practices do go wrong, what is needed, according to Ward and Wells, is a retrieval of the true and reliable practices of formation. By this argument, the church already knows what is necessary for good formation, even if this is sometimes forgotten or badly executed. Where Christians' desires are distorted, this is the result of having been captured by problematic cultural and socio-economic trends in their life outside the church. The possibility of this distortion having been passed on through – or even generated by – the faithful enactment of the church's practices is not seriously entertained. Rather, what is pictured is 'a seamless flow of offering and receiving love and mercy in the Church', and in this flow, 'worship makes disciples faithful, and ... faithful disciples renew worship'.[66]

The world as site of ethical malformation

Alongside these tendencies runs a minimal account of the potential for formation for good action as a Christian outside the practices of the church. Here we see the other side of the disjuncture between formation in the church and in the world: not only is the church almost exclusively the site of good formation, but the world is the site of distortion and malformation.

While Ward is clear that the material practices of the church – 'in all its concrete locatedness *and* eschatological significance' – is the context of this formation, this is not set in wholesale opposition to the formation offered by the world.[67] Ward's eschatological ecclesiology carries within it an understanding of the relationship between church and the world that moves beyond a construal of the two as opposed realms of activity. Rather, the church is the 'public and material manifestation of that which transcends the world'.[68] As such, it is implicated in both reflection and critique, being *within* the world while also seeking to address the world through actions and speech from a point *beyond* it. By this construal, the church 'names an unfinished project' and the world 'names a certain conception of global living constituted from a specific standpoint'.[69] In keeping with this, while he identifies the church as the body of Christian action, Ward locates Christian action within the Spirit's divine action in the world, not just within ecclesial practices.[70] Ward also finds resources for shaping the Christian's imagination in 'secular' art and literature, as part of his proposed 'engaged systematics' – an approach to theology that starts with 'the human condition as we understand and recognize it through and in our social engagements'.[71] In like manner, he argues that our understanding of the nature of ethical life 'can be deepened by molecular biology, epigenetics, and an investigation into sensing itself'.[72] This is in keeping with his underlining, at points, of the way in which self-centred and divine desires are 'commingled' in the concrete ecclesial body, which ought therefore to be 'humble' in its judgements and 'open-ended' in its narrative.

However, this is not fully carried through, and at other points Ward comes close to identifying the concrete church with the 'heavenly city', and thus putting 'church' and 'world' into stark opposition'.[73] So, while Ward insists on the need for theology to respond 'positively and also critically to the postmodern city', the emphasis ends up falling on the negative. Ward's engaged systematics also ends up primarily in service of diagnosing the distortions of desire – rather than in identifying gifts the Christian tradition needs to receive.[74] After all, it seems that attention to the world is ultimately in order that Christians 'will be better equipped to recognize the nature of discipleship demanded of them and to see what it is they have to contest'.[75] This all combines to throw into doubt the extent to which the church, for Ward, should truly be open to receiving the challenges and gifts brought by other bodies – and the extent, therefore, to which these bodies can be sources of Christian ethical formation.

This ambivalence about the world having any formative goodness to offer can also be seen in Wells' work. At the heart of Wells' account of formation through improvisation is an emphasis on the importance of what he calls 'overacceptance'. This names an attitude of consistently treating the actions of others as 'offers' to be 'accepted' (rather than 'blocked'). For Wells, saying 'yes' to the offers of grace encountered through deep engagement with the world leads to adventures, whereas saying 'no' (which can take the form of either passive or active blocking of offers) leads to security but also stagnation.[76] As we have seen, Wells suggests that 'the Church finds itself more often in the role of receiver [of offers of grace] than of giver'.[77] Indeed, this involves becoming aware of 'those who are not gathering together', and those gifts the *ekklesia* are not receiving.[78] This posture of openness to the gifts that might be received is rooted in attention to the world: 'If disciples are to listen to God they must learn to be attentive in other relationships too', and so 'life becomes a ministry of listening (and watching) for revelation' amid the unexpected events of life.[79]

The suggestion here is that we learn to attend to God through also attending to other people, as well as learning to pay attention to one another as a result of the way we seek to pay attention to God. This sense of how attention plays out in encounters outside the established practices of the church is most strongly drawn out in Wells' account of being formed *through* improvisation, in which attention is understood as 'relaxed awareness' (or *disponibilité*).[80] In this state of awareness, he argues, 'the actor senses no need to impose on the outside world or on the imagination; there is openness to both giving and receiving' gifts in every new ethical situation.[81] The gifts received come 'direct from God', 'from the fellowship of faith', and 'from strangers' – and there is no hierarchy between these, for all are essential to the life of the church.[82] It is on the basis of this expectation of receiving gifts outside the church that Wells argues for each new celebration of the Eucharist beginning 'with a sense of what has been discovered, where God has been met in the time since the last gathering'.[83] Being brought into God's story reconfigures the Christian's imagination and the church comes to see that 'We are not the answer to the prayers of "the despised and rejected of the world", but that they are the answer to ours.'[84] So, the life of the church involves learning to recognize and receive gifts from beyond its doors, discovering 'the abundant grace of God in unexpected ways' and so learning to better attend to the ways God is at work.[85]

However, while Wells' account of improvisation contains an affirmation that gifts from God can be found in life out in the world, and that these encounters are an indispensable part of Christian ethical formation, there is a clear expectation that what is encountered – however puzzling, awkward, or surprising – can be slotted into the story that is already known. So, while there is space here for surprise, there is nonetheless still an expectation that the surprise will not shake the framing narrative. If the Christian community should choose to actively 'receive' offers 'in the light of a larger story' which 'stretches from creation to eschaton',[86] then improvisation is ultimately ordered towards re-narrating the particular 'offer' received in terms of the larger story one already knows. This continuing story structures discernment: what is fitting within this story, which is already known, can be accepted and 'reincorporated'.[87] This manner of finding a way of (re-)telling the particular story one is offered to make it part of this larger story is described by Wells as 'a way of accepting without losing the initiative'.[88] So, it seems to be that improvisation out in the world is to take place only because of the storied practices found in the church. There is, in other words, an overarching confidence that one already knows the shape of the story of God and God's people, if not all the particulars of events.[89]

This ambivalence in Wells' account about the possibility of the world having any formative goodness to offer can also be seen in his discussion of catechesis. Wells describes the child catechumen as 'a mass of unformed urges and skills and ideas and desires', which need to be shaped into 'membership of the body of Christ'. The adult catechumen, meanwhile, is described as having 'already made commitments and developed dispositions and formed habits and fostered relationships that reflect the partial and fallen nature of a life spent, like Jacob, wrestling for identity with the angel of God'. This means, Wells argues, that for the adult 'the role of catechesis is to lead the catechumen to repentance, to recognising the lies and deceit wrapped up in a story that seeks to airbrush God out'.[90] The implication is that it is in the church that encounter with the Holy Spirit begins and positive ethical formation follows. Wells does see the 'honest scrutiny' brought to bear upon ecclesial practices by the catechumen as a gift to the church.[91] However, it is a gift in the sense of prompting *rediscovery* of things the church knew but has forgotten. Such a rediscovery of what was already known is not the same as coming to see something new. There is not an expectation that those who are not yet members of the church may reveal, and fulfil, a lack of which we were not even previously aware – and that this could be part of the way God's gifts are disclosed.

While both Ward and Wells offer us resources for thinking about how the world outside the church may be positively formative and have gifts that the church needs to receive, it seems that, ultimately, both see our ability to discover God's abundance in unexpected ways *outside* the church to depend on having been formed in the right way *in* the church. As Wells argues, '[Christian and liturgical] practices are gifts to the Church not only in themselves, but also in that the Church, in seeking to be the kind of community that can perform these practices well, discovers the abundant grace of God in unexpected ways.'[92] So, regular participation in corporate ecclesial practices and private practices of prayer mean that Christians trust their instincts, having had their imaginations formed in the habits of the Christian story and therefore being able to take the right things for granted.[93] In Ward's account of prayer as the place where the Christian learns to pay attention to the work of God in the world we see a similar emphasis. From this we see that it is the practices of the church that enable one to recognize what is out in the world that is, or has the potential to be, a gift – and these practices are not themselves open to being reshaped by that which is encountered outside the church.[94]

Conclusion

We have now filled out the dominant account of ethical formation through participation in the church through looking at the contours of the account in the thought of Ward and Wells.

Through this engagement we have seen how this kind of trust in the formative practices of the Church means that possibility – or even the inevitability – of malformation through participation in ecclesial life receives little sustained attention and the formative potential of the practices of the church is never seriously doubted – if they are undertaken seriously and consistently enough. Seeing already extant practices as the solution means that the problem of ethical malformation (whether in the world or in the church) ends up being misdiagnosed: it must be the kind of disordering capable of being identified and rectified by these practices that we already have and know how to enact. We can fairly say that the need for the church to be subject to ongoing correction has also tended to be downplayed in accounts of Christian formation, and is a dynamic in need of greater theological attention.

A further consequence is the suggestion that God is to be encountered only, or mainly, within established ecclesial and Christian practices. This includes a tendency to speak of Christians being formed as Christians almost exclusively in the church, from which Christians then undertake wider ethical action. So, there is very little suggestion that the church's ethical and political vision should itself be formed through engagement with the world – or, more fundamentally, that the church and its members might need to receive from the world in order to become what they are called to be. Altogether, this limits how we understand God's ways with the world and so, too, where and how we expect to encounter God.

We are in search, then, of a way of thinking about ethical formation that does not 'round up' the practices of the church to being basically good – with sin as an add-on to this picture – and in which the receiving from the world is intrinsic to the process of being formed for good action.

Notes

1 A related but distinct trend has been a growing consensus that Christian formation includes being formed to belong to the political community of the church, and so being a Christian is an inherently political identity. We will return to this second trend in Chapter 6.

2 A central locus of these discussions has been the relationship between justice and the liturgy. See, for example, Gerard Moore, 'Let Justice Find a Voice: Reflections on the Relationship between Worship and Justice', *Worship* 90 (May 2016): 206–24. See also Christian

Scharen, *Public Worship and Public Work: Character and Commitment in Local Congregational Life*, Virgil Michel Series (Collegeville, MN: Liturgical Press, 2004), pp. 20–6. For an Anglican perspective on this relationship, see Mark Earey, Ruth Meyers and Carol Doran, eds, *Worship-Shaped Life: Liturgical Formation and the People of God* (Harrisburg, PA: Morehouse Publishing, 2010).

3 MacIntyre summarizes this formative process thus: 'The flourishing of the virtues requires and in turn sustains a certain kind of community, necessarily a small-scale community, within which the goods of various practices are ordered.' Thomas D. D'Andrea, *Tradition, Rationality, and Virtue: The Thought of Alasdair MacIntyre* (Abingdon, Oxon: Routledge, 2006), quoting the preface to the Polish edition of MacIntyre's *After Virtue*.

4 Christian Scharen has charted the retrieval of Thomistic understandings of learning through bodily practice that took place through the Protestant recovery of Aristotelian virtue ethics. This retrieval of Aristotle and Thomas bore MacIntyre's influence, but has also been resourced through other streams of thought – including that of H. R. Niebuhr. Scharen, *Public Worship and Public Work*, pp. 26–7. For more on Anglophone Protestant theologians' adoption of the category of 'practice', see Lauren Winner, *The Dangers of Christian Practice: On Wayward Gifts, Characteristic Damage, and Sin* (New Haven, CT: Yale University Press, 2018), pp. 168–80.

5 See, for example, Stanley Hauerwas, 'The Virtues of Alasdair MacIntyre', *First Things* (October 2007).

6 James K. A. Smith, *Desiring the Kingdom: Worship, Worldview, and Cultural Formation* (Grand Rapids, MI: Baker Academic, 2009) and *Imagining the Kingdom* (Grand Rapids, MI: Baker Academic, 2013).

7 Rod Dreher, *The Benedict Option: A Strategy for Christians in a Post-Christian Nation* (Waco, TX: Sentinel, 2017), and Shane Claiborne, Jonathan Wilson-Hartgrove and Enuma Okoro, eds, *Common Prayer: A Liturgy for Ordinary Radicals* (Grand Rapids, MI: Zondervan, 2010).

8 On formation in the context of ministerial training, see for example: Sue Groom, 'The Language of Formation in Official Church of England Documents', *Anglican Theological Review* 99, no. 2 (2017): 233–54; Jeff Astley, Leslie J. Francis and Colin Crowder, *Theological Perspectives on Christian Formation: A Reader on Theology and Christian Education* (Leominster; Grand Rapids, MI: Eerdmans, 1996); Jeremy Worthen, *Responding to God's Call: Christian Formation Today* (Norfolk: Canterbury Press, 2012). This concern also informs ongoing debates over residential versus context-based training – for

ETHICAL FORMATION IN THE CHURCH?

instance, arguments for the continued importance of residential training emphasize the formative nature of community living and of daily rhythms of corporate worship. See also 'Church of England Vision for Education: Deeply Christian, Serving the Common Good' (Autumn 2016), *Church of England*, https://www.churchofengland.org/sites/default/files/2017-10/2016%20Church%20of%20England%20 Vision%20for%20Education%20WEB%20FINAL.pdf, accessed 04.08.2022. This approach to formation also crops up in other Anglican spheres – for example, in the pastoral letter from the House of Bishops written ahead of the 2015 general election: 'Who is My Neighbour? A Letter from the House of Bishops to the People and Parishes of the Church of England for the General Election 2015' (2015), https://www.churchofengland.org/sites/default/files/2017-11/whoismyneighbour-pages.pdf, accessed 04.08.2022.

9 Worthen, *Responding to God's Call: Christian Formation Today*, pp. xi–xiv.

10 The thought of Wells and Ward cannot, of course, be reduced to the features of this account, and in the next chapter I will pick up threads in their thought that offer possibilities for extending and going beyond this dominant account.

11 It is worth noting that while much of Wells' work is framed by a concern with recasting understandings of the discipline of ethics, my interest is focused around his account of the formation of Christian ethical identity.

12 Samuel Wells, *God's Companions: Reimagining Christian Ethics* (Oxford: Blackwell Publishing, 2006), p. 2.

13 Stanley Hauerwas, *A Community of Character: Toward a Constructive Christian Social Ethic* (Notre Dame, IN: University of Notre Dame Press, 1981), p. 91.

14 Hauerwas, *A Community of Character*, p. 95.

15 Hauerwas, *A Community of Character*, p. 91.

16 Samuel Wells, *Transforming Fate into Destiny: The Theological Ethics of Stanley Hauerwas* (Carlisle: Paternoster Press, 1998), p. 41.

17 Wells, *God's Companions*, p. 68.

18 Samuel Wells, *Improvisation: the Drama of Christian Ethics* (Grand Rapids, MI: Baker Academic, 2018), p. 57.

19 Stanley Hauerwas and Samuel Wells, eds, *The Blackwell Companion to Christian Ethics* (Malden, MA: Blackwell Publishing, 2004), p. 18.

20 Hauerwas and Wells, *Christian Ethics*, p. 18.

21 Wells, *God's Companions*, p. 67. This is also reflected in Wells' description of catechesis as 'the process by which the Church invites the Holy Spirit to form the character of its catechumens and to prepare

them for baptism'. The implication is that this is where the catechumen's formative encounter with the Holy Spirit begins: in a practice of discipleship within the church (p. 64).

22 Such that the 'the disciple becomes part of Christ's body'. Wells, *God's Companions*, pp. 24–5.

23 Wells, *God's Companions*, pp. 24–5.

24 Graham Ward, *Cities of God* (London: Routledge, 2000), p. 173.

25 Ward, *Cities of God*, p. 154.

26 Ward, *Cities of God*, p. 174.

27 James K. A. Smith, *Introducing Radical Orthodoxy: Mapping a Post-secular Theology* (Grand Rapids, MI: Baker Academic, 2004), pp. 246–7.

28 Graham Ward, *The Politics of Discipleship: Becoming Postmaterial Citizens* (Grand Rapids, MI: Baker Academic), p. 280.

29 Graham Ward, *Cities of God* (Abingdon: Routledge, 2000), pp. 259, 95. In the task of discovering 'what it is [we] say when [we] say "Christ"', we are 'continually being opened up' precisely as we engage in 'acts of following'.

30 Ward, *The Politics of Discipleship*, pp. 280–1.

31 Ward, *The Politics of Discipleship*. The Christian (the 'layperson' particularly, Ward suggests) 'is continually called upon to pray for discernment; and allow the world within which they engage to permeate those prayers, that it might be redeemed' (p. 283).

32 Ward, *The Politics of Discipleship*, pp. 16–17. In this way, Ward's sense of the necessity of encounter in changing the cultural imaginary is in a similar vein to the contingency in Wells' account of improvisational response.

33 Wells, *Improvisation*, p. 46. Yet, Wells fears that the language of performance gives the impression: a) that 'the script provides a comprehensive version of life'; b) that all of the church's narrative is contained in the Bible; c) that there is a golden era to be recreated; and d) that the world should not be deeply engaged with (pp. 62–3). For this reason he proposes improvisation.

34 Wells, *Improvisation*, p. 77. Wells draws this distinction on the basis of there being two stages in the moral life: the stage of 'the moral situation', requiring 'the ordinary imagination to respond from habit and instinct' and, prior to this, the stage of 'moral formation, requiring 'the creative imagination to form character through moral effort' (p. 104).

35 Wells, *Improvisation*, p. 128.

36 Wells, *Improvisation*, p. 82.

37 Wells, *God's Companions*, p. 12.

38 Wells, *Improvisation*, p. 104.

39 Wells, *Improvisation*, p. 68.
40 Wells, *Improvisation*, p. 67.
41 Wells, *God's Companions*, p. 66.
42 Wells, *God's Companions*, p. 83.
43 Wells, *God's Companions*, pp. 18–19.
44 As James K. A. Smith puts it, Ward's theological project hinges on recovering the centrality of *eros* and desire for theological reflection, 'by first unhooking it from its reduction to sexual desire and then reconceiving the ecclesial community as a community of desire'. *Introducing Radical Orthodoxy*, p. 126.
45 Graham Ward, *Christ and Culture* (Oxford: Blackwell, 2005), p. 79.
46 Smith, *Introducing Radical Orthodoxy*, pp. 187–8.
47 Ward, *Cities of God*, pp. 238–9, 259–60.
48 Al Barrett, *Interrupting the Church's Flow: A Radically Receptive Political Theology in the Urban Margins* (London: SCM Press, 2020), p. 88; referencing *Cities of God*, pp. 75, 76, 56, 59–60; *The Politics of Discipleship*, pp. 83, 96; *Christ and Culture*, pp. 79, 263–6.
49 Ward, *Politics of Discipleship*, p. 267. See also: *Christ and Culture*, pp. 79, 263–6.
50 Ward, *Cities of God*, p. 76. We should note here Christianity's role in this distortion of desire: global capitalism's comprehensiveness is parasitic, Ward argues, on 'the global logic of Christianity, which forever saw other nations beyond its borders that lacked the gospel'. It is therefore no accident that postmodern desire is a parodic distortion of Christian desire. *Cities of God*, pp. 90–1, 96.
51 Smith, *Introducing Radical Orthodoxy*, pp. 187–8.
52 Barrett, *Interrupting the Church's Flow*, p. 89.
53 Ward, *Cities of God*, pp. 172–3. Ward is drawing on the Augustinian distinction between *uti* – 'use' – and *frui* – 'enjoyment'.
54 Ward, *Cities of God*, p. 76.
55 Ward, *Christ and Culture*, p. 266.
56 Smith, *Introducing Radical Orthodoxy*, pp. 238–9.
57 Ward, *Christ and Culture*, p. 266.
58 Wells, *Improvisation*, p. 19.
59 Wells, *God's Companions*, p. 10. See also for discussion of sin in the Church: *God's Companions*, pp. 113–24; *Improvisation*, p. 19.
60 Wells, *God's Companions*, pp. 142–3.
61 Wells, *God's Companions*, p. 88.
62 Ward, *Cities of God*, p. 70.
63 Ward, *The Politics of Discipleship*, pp. 265–6.
64 Ward, *Cities of God*, p. 70.
65 Indeed, as Lauren Winner has shown, to speak of 'Christian prac-

tices' at all risks conjuring up the illusion of a pure and stable set of practices internal to the church, which are to be commended and recovered from a rosy Christian past. While I continue to use the language of 'practices' in describing modes of Christian formation, I do so without any desire to deny that practices are (a) contextualized and (b) that they 'carry with them their own deformations'. Lauren Winner, *The Dangers of Christian Practice* (New Haven, CT: Yale University Press, 2018), pp. 167–9, 180.

66 Wells, *God's Companions*, p. 11.
67 Ward, *Politics of Discipleship*, p. 184. Emphasis is my own.
68 Ward, *Politics of Discipleship*, p. 24.
69 Ward, *Politics of Discipleship*, p. 27.
70 Ward defines Christian action as 'a praxis that participates in a divine *poiesis* that has soteriological and eschatological import'. Ward, *Politics of Discipleship*, p. 201.
71 Graham Ward, *How the Light Gets In: Ethical Life I* (Oxford: Oxford University Press, 2016), p. 147.
72 Ward, *How the Light Gets In*, p. 295. In this vein, Ward also undertakes a sustained engagement with biology as illuminating creation's teleology (pp. 291–3).
73 Barrett, 'Interrupting the Church's Flow', p. 17. Barrett further argues that it is this ambivalent description of the church itself that renders precarious the extent to which Ward's church is open to the challenge of its 'others' (p. 28).
74 For instance, Ward draws on Chaucer's *The Book of the Duchess* and Daniel Myrick and Eduardo Sánchez's *The Blair Witch Project* to illuminate the 'lost and alienated' human condition, *How the Light Gets In*, p. 147. This has the effect of pointing the reader back to ecclesial praxis as the source to be drawn on in developing a socially transformative theological imaginary.
75 Ward, *Politics of Discipleship*, p. 33.
76 Wells, *Improvisation*, pp. 103, 108. Against this account of improvisation, then, sin is understood as 'the refusal to keep the story going ... It is closing one's heart to grace' (p. 115).
77 Wells, *Improvisation*, p. 128.
78 Wells, *Improvisation*, p. 82.
79 Wells, *Improvisation*, p. 87.
80 Wells, *Improvisation*, p. 80.
81 Wells, *Improvisation*, p. 80.
82 Wells, *God's Companions*, p. 83.
83 Wells, *God's Companions*, p. 222.
84 Samuel Wells, *A Nazareth Manifesto: Being with God* (Oxford: Wiley, 2015), p. 96.

85 Wells, *God's Companions*, p. 83.
86 Wells, *Improvisation*, p. 160.
87 Wells, *Improvisation*, p. 147.
88 Wells, *Improvisation*, pp. 131–3.
89 Wells cautions his readers: 'Do not assume others will see Jesus' face in you: go, and expect to see Jesus' face in them.' *Nazareth Manifesto*, p. 96. Yet, a question remains here: is this the face one already knows – or do others teach us to see more of the face, or to see it differently? It does seem that it is, for Wells, a face one already knows, which one has been reliably taught to recognize by the church.
90 Wells, *God's Companions*, p. 65.
91 Wells, *God's Companions*, p. 64.
92 Wells, *God's Companions*, p. 83.
93 Wells, *Improvisation*, pp. 81–2.
94 We will explore this further in Part II, but it is worth noting for now the contrast that is set up between acknowledging the church's deep flaws and attending to God's gifts. There is little sense here that being brought to a new awareness of its role in oppression could in fact be a gift to the church – one that it desperately needs to receive.

2

Formation by the Spirit through Doubt and Disruption

In the last chapter, we identified some problems with the dominant theological account of Christian ethical formation. In this chapter, I am picking up some of the generative shoots I noted in Ward and Wells' accounts of formation and developing them into an approach to Christian ethical formation which is better able to reckon with the complexities of participating in the life of the church and in the world. I make two main claims: first, that Christian ethical formation centrally involves cultivating doubt about our desires (and about the ability of any practice to unproblematically form our desires); and, second, that Christian ethical formation requires openness to surprising encounters with the Spirit out in the world.

I begin by highlighting doubt as a central discipline in Christian formation if we are to grapple with the often malformed practices of the Christian tradition. To be capable of ethical formation, Christian practice needs to be made open to correction and supplementation – including from spheres of life not traditionally looked to as sources of spiritual formation, such as everyday social relations.

This attention to everyday sociality leads to a richer, more abundant account of the Spirit's work in Christian formation. I underline the need for an attentive openness to the work of the Spirit in the world, identifying receptivity to unexpected gifts of the Spirit as a central ethical discipline. This discipline includes the expectation that the gifts that are encountered in the world will reshape the practices of the church.

The ethical discipline of doubt

In arguing for the central importance of learning to doubt, I am responding to the tendency identified in the previous chapter towards overconfidence in the formative potential of ecclesial practices – including a reliance on established praxis to correct the malforming presence of sin in the life of the Christian and of the church. In the dominant account I described, I identified an account of the given-ness of the practices of Christian tradition which translates into a confidence that we know what to do in order to be formed properly (even if we never do these things perfectly). Failures of formation, by this account, stem from imperfectly enacting the given practices. As I have indicated, I think this account of formation is too confident about our ability to recognize the presence of sin – to identify where and how our desires are being distorted. The remedy proposed is therefore also insufficient. By circumscribing sin as something that can be identified and remedied by known praxis, we end up with a stunted understanding of formation.

In the previous chapter, we saw that desire plays a central role in the dominant account of Christian formation. Here again, desire is central to the account I develop of ethical formation: in particular, I am suggesting that we should more strongly emphasize the difficulties of desiring God, and so give a fuller account of the obstacles to the re-formation of desire. Wrestling with these difficulties radically destabilizes the confidence that can be placed in any Christian practice as a reliable source of ethical formation. In this, I am taking a negative theological approach and positing it as an ethical practice (not just as a linguistic technique for dealing with an epistemic problem, as the negative tradition has sometimes been cast).[1]

This negative emphasis underlines that there is a fundamental limitation in any finite creature's attempt to be formed in desire for 'a God who transcends knowledge and experience'.[2] Grappling with what it means to desire a transcendent God necessarily generates doubt about the knowledge of God and love for God that we *think* we have, in part because of the inadequacy of language to properly frame knowledge and love of God. Our ability to properly form our desire for God is made yet more difficult by the fact that our understanding of God and what it means to love God (and to be loved by God) is limited not only by our finite desire in the face of God's transcendence, but also by the ways in which our desire for God goes wrong. According to the negative theological tradition, the main way that our desire for God tends to go wrong is in our tendency to treat God as 'something' that can be 'possessed'. This attempt to tame the transcendent God can be seen, for example, in approaching God in terms of what we can get out of God (including the aim of attaining Christian virtue). Denys Turner identifies at the root of all possessiveness 'the ultimately possessive desire to be a self: the desire that there should be at my centre not that unnameable abyss into which, as into a vacuum, the nameless Godhead is inevitably drawn, but an identity that I can own, an identity which is defined by my ownership of it'.[3]

To this account of the difficulty of attending to God, we also need to add the difficulty we experience in receiving God's attention. Rowan Williams underlines the necessity of continual openness to the judgement of Christ, who stands apart, utterly other.[4] Here an understanding of what it is to be formed as a disciple of Christ must recognize his untameable alterity. For while union with Christ is the first and last word on Christian identity, 'His solidarity is no uncritical endorsement of lives and attitudes opposed to God's love: it includes his confrontation and critical dialogue with the religious and political leaders of the nation and his prophetic woes on the cities that rejected his message.'[5] Christ's gaze of judgement destabilizes settled traditions and their stable practices, and means that there should be a pattern of 'reversal and renewal' – led by rhythms of self-inspection and penitence – in the ethical development of the disciple.[6] The rupture of coming to a new and unanticipated awareness of one's sinfulness, and the reweaving that follows are not, therefore, aberrations or diversions from the process of formation, but rather are at the heart of discipleship.[7]

While receiving God's attention is shattering, it is also unifying. This is what leads Williams to claim that: 'Real dependence on God's grace, real apprehension of God's free action to make us righteous in his eyes, is more evident in the unconsoled endurance of inner turmoil and darkness than in bland confidence that all has been achieved, since the sense of inner darkness turns our attention away from what our minds can register, contain, and be confident of, towards the utterly mysterious love of God.'[8] The divine gaze is not only what shatters all premature attempts to unify and finalize the self, but also what holds our identity together. We can see in the work of Ward and Wells an affirmation that Christian identity is held by the divine gaze (which in turn makes possible our attention to one another), and also an emphasis on Christ's unsettling alterity.[9] Developing a more negative emphasis allows us to perceive more fully the way divine attention breaks in and unsettles stability in the Christian life, and to see that an ongoing unsettling is at the core of Christian formation. By this account, even this unifying dimension is also radically destabilizing because it is not in our control.

We are called, then, to put aside the attempt to discover a 'true' self that we can possess. As Williams puts it:

> You have an identity not because you invented one, or because you have a little hard core of selfhood that is unchanged, but because you have a witness of who you are. What you don't understand or see, the bits of yourself you can't pull together in a convincing story, are all held in a single gaze of love. You don't have to work out and finalise who you are, and have been; you don't have to settle the absolute truth of your history or story. In the eyes of the presence that never goes away, all that you have been and are is still present and real; it is held together in that unifying gaze [of] the divine observer, the divine witness.[10]

In the face of this destabilizing attention, we all too often 'crave to be a something of ourselves, to be a something with which we can love God, to possess "means" through which we can approach God, to know ways of our own to God'.[11] There is a sense, then, in which our selves can get in the way of learning to pay and receive attention, instead driving us into attempts to achieve finalizable understandings of God and ourselves in relation to God – turning God into what God is not, and turning ourselves into what we are not.[12]

This description of what is going wrong when desire for God is malformed chimes with Ward and Wells' descriptions of the distortions of desire. Wells, for example, accounts for sin as an impulse to turn away from God's abundance 'out of a sense of self-protection': a misplaced impulse towards the 'preservation of identity in the face of a tidal wave of glory'.[13] When we frame this in a wider emphasis on the formative importance of recognizing our limits, this helps us to see more clearly the human propensity to try and protect against God's discomfiting yet ultimately unifying attention.

In thinking about the need to recognize the limits within which desire for God is formed, we also need to reckon with the human propensity to deceive ourselves about what it is we desire. We have seen from Wells that self-deception is part of the mix when thinking about how desire goes wrong, and the need to structure practices of repentance in this light.[14] We are not only limited in our knowledge of God but also in our understanding of ourselves; the clouded nature of our knowledge extends even to our own desires and motivations. So, the problem posed by sin for the formation of desire is not just that we have limited or bad desires, but also that we do not even know *what* our desires are. All too frequently, we fail to acknowledge the need for ongoing struggle against self-deception – particularly when it comes to our own desires and motivations. Because we do not know even our own desires very well, we therefore need to bring to bear on our thinking about formative praxis an awareness of our tendency to deceive ourselves.

There are analogous limits in relation to our knowledge of and desire for the good of those around us, and Janet Soskice notes that some Orthodox theologians suggest 'that to say "man is in the image of God" is to say that "man is mystery" because God is mystery'.[15] This means that there is a proper kind of *apophasis* that we ought to accord to each other, as there is a sense that in standing in front of another we stand on holy ground.[16] The mystery of the other means that we do not know what they apprehend of God's mystery – what has been revealed to them. We need, therefore, to apply the same – or at least, a similar – 'negative' or contemplative approach to social relations as we have to our relation with God.

However, humanity's possessive tendency crops up again here. It can be manifested in an inattentive sense of superiority to other people: the egotistic deception that we already know what the other knows and that they have nothing of worth to give to me – that I have nothing to learn from them. This extends also to the accounts that others give of God. This kind of inattention can also take the form of seeing the other in relation to how they can fulfil my needs and desires.[17] Any one person's ability to recognize the good or harm of a practice is therefore limited.

If we apply this to established Christian practices – whether the liturgical practices of the church or those practices named as 'spiritual practices', such as contemplative prayer – we are forced to reckon with the possibility that even in the practices that we have received as most reliable (the established practices of Christian tradition), we can be deceived by ourselves about how these are forming us and our desires. We can think we are seeking God, when we may, for example, be seeking an 'experience' of encountering God.[18] Moreover, even in practices where we are not being deceived about our desires, we may be failing to recognize how these practices are harming others.

This all leads me to make a recognition of our limits a cornerstone of how we should think about ethical formation. Our ability to know and enact what it is we need to do to be formed well is fundamentally limited – more so than we will ever fully recognize. As we have seen, this limitation stems both from finitude and from sinfulness. This capacity for misrecognition and self-deception about the content and goodness of our desires leads, then, to an important role for the discipline of doubt.

The kind of doubt I am advocating for questions the capacity of any established practice (or set of established practices) to properly form love for God and for those around us. Such doubt involves doubting the goodness of our desires, as well as cultivating doubt over what we can even know about our desires. To doubt in this way attunes us to the damage that may be being wrought despite our attempts to be formed ethically. This is not to advocate a withdrawal from participation in the practices of ecclesial life. Rather, this kind of uncertainty about the formative potential of practices received through the Christian tradition (both individually and corporately) should render these practices open to ongoing revision and supplementation – as we will return to in Part II.

Emphasizing doubt as a central formative practice also has implications for how we understand the role that can be played by social relations in ethical formation. As Wells in fact argues, seeing the creaturely limits we each have as a gift, rather than as a lack, opens up the opportunity for creatively receiving from one another. We also saw in Chapter 1 an emphasis on how attention to God will flow into attention to those around us.[19] Here, I am suggesting that if we extend Wells' insight we will see that flow of attention can also go in the other direction – and that this is significant for ethical formation. I am by no means contesting that practices such as listening to Scripture and contemplative prayer can train our ability to also attend to those around us. However, when these established practices are isolated as *the* mechanisms for the reconstruction of desire this ends up pulling away from the ordinary stuff of social interaction, and the gifts therein.

We have noted that a 'negative' approach to social relations requires us to accept the mysterious opaqueness of the other. Accepting this opaqueness has implications for both our understanding of others' desires and our own desires. As we have seen, we do not know even the shape of our own desires very well. Indeed, we will misread our desires until we are confronted with the desires of others. As Williams puts it, if everybody else was taken away, finding out who we are in the eyes of God would be an even longer and more painful journey.[20] We are, as Williams says, 'our limits', not simply in the sense of having a particular location, but in the sense of being material and historical – shaped by all manner of forces in a specific history, in a tangle far too dense for us to tease out our identity with any completeness. We inevitably see only some of the factors that shape our vision and our desire and make us who we are. We discover more of that tangle not by introspection alone, but also as a result of interactions with others that bring different strands to the surface. Our ability to perceive what we desire and whether that might allow for the flourishing of others and of ourselves is necessarily formed, therefore, through others, as 'the barriers of egotistic fantasy are broken by the sheer brute presence of other persons'.[21] We require the perspective of others to know ourselves.

Recognizing our own limited ability to know and understand ourselves (and what is going in our formation) in this way reveals the incompleteness of any one voice, and the need for it to be brought into robust conversation with others in order to be challenged and supplemented. The mystery of the other means that we need to be open to receiving insights from them. There is what we might call an anticipatory soul posture being cultivated here, in which we expect to encounter God in formative ways through those around us.

So, we can see that social relations should not be understood to be separate from the kind of non-possessive attention to God that, I have suggested, we should be seeking; rather, quotidian social practices can also lead into deeper knowledge and love of God. This is partly so because of the way that the opaqueness of others acts as a check on false images of God, others and ourselves and leads us to continually renegotiate our sense of who we are before God. Yet this is not a picture of negotiation that starts from clear and fixed positions;

rather, we discover who we are through ongoing interaction. An awareness of our limits can result, then, in making other people intrinsic to learning to lovingly attend – to God, ourselves and to others.

It is worth saying a word here about power relations and the limits of receptivity. There are violent and oppressive ways in which we relate to one another, and not all attention is generous and aiming at the other's unfolding and flourishing. So, I am not proposing receptivity towards others' attention as a stable virtue, irrespective of context. There is thinking to be done about how we discern what is to be received (and about the tension between the way reception rests on both trust *and* on openness to surprise). Nonetheless, I think a posture of openness to receiving unexpected gifts through being the object of others' attention can still be affirmed as central to Christian ethical formation. Practising this kind of doubt reshapes our relationship to God and those around us, rendering us more receptive to receiving God's loving attention (the basis of Christian identity, out of which flows all ethical action – the ability to desire and act for the good of others and for ourselves).

Shared attention

I am arguing here that being attended to – learning to be objects of attention – can be a central part of the process of learning to desire God. More specifically, I think that being attended to by others can make us aware of divine attention: there is a sense in which we mediate God's attention to one another. One way in which this can happen is through a negative, or contemplative, approach to social interactions allowing situations to be reframed in a way that opens us up to receiving God's loving attention (and so also to returning it).

We see an instance of what this might look like in Stuart Jesson's extension of Simone Weil's account of attention, in which he seeks to move attention beyond the 'private operation of the individual "soul"' to being something that can be shared and where there can be a 'joint subject' of attention.[22] In the context of Weil's work on suffering and compassion, Jesson makes the argument that in understanding attention as being, in some cases, 'an irreducibly social phenomenon', compassion might, in turn, also be thought of as something that can be shared. The term 'joint attention' refers to the capacity to be aware of *another's awareness* of the object of *one's own awareness*, and involves shared orientation to that object of attention. Compassion, meanwhile, concerns questions, whether it is asking what Weil calls 'the redemptive question' – 'what are you going through?' – or listening compassionately to the question 'why is this happening to me?' As Jesson puts it: 'If I ask "what are you going through?", then I must learn to pay attention not just to the other, but to that which the question "why am I being hurt?" directs me; I must learn to pay attention *with* the questioning other.'[23]

Jesson illustrates the relationship between joint attention and compassion in his account of being unemployed and having, after a long series of unsuccessful attempts, failed once again to get an interview for a much-desired job. He describes a series of encounters with friends who, in various ways, fail to join in with *his* attention to his situation. He then describes an encounter in which attention and compassion are shared:

> Finally, let us say that the friend works part-time in a job which is tolerable, but not ideal, and has two children, the youngest of which has recently been diagnosed with a cancerous tumour on her leg at the age of three, and has been undergoing chemotherapy. I bump into my friend whilst walking in the park: I am there to try to lift my depressed mood; she is out with her youngest child. She asks how I am, and I briefly explain, looking down and largely avoiding her gaze. When I finish, my friend grimaces slightly, nods, and says 'that's rough'. She does not have to make it clear to me that she sees how frustrating the situation is (I do not reflect on this at the time, but for some reason, I sense that

intuitively). After replying with a brief agreement, I look over at her three-year-old daughter, who is engrossed by a nearby tree stump, which she is, with some effort, climbing on and then jumping off. We are silent for a short while, then I say: 'she's pretty great, isn't she?' My friend smiles. We watch silently for a short while. Then my friend looks back at me, and says 'you'll be ok, you know.' I nod, and reply: 'I know. Thanks.' There is another pause, filled with the sound of my friend's daughter talking to herself, and then we leave each other. I go home feeling lighter and calmer, although still frustrated.[24]

The thing that has changed here for Jesson is 'the simple fact that I sense that someone else has attended to the problem that I am concerned with, in the *way* that I am concerned with it'. It is this that somehow alters the significance that the situation has for him. His friend's attention to and *with* him changes his experience of his current situation 'only because she does not try to change it, but enters into it as it is': 'She does not force her hope on to me as a consolation that should drive away my initial reaction, but because we are attending jointly (to my troubles, to her daughter), her own hope, in the face of her own fears—which are deeper, and more serious—affects me, and it bleeds into my own.'[25]

This willingness to enter into another's situation on their terms involves generously attending to it, putting aside one's own agenda and the desire to 'tidy up' their suffering. In the sharing of attention, consolation is generated and the troubling situation is seen in a subtly different light, refracted through the other's attention to it. We might understand the experience of compassion and consolation that emerges through this sharing of attention as an experience of God's loving attention, which the presence of the other person enables us to receive in a new way.[26]

We can get a further sense of what receiving God's loving gaze through sharing attention might look like in Jessica Martin's description of her experience of attending a support group for the relatives of addicts. In this context attention is again given to one another and together to common sorrow:

> Nothing dramatic has happened, but the space left by our collective silences is still there, light filtering through cloud cover in a big sky. Held in the large space made somehow between my hands is every intractable situation I have encountered that day, and will encounter (the same ones, and new ones) tomorrow and the next day. I am not being required to solve anything, or to perform great feats of faith or marathons of nagging the divine with this or that trouble. But, just for today, I have been given the strength to hold them all towards the unsettling compassion of the Person I let myself encounter from time to time, who stands waiting in the silences, still knowing griefs, still carrying sorrows, stilling tempests, sanctifying the moment.[27]

Martin affirms that we live in, and through, an unceasing divine attention to the existing materials of one's own life, and the life of each and every other, in the world – to each of our specific histories, our particularities, our existing capacities and possibilities. So, our learning to attend is as those who are recipients of this attention, who must learn to share in this attentiveness (both to ourselves and to others). We have seen that coming to understand our being as contingently dependent on being open to disruption by God means that we should carry this openness to contingent disruption into our social relations. This is expressed in both who one pays attention *to* and who one is prepared to receive attention *from*. Core to this way of understanding what it means to lovingly attend to God, then, is an openness to coming to see things in new and surprising ways, from perspectives that are not initiated or willed by oneself.

I have been arguing here that there are resources in a negative theological approach for understanding social relations and interactions as sites where loving attention to God can be trained, in ways that mirror, add to, and sometimes challenge what takes place in more recognized ecclesial and spiritual practices. The significance of receiving attention that is offered by those around us has often been overlooked in accounts of formation. Yet this kind of reception discloses something crucial about God's action in the world, holding within it the expectation that God's ongoing work of forming Christians for good action happens also through those around us.

Attending to findings of the Spirit

This attention to everyday sociality has the potential to lead to a richer, more abundant account of the Spirit's work in Christian formation. We saw in the dominant account of Christian formation an expectation that the world will primarily be a site of malformation. Where engagement with the world yields insights or wisdom, these gifts tend to be understood as a rediscovery of things the church knew but has forgotten. This sits alongside the expectation that what is encountered – however puzzling, awkward, or surprising – can be slotted into the contours of the storied community that is already known. So, there is not really an expectation that encounters in the world may reveal, and fulfil, a lack in one's own Christian formation and in the formation of the church of which one was not even previously aware – and that this could be part of the way God's gifts are disclosed. Additionally, being able to discover God's abundance in unexpected ways *outside* the church depends, in the dominant account, on having been formed in the right way *in* the church. There is not much of a sense in the dominant account of formation that the practices we rely on for formation should themselves be held open to disruption and re-formation by the work of the Spirit.

Consonant with the critique I have offered of the dominant account of Christian ethical formation, Daniel Hardy argues that the church 'has become over-concentrated on its inner meaning', and Christians need to learn better 'how to persist with our task in the world'. This task involves being part of the 'Opening up of the true potential and resources of human life', and Hardy identifies liturgy as one way of drawing people deeper into the creative life of God. However, he stresses that the ability to draw people deeper in this way is not the exclusive possession of the church. For 'the presumed sufficiency of human wisdom, discernment and power', including in ecclesial life, 'must give way to the Spirit of God, that which searches the very depths of God and human life and gives knowledge of God and of the true possibilities of humanity'.[28] In a similar vein, and influenced by Hardy, Ben Quash argues that an overemphasis on the 'givens' of the Christian faith risks cutting us off from new experiences and what we might learn from them, for such an overemphasis 'supposes that we already have a sufficient grasp of just what those givens really are and mean'.[29] There is a need, therefore, to recognize that, for Christians and for the church to become who they are called to be, we must look for where God is at work beyond the practices of the faith we have already received.

The activity of the Spirit in the world

In focus here is how the activity of the Spirit might encourage Christians to expect to be formed ethically outside the church, and the kinds of practices this might require. While I will be primarily discussing this in relation to Hardy and Quash's thought, it is worth noting that these two are not alone in identifying the Spirit at work beyond the church. It is certainly true that the work of the Spirit has tended to be associated very closely with the church.[30] Nonetheless, throughout the twentieth and twenty-first centuries, in particular, a growing number of theologians have argued that the Spirit is present in social movements for justice; in the community of human and non-human creation; in faithful adherents of other religions; and in 'non-Christian' art, among other spheres of life.[31]

Hardy proposes that we think of the work of the Spirit as 'a kind of turbulence which – as they accept their weakness in fear and trembling – pushes human beings ever more deeply into the deeds of God'.[32] Sharing in the inexhaustibly vital movement of God in the world means that Christians should live, Hardy argues, with an ongoing expectation that the Spirit will be 'pressing us into the surprising depths of God and God's purposes for human life'.[33] Quash likewise speaks in dynamic terms of 'the God who takes us over new horizons', who, as we follow, is always pressing ahead of us. Yet, this is also a God of 'perpetual Advent', who is always approaching and giving. The paradox of experiencing God as both departure and arrival means that, 'God is manifest in an otherness from us, an independence of us, that breaks our idolatrous hold on God – and will often feel like "departure." But this thrill is also ... the thrill of the lover's approach.'[34] So, by this account, the Christian should expect to encounter the work of the Spirit bubbling up in the world in surprising and sometimes discomfiting ways.

We will now consider what this understanding of the Spirit's ways with world means for Christian ethical formation, drawing on Hardy's terms 'intensity' and 'extensity', and Quash's categories of the 'given' and the 'found'. Hardy writes of the dynamic activity of God in the world, and the human response to this, in terms of 'intensity' and 'extensity'. The precise meaning of these terms is hard to pin down in Hardy's thought, but 'intensity' means something like 'God's self-movement of love towards the world': an inexhaustible creative and redemptive movement that we can know ever more intensely and fully. 'Extensity', meanwhile, can be understood as connoting the manifoldness of the life of God, as expressed and found in the endlessly different particularity of all that is encountered in life in the world.[35]

For Hardy, by the movement of the Spirit of Christ, intensity and extensity are held in dialogical relationship. The meeting of the intensity of faith and the extensity of life, 'force[s] faith deeper and make it more unshakeable'. For, the issues of life in the world today (such as the concerns of political life) are not a distraction from discipleship, but rather are the medium by which our understanding of what it is to live in the movement of God's love is renewed and redeveloped 'in all its demandingness'.³⁶

While Hardy's work emphasizes the demanding nature of the task of keeping intensity and extensity in relationship, Quash more fully draws out the joyful side of encountering the movement of the Spirit. Quash talks about this dynamic of stumbling across gifts of the Spirit in the world as 'finding'. He writes that

> the Spirit is the one to be 'found' over and over again, and in the finding of the Spirit one realises oneself as, in fact, caught up in a trinitarian dynamic, in which the Son who shows us the Father is redelivered to the Church by way of its active, imaginative engagement with the events of history.³⁷

So, 'The life of Christian discipleship ... "is about recognising how much more there is than we have ever seen before and about being attracted by it and lifted up to it".'³⁸ This resonates with Wells' account of ethical formation as a dynamic process of rediscovery: 'a dynamic, spiralling process of constant repetition, transfer, and restoration of meaning, of things never being the same again and other things being rediscovered, ever new'.³⁹ However, the pneumatology that Quash offers allows us to go further than just 'rediscovery' in accounting for the Spirit's work in formation.⁴⁰

For both Hardy and Quash, there is a sense of provisionality to the Christian life which is grounded in a belief that the structure of creation is one of ongoing formation. As Williams likewise argues: 'Creation, then, is the realm in which good or beauty or stability, the condition in which everything is most freely and harmoniously itself in balance with everything else, is being sought and being formed.'⁴¹ This is quite a radical point, in relation to significant swathes of the tradition: the good of creation is not simply given (and then fallen away from and regained), but is rather always ahead, not yet fully given. We should expect, therefore, to continue to receive the gifts of creation in the places, and among the people, we are located. This is how we grow.

This unfolding of the 'ever more' happens, for Quash, through relating the 'given' to the 'found'. He is working with a distinction between these two terms whereby the given is described by analogy as the backpack that God has stocked for us for our journey, and the found as those things that God places in our path ahead of us.[42] Through finding, Quash argues, 'God is constantly inviting human beings to relate the given to the found': inviting us to be attentive to the findings that the Holy Spirit is offering us, in light of the things we have already received from God.[43] Broadly speaking, for Quash, the given happens in canonical Christian tradition, including the gathered practices of the church, and the finding 'out' in the world.[44] While 'the givens of Christian faith will help to order and illuminate newly ordered experiences or challenges', this is not the full story. For, 'found things, conceived as gifts of the Holy Spirit who unfolds all the riches that are in Christ, can and must reconfigure, unlock and amplify what is already held true by the Church'.[45] This makes it clear that Christian faith does not grow only through grappling with the difficulty and suffering of the world, but also through stumbling across joyful gifts of the Spirit in unexpected places and carrying them back into a church that will be challenged and changed by them.[46]

Understood in this way, there is an invitation at the heart of discipleship to relate life in the world to the faith one has received so as to deepen and strengthen this faith, leading one further into the life of God.

Practices of openness to the Spirit

There is a need, then, to make oneself open to encounters with the Spirit if one is to grow as a Christian. But how do we do this? How might we be more attentive to the work of the Spirit who helps us grow as Christians? I suggest here that being open to receiving from the Spirit involves disciplining ourselves in certain sorts of practices. However, I should be clear that I am not arguing that there is a particular posture which guarantees proper discernment of the Spirit's movement. There are postures, processes, practices, which can put us in a position of openness towards the ongoing discovery of the Spirit, but, while these are important prerequisites, they are not guarantees that we will recognize encounters with the Spirit. This is not a stance that we can simply will into existence on our own resources, but rather through being impelled, shaped and continually taught by the Spirit. In what follows, I outline what these postures might be that keep us open to recognizing and being formed by encounters with the Spirit.

Anticipative openness to surprise and to rethinking the familiar

First, a posture of anticipation and openness is necessary to notice and receive the work of the Spirit. As Quash argues, the Christian life is one 'in which love is always concretely and particularly taught and learnt – not in universal and abstract principles – and it requires a response to what is found in front of you, under your nose, here and now'.[47] This attentive responsiveness to 'the surprising possibilities of the present moment' – learning to see the particularities of our lives as sites where God is, whether or not we recognize the divine presence – is thus central to the process of discipleship.[48] These sites will include those who are strange to us.[49]

This openness to encountering God in surprising ways out in the world runs alongside an openness to rethinking and reshaping those things that are familiar to us: the givens of Christian life. These restless, 'extensive' journeys outwards carry with them the expectation that what one encounters out in the world will drive one back into what one has already been given through the church. For, as we saw above, it is as we open ourselves up to the Spirit that 'the steadfastness and quality of our faith will grow as we confront the tasks of understanding and living in this world'.[50]

We should expect that redeveloping faith in response to the demanding issues of life will lead into new convictions of sin. For in understanding the found as a genuinely new thing given by God, we draw attention to the fact that, as Williams argues, there is a danger of 'theologizing what is "given" as if the given represented the finished, the fixed'.[51] In expecting discipleship to involve coming to new understandings of the 'givens' of faith, we should expect this to include new understandings of how we have been faithless – twisting the faith we have received to serve our own interests. The 'findings' through which we are led to realize how far we have strayed from the faith we have been given will often lie outside the church (as we will explore further in Chapter 6).

Rethinking the familiar requires, then, engaging movements and ideas from beyond the church that help Christians to rethink their own faith community. In this way, we are to expect that discipleship will involve coming to new understandings of what we have been given in the faith, as, through our following, we stumble across new findings on the path. This re-formation takes the form of both unlocking a greater depth of meaning within established practices and also bringing to our attention where those practices stand in need of revision. This is all part of the task of relating the given to the found.

Discerning the work of the Spirit

This expectation of new and unfamiliar encounters with the Spirit raises the question: How do we know that it is the spirit of God that we are encountering in these novel and surprising ways? In learning to discern the presence of the Spirit, we must start with what we are told of the Spirit by Christ in Scripture. We are told in John's gospel that the Spirit is the spirit of Christ, who interprets and illuminates Christ for us: 'He will take what is mine and give it to you' (John 16.14). As we have seen in Quash's argument above regarding the Spirit redelivering Christ to us, we are therefore to expect a distinctively

Christic pattern to the work of the Spirit. Thus, not all novelty should be attributed to the Spirit. Quash writes that:

> The Spirit's characteristic way of being generative ... is a power of continual 're-formation' in the lives of believers, both as individuals and as communities. The form that is continually 're-formed' is, of course, Christ-like, and the process of re-formation happens participatively, as creatures find Christ taking place within and among them by virtue of their sharing in and with his living example. The Spirit is the medium of this participation.[52]

The re-formative 'spiralling' work of the Spirit in interpreting Christ is recognizable, therefore, but it also never comes to a resting place.[53]

This is expressed in Hardy's discussion of how an expectant and discerning posture of openness to the Spirit can be formed through the Anglican daily offices. In the context of a sermon preached during evensong, Hardy argues that 'What we are doing right here and now should be seen ... as the Spirit pressing into the surprising depths of God and God's purposes for human life and the hope they bear for the future of the world.' In the daily offices, both Old and New Testaments, as well as the Psalms, are heard twice a day. The canticles guide the hearers, Hardy argues, in their response to Scripture – in this way the offices provide a window into the Bible, guiding an expectation of how God continues to disclose the meaning of Scripture through the lives of the faithful. The Creed and sermon deepen this 'intensive' awareness of God's actions and purposes. All in all, this exposure to God's interactions with the world should shape how we imagine and expect the Spirit to move in the world.[54]

If the postures of expectant anticipation described here, which can be developed in certain ways through church practices, are appropriate preconditions for being drawn into new findings by the Spirit, then taking this stance really does matter. Yet, even the nature of these postures is something we go on learning from others (they are both given and continually found). So, we should not take Hardy's argument here to mean that Christian formation will take place through simply repeating the practices we already have; rather, we should expect this ecclesial practice to propel Christians outward to encounter the Spirit at work (in often surprising ways) in the world – including in ways that reshape familiar ecclesial praxis. The imagination is shaped by hearing in Scripture of God's ways with the world, but it is not fixed within the bounds of what is described there.

Conclusion

In this chapter, we have seen that the problems I underlined in the dominant account of ethical formation are not necessitated by that approach. It is often overshadowed in these accounts, but there are nonetheless hints and suggestions of a more doubting and disrupted sense of formation, which I have drawn out and further developed here. Taking these shoots in a more apophatic direction has led to a richer, if somewhat messier, picture of how Christian ethical formation does and should happen.

In my attempt to account for what is involved in ethical formation, I have made my starting point a recognition of the propensity of Christians to be ethically malformed, rather than adding this sinfulness onto a largely complete picture of the dynamics of formation. I have come to argue that recognizing the practices of the church as not wholly reliable nor finalizable sources of ethical formation is not a threat to Christian formation – rather, paying attention to the flawed nature of ecclesial praxis leads us to a richer account of what it means to live receptively as a finite creature. I have identified doubt as a practice that helps to reveal our limits, and so train us to lovingly attend to God – which fundamentally lies in learning to receive God's loving attention. I have further argued that this formative discipline of doubt is connected to an attentive openness to the work of the Spirit in the world, identifying receptivity to unexpected gifts of the Spirit as a central ethical discipline. Expecting that the world too will be a site of Christian ethical formation includes the anticipation that the gifts that are encountered in the world will reshape the practices of the church.

So, what might these kinds of new and surprising encounters with the Spirit in the world look like? And how might the church be structured towards openness to this kind of formative encounter? It is to these questions that we turn in Part II.

Notes

1 David Newheiser, *Hope in a Secular Age: Deconstruction, Negative Theology, and the Future of Faith* (Cambridge: Cambridge University Press, 2019), p. 40.

2 David Newheiser, 'Introduction: The Trials of Desire' in *Desire, Faith, and the Darkness of God: Essays in Honour of Denys Turner*, ed. Eric Bugyis and David Newheiser (Notre Dame, IN: University of Notre Dame Press, 2015), 1–9 (p. 3).

3 Denys Turner, *The Darkness of God: Negativity in Christian Mysticism* (Cambridge: Cambridge University Press, 1995), p. 184.

4 See, for example: Rowan Williams, 'Different Christs?' in *Open to Judgement* (London: Darton, Longman and Todd, 2002), pp. 105–11.

5 Rowan Williams and Richard Bauckham, 'Jesus: God with Us' in *Stepping Stones*, eds C. Baxter, J. R. W. Stott and R. Greenacre (London: Hodder and Stoughton, 1987), p. 35.

6 Medi Volpe, *Rethinking Christian Identity: Doctrine and Discipleship* (Oxford: Blackwell, 2012), p. 59.

7 There are, of course, dangers to commending rupture and shattering of self, to which feminist theologies are particularly well attuned.

8 Rowan Williams, Kenneth Stevenson and Geoffrey Rowell, eds, *Love's Redeeming Work* (Oxford: Oxford University Press, 2001), p. 8.

9 See, for example, Graham Ward, *Politics of Discipleship* (London: SCM Press, 2009), pp. 280–3.

10 Rowan Williams, *Being Disciples: Essentials of the Christian Life* (London: SPCK, 2016), p. 29.

11 Turner, *The Darkness of God*. But, as John of the Cross teaches us, 'The land of the Spirit is a land without ways', p. 246.

12 Rowan Williams, *Silence and Honeycakes* (Oxford: Lion Books, 2004), pp. 47–8.

13 Samuel Wells, *God's Companions: Reimagining Christian Ethics* (Oxford: Blackwell Publishing, 2006), p. 7.

14 See, for example, Wells, *God's Companions*, pp. 87, 142–3.

15 Janet Martin Soskice, *The Kindness of God: Metaphor, Gender, and Religious Language* (Oxford: Oxford University Press, 2007), p. 39.

16 Williams, *Being Disciples*, p. 64.

17 Or, as Simone Weil argues, inattention to the other can involve cushioning oneself from any real encounter with their suffering by, for example, 'seeing the suffering other as representative of a class of people defined by such suffering; thereafter, their situation no longer seems surprising'. Stuart Jesson, 'Compassion, Consolation, and the Sharing of Attention' in *Simone Weil and Continental Philosophy*, ed. A. Rebecca Rozelle-Stone (Lanham, MD: Rowman and Littlefield, 2017), pp. 121–42 (p. 121).

18 Turner writes of the revenge of the possessive self that is threatened by the vacuum of detachment – attempting to make the vacuum itself an object of experience through reproducing the vacuum in a specialized set of 'spiritual' experiences of it. Turner, *The Darkness of God*, p. 209.

19 For example, Ward, *The Politics of Discipleship*, p. 280, and Samuel Wells, *Improvisation: The Drama of Christian Ethics* (Grand Rapids, MI: Baker Academic, 2018), p. 82.

20 Williams, *Silence and Honey Cakes*, p. 49.

21 Rowan Williams, *The Wound of Knowledge* (London: Darton, Longman and Todd, 2014), p. 107. See also Mike Higton, *Difficult Gospel: The Theology of Rowan Williams* (London, SCM Press, 2004), p. 124.

22 Jesson, 'Compassion, Consolation, and the Sharing of Attention', p. 122.

23 Jesson, 'Compassion, Consolation, and the Sharing of Attention', p. 125.

24 Jesson, 'Compassion, Consolation, and the Sharing of Attention', pp. 131–2.

25 Jesson, 'Compassion, Consolation, and the Sharing of Attention', p. 132.

26 Attention should shape, then, both the one attending and the one being attended to. As Tim Jenkins argues, the act of seeking to comprehend others 'cannot be a kind of passive act leaving one or both sides unchanged'. Timothy Jenkins, 'Fieldwork and the Perception of Everyday Life', *Man* 29, no. 2 (1994): 433–55 (p. 445).

27 Jessica Martin, 'Attention' in *Praying for England: Priestly Presence in Contemporary Culture*, eds Samuel Wells and Sarah Coakley (London: Continuum, 2008), pp. 107–24 (pp. 123–4).

28 Daniel Hardy, *Wording a Radiance: Parting Conversations About God and the Church* (London: SCM Press, 2010), pp. 32–3; Daniel Hardy, 'A Magnificent Complexity' in David Ford and Dennis Stamps, eds, *Essentials of Christian Community* (Edinburgh: T&T Clark, 1996), p. 337.

29 Ben Quash, *Found Theology: History, Imagination and the Holy Spirit* (London: Bloomsbury T&T Clark, 2013), p. 1.

30 As reflected, for example, in the third portion of the Nicene Creed, which is dedicated to the work of the Spirit and focuses on the realm of the church, and in the writings of Irenaeus and Hippolytus, for example. Veli-Matti Kärkkäinen, *Pneumatology: The Holy Spirit in Ecumenical, International, and Contextual Perspective* (Grand Rapids, MI: Baker Academic, 2002), p. 109.

31 See, respectively, the work of Jürgen Moltmann, José Comblin, Nimi Wariboko, Amaryah Armstrong, Tim Gorringe; Sallie McFague and Elizabeth Johnson; Joseph Pathrapankal, Karl Rahner and Clark Pinnock; and Beth Dodds. It is evident, then, that this is a concern that spans geographic location and denominational affiliation, as well as spanning theological sub-disciplines. One reason for this shift relates to the primary metaphor that one uses for the Spirit. Classically the West has thought in terms of love while the East has thought in terms of life. By thinking about the Spirit in terms of life, contemporary western theology has found resources to think about the Spirit outside the meters of the church. The work of Jung Young Lee and Wolfhart Pannenberg offer particularly striking examples of this association of the Spirit with the giving of life.

32 Daniel Hardy, *Finding the Church: The Dynamic Truth of Anglicanism* (London: SCM Press, 2001), p. 233.

33 Hardy, *Finding the Church*, pp. 232–3.

34 Quash, *Found Theology*, p. xvii.

35 Julie Gittoes, 'Where is the Kingdom?' in Julie Gittoes, Brutus Green and James Heard, eds, *Generous Ecclesiology: Church, World and the Kingdom of God* (London: SCM Press, 2013), pp. 98–119 (p. 103). Indeed, Hardy sees 'God's life at its fullest' as 'an engagement with the extensity and manifoldness of the world for the sake of bringing it to the perfection appropriate to it in the purposes of God', Hardy, *Finding the Church*, p. 159. For Hardy, the churches of the Anglican Communion, in their diverse immersion in different contexts yet united relationship, 'are an effective sign of the intensity of God's life and purposes engaging with this extensity and manifoldness' (p. 159).

However, we should note with Gittoes that: 'there is a risk inherent within the gift of creaturely freedom that in being drawn outward we are in danger of losing God's presence with us', Gittoes, 'Where is the Kingdom?' p. 103.

36 Hardy, *Finding the Church*, p. 236.
37 Quash, *Found Theology*, p. xvi.
38 Quash, *Found Theology*, p. 249.
39 Wells, *God's Companions*, p. 46. Similarly, Ward argues that in the task of discovering 'what it is [we] say when [we] say "Christ"', we are 'continually being opened up' precisely as we engage in 'acts of following'. Ward, *Cities of God*, pp. 95, 259.
40 There are echoes here of a central sensibility in T. S. Eliot's *Four Quartets*, in which Eliot writes of returning to the place where one began one's journeying and knowing it again but as if for the first time (a sense Quash names as 'vertiginous at-homeness'): 'We shall not cease from exploration, and the end of all our exploring will be to arrive where we started and know the place for the first time', T. S. Eliot, 'Little Gidding' in *Four Quartets* (London: Faber and Faber, 2001); Quash, *Found Theology*, p. 240.
41 Rowan Williams, 'Good for Nothing? Augustine on Creation', *Augustinian Studies* 25 (1994), 9–24 (pp. 17–18).
42 Quash, *Found Theology*, p. xiv.
43 Quash, *Found Theology*, p. xiv.
44 Quash, *Found Theology*, p. 17.
45 Quash, *Found Theology*, p. xiv. See also Hardy, *Finding the Church*, p. 234.
46 This extends Wells' expectation of receiving gifts outside the church, which leads him to argue for each new celebration of the Eucharist beginning 'with a sense of what has been discovered, where God has been met in the time since the last gathering.' Wells, *God's Companions*, p. 222.
47 Hardy, *Finding the Church*, p. 24.
48 Hardy, *Finding the Church*, p. 282.
49 This is a theme discussed by Rowan Williams in his lecture on 'Encountering the Other' (Autumn 2018) given at St Martin-in-the-Fields, https://www.stmartin-in-the-fields.org/rowan-williams-encountering-the-other/, accessed 04.08.2022, and by Charles Mathewes in *A Theology of Public Life* (Cambridge: Cambridge University Press, 2007), pp. 71–2.
50 Hardy, *Finding the Church*, pp. 236–7.
51 Rowan Williams, 'Trinity and Revelation' in *On Christian Theology* (Oxford: Blackwell, 2000), pp. 131–47, 132.
52 Quash, *Found Theology*, p. 28.

53 As Williams argues, 'For the event of Christ to be authentically revelatory, it must be capable of both "fitting" and "extending" any human circumstance; it must be re-presentable, and the form and character of its re-presentation are not necessarily describable in advance', 'Trinity and Revelation', pp. 142–3. Quash is particularly influenced by Williams' account of the spiration of the Spirit: conceiving of the Spirit as 'spiralling generatively forward in history, helping the Church to think ever more deeply about the meaning of its own thought and practice'. Quash, *Found Theology*, p. xv.

Arguing in this way that the church should expect good to be found on the other side of its walls, does not mean, as Mike Higton makes the point, 'that church will make no rules, have no policies, and draw no boundaries'. Nor is this a denial that learning to be the people of God depends in important ways on the ecclesial community, constituted by the Spirit (although not the Spirit's fixed domicile). However, it does mean that 'the church will have to operate its policies, and police its boundaries, in the recognition that it neither thereby creates a sterilised environment within which everything is guaranteed to be good, nor erects a pale beyond which everything is guaranteed to be bad', Mike Higton, 'The Ecclesial Body's Grace: Obedience and Faithfulness in Rowan Williams', 'Ecclesiology', *Ecclesiology* 7 (2011), 7–28 (pp. 17–18).

54 Hardy, *Finding the Church*, pp. 232–3.

PART II

Ecclesial Formation

In the discussion above, the church has emerged as a body in need of ongoing ethical and political formation (not just its members). Such a vision of the church is needed because accounts of a basically finished church do not richly account for Christian formation. Having seen that the church cannot just be understood as a reliable site of formation (in Chapter 1), and that there is a need for those practices to be made open to doubt and disruption as part of ethical formation (in Chapter 2), we therefore move in this part to think about the church as a body that is in need of formation itself, rather than just being understood as a site of formation of individuals. So, the focus shifts here from the formation of individuals within the body to the ongoing formation of the body itself.

If we do not have such a picture of a basically finished church which is capable of providing the formation we need, what do we put in its place? How can we think about the church itself as a body needing to be formed (and to go on being formed), especially at the level of polity?

In Chapter 3 we are thinking about how we have to structure the polity of the church to make it open to ongoing formation. What is the basic picture of the church we need to be working with in order to have this expectation of ongoing formation? Then, in Chapter 4, we explore how the church needs to be subject to ongoing formation – in part because of the ongoing struggle with sin within the life of the church. From Part I we have seen that there is a need to account better for how malformation can occur through the practices of the church – and this is what we look at in Chapter 4. In so doing, we see that the ongoing formation of the church will involve ongoing conviction of the church in unexpected ways. In Chapter 5 we therefore look at what the kind of processes and practices are that can put the church into a position of openness to ongoing discovery of sin. Having seen that we should expect that part of the ongoing formation of the church to be this ongoing discovery of how the church is being malformed and is ethically malforming, this leads us to ask how we make the church open to recognizing these malformations. What are the practices through which the church can make itself open to what I name as 'troubling gifts' of the Spirit?

In the process of responding to these questions, I develop an ecclesiology: an account of the basic dynamics and structures that the church needs if it is to be formed in this way. Instead of looking at the sinfulness and brokenness of the church as an afterthought, or as a topic that comes as a caveat *after* the description of what the church should be, I place it right in the heart of my account.

In engaging with ecclesiology, my focus is on the ways the different needs, desires, gifts, and challenges of members are negotiated in the common life of the church (including the different ways this common life is envisaged), and the ways that power is exercised in these negotiations. In other words, my interest here is with the political character of church life – in its structures, practices and relationships, and the ways these are contested and negotiated.[1] Attending to these is crucial in accounting for the church both as a body whose life is politically formative, and as a political body whose formation is ongoing.[2]

Notes

1 As a result, I do not engage deeply with the field of liturgical studies, as this field of scholarship does not tend to be oriented by the same concern for the political in the analysis of ecclesial practices.

2 As Luke Bretherton has highlighted, there is a tendency for the political life of the church to be discussed in terms of realms of institutional authority, rather than through attention to the negotiation of power through relationships. *Christ and the Common Life: Political Theology and the Case for Democracy* (Grand Rapids, MI: Eerdmans, 2019).

3

The Form of Church Polity

This chapter begins the search for an account of the church in which its life is understood as resting upon ongoing formation. I identify three sets of twin callings that shape (or *should* shape) the negotiation of life in the ecclesial polity, and so help us to think through how this body should be formed: as an *oikos* (a household or family dwelling place) and a *polis* (a city or other abode of a political community); in confidence and humility; and through gathering and scattering. The first set of callings is drawn from scriptural descriptions of the early church, while the second and third set are more particular to theological descriptions of Anglican polity.[1] These dynamics give us a picture of a church in which we say both that the church is called into being by God, *and* that the church remains unfinished and incomplete. In fact, we affirm the church's incompleteness precisely because of its vocation.

It is worth noting at the outset that the difficulty in overlaying accounts and in finding resonant language to speak of Anglican polity is compounded by the diverse manifestations of polity on which these accounts reflect and which they seek to describe.[2] At the same time, we must also bear in mind that these accounts do not just replicate what is happening on the ground – rather, normative statements are being made about what the church *ought* to be. Furthermore, these accounts of polity are themselves in play, forming how polity is enacted. So, in saying, as I will below, that an account of the church as humble is important for conceptions of Anglican polity, this is not to say that the Church of England *is* a particularly humble church. Rather, I am saying that this is an understanding of the church that has often been articulated (by certain academics and clergy) and this sustained articulation has come to shape its members' self-understanding of what it is to be the Church of England. It has come to be part of how we understand ourselves, and so has come to form polity in certain ways – even if, at times, this is only through blinding members of the Church of England to their failure to realize these callings.

The church as both *oikos* and *polis*

We begin by briefly looking at the language used to describe the political character of the nascent church in the New Testament. In particular, it is worth noting how the language of *polis* is intrinsically tied to that of *oikos* when used to describe the community of the church, in such a way that both terms are reconceptualized. In the new creation of the church, these previously unreconciled 'linguistic worlds' are combined.[3] As Bernd Wannenwetsch stresses, this is a deliberate combining, not simply an incidental placement next to one another. These are not just alternative pictures of the church – rather, both are united and, in this uniting, fundamentally transformed: Christians become 'fellow citizens in the household of faith'.[4] This means we should expect the relationships between Christians who understand one another to be siblings in the faith to nonetheless have a political character and, at the same time, that the social and political life of the church will retain the character of kinship relations.

How, then, do these twin dimensions of ecclesial polity play a role in accounting for the church as a body that requires ongoing formation? Why is it important to pay attention to the political *and* familial character of relationships in the church as part of the church becoming what it is called to be?

We begin by exploring the use of the language of the civic *polis* to describe the church. Dorothea Bertschmann notes that, while the term *politeuma* has often been understood as evoking full belonging to a distant country, it also has 'more active, dynamic, and political connotations', signifying 'political actions' in the present.⁵ Rowan Williams adds to this sense of the active political life of the church through drawing out the implications of the language of *ekklesia* (a public assembly of the people), and the way this recasts the church as the civic assembly of a new social order. As the citizens' assembly the church is 'not a private group, not a transcendental worshipping community in heaven, but a civic fact': it is 'a place where members of a civic society exercise their civic dignity ... in a common life that seeks to conform itself to the purpose, in this case, of God'.⁶ Luke Bretherton also comments that, by drawing on classical usage, the New Testament authors convey that 'it is active and virtuous participation or communion (*koinÐnia*) in the people that is a condition for fulfilling what it means to be human'.⁷ This all combines to give us a sense of life in the ecclesial polity as irreducibly participatory, with the form of the *polis* depending upon each member's ongoing active negotiation of common life. Consequently, the church is always in a process of formation.

The *telos* of the ongoing formation of this political community can be seen in the way in which the church can be described as a household. To understand the church as a household expresses the idea that it is a community held together by, and whose distinctiveness lies in, each member's relationship with a single person: it is, as Williams puts it, 'the kinship group of Jesus of Nazareth'.⁸ So, the church's membership is constituted by sharing in the circulation of a life.⁹ In seeking to better understand the way the church is formed by political contestation and negotiation, we must not lose sight, then, of the impossibility of speaking of the church as if it has a free-standing life aside from the life of Christ – as if membership can be reduced to visible participation. Rather, as Williams puts it, 'Kinship is a bare fact about belonging together: commonality as the Church is not based on an agreement that has been brokered, but is about the simple fact that you and the person next to you both belong to someone independent of both of you.'¹⁰

Because this household is a kinship of belonging to Christ, this household is radically open for, as Williams writes, 'the "limits" set by Jesus are as wide as the human race itself'.[11] So, the familial character of the church should disrupt previous kinship ties. Recognizing how kinship with Christ cuts across all other 'natural' ties of belonging is important not only for the ordering of life 'inside' the church, but also for the relationship between the church and the world, which is, as Julie Gittoes notes, undermined by the imposition of 'false limits' (as we will explore further in the following chapter).[12] Just as it is important to note that the church being a *polis* does not mean it possesses and controls a territory, understanding the church as *oikos* is not to render it a closed and static community. As such, the church's character as *oikos* likewise entails that it is always undergoing a process of formation. This reconceptualization of both spheres in their uniting, then, gives us an outline of the form of ecclesial life to which we are called – and of the types of relationship involved in being formed by that calling.

Confidence and humility

In making the case that the church has a proper confidence, I have in view a confidence which is not about the correctness of the church's history, traditions and institutional structures, but about its vocation to be the convoked, convened body of those who have answered the call to inhabit the new creation (as Williams names it).[13] In this way, Williams relates the proper confidence of the church to its identity as a household: a household, or habitat, is where we know we abide. It is (or should be) where we know we are always welcome to return (including to be fed), and to which we know we can invite others (for example, to share our food). So, confidence in the church is fundamentally about 'where we know there is food, and how we keep the door open'.[14]

In offering a place to return to and invite others to, the church shows forth the life of Christ. In doing so, the church inevitably holds a particular place in the world. It is to be a place where people know that certain dimensions of their humanity belong most deeply, as these are brought more fully to life through being centred in the unique events surrounding the living, dying and rising again of Jesus of Nazareth.[15] Yet this place that is a distinctive form of life in the world, capable of inviting and resourcing, is not something to be possessed and defended. While the church's calling leads it to seek a place and a voice in society, this is not to be a specially protected place. Indeed, Williams ventures, the distinctive characteristic of the place of Christ is precisely that it does not seek to be a protected form of life.[16]

It follows, then, that the church's confidence in its calling should oblige it to think critically and to work hard at being faithful to this calling. In other words, intrinsic to the confidence of the church is humility. Two central aspects of this humility are the recognition of the provisionality of its institutional structures and the acknowledgement of its ongoing need for penitence.

In claiming a provisionality for the church, I am extending the provisionality involved in Christian ethical formation that we saw in the previous chapter to an ecclesiology that is also resistant to being finalized or completed. Julie Gittoes underlines this always incomplete nature of the church, arguing that 'As it refers all social meaning to the truth of God, the Church is much more conditional than is recognised by those who suppose it is somehow complete and perfect.' She continues: 'Whatever grasp it has of the truth of God, it still needs the deepest formation.'[17] By this way of thinking, the confidence of the church is rooted in its need for ongoing formation.

As we saw in Chapter 2, recognition of our always partial and imperfect grasp of what it means to love God and those around us leads to an awareness of the need for openness to being surprised – especially from sources which seem unlikely. This posture of openness to surprise in the life of the church should include the expectation of ongoing correction. Williams has remarked that he has often thought that there should be a fifth mark of the Church: 'I believe in one, holy, catholic, apostolic, *and repentant* Church', and Peter Sedgwick goes so far as to claim that, central to Anglican polity, is the understanding of the Church of England 'as a body that can and does err'.[18] Whether the Church of England is willing to enact this idea in practice, we should nonetheless note here that the church is constituted as a body by forgiveness and, as such, ought to be marked by ongoing patterns of penitence. These patterns of rupture and recognition, reversal and renewal, are essential to ecclesial polity.

It is these penitential patterns that allow the church to become a sacramental sign. As Williams suggests, the church 'becomes sacramental as a whole when it penitently redescribes itself in the light of the self-giving of God'. In its penitence:

> it surrenders the power of deciding what it is in human terms alone. It establishes its identity as 'mystery' by admitting that it is humanly ambiguous – capable of failure and sin – and so also a sign that encodes as well as revealing. Its sacramental character is in its confession that it participates in a humanity still in process of enlightenment and transfiguration, still absorbing the effect of the divine act in Christ. ... it is a sacramental sign in its admission of poverty in respect of God: it has nothing to do or say that can reveal God except the admission of dependence on God in Christ.[19]

So, we see here again that a choice between the church as confident or humble is a false one: for, 'our real confidence, our ultimate security, is our radical insecurity in the presence of Christ, who is alone our security'.[20] It is this ultimate confidence that should allow the church to examine itself and confront the profound ways its life goes wrong. It is this posture of humble confidence which should also orient the church's discernment of 'the engagement of the triune God with the world', which we now consider.[21]

Gathering and scattering

When we think about the church, we tend to have in mind its gathered life, all that happens when Christians gather in worship. However, it is important for us to locate the life of the church in both its gathering and scattering. Oliver O'Donovan notes that the life of the early church was located in the daily movement *between* the temple and the households of members of the early church,[22] and this sense that the life of the church does not only happen in the gathered practices of the church is important for our understanding of the church and Christian formation today. In this section, I make the claim that the gathered life of the church depends on the gathering up of its scattered life – and, in particular, of what is experienced of God in its scattered life. In contrast to the ecclesiology of the dominant account of Christian ethical formation, we need to work with a rhythm of Christian life as involving gathering and scattering, moving between church and world. In this rhythm, the church's gathering has to be shaped by the scattering as well as its scattering by its gathering.

I have already engaged with Hardy's account of the Spirit's 'intensive' and 'extensive' movement and suggested that Christian ethical formation lies in the relationship between these two. As Gittoes makes clear, this ongoing pattern of movement between the 'intensive' moments of the church's gathered life and 'extensive' moments of its scattered life is also necessary for the church to become what it is called to be: 'The Church cannot fulfil [its] call to embody God's purpose apart from worship; nor can the Church be itself if it neglects the call to participate in the world.'[23]

The church is often pictured as pre-eminently gathered at the Eucharist. As Gittoes, Green and Heard write, inspired by Hardy, the Eucharist 'establishes [the church's] calling as society – a Church formed by the intensity of worship and the extensity of mission, witnesses to a God of salvation, the limits of whose generous love we cannot identify.'[24] In the Eucharist, we find perhaps the fullest instance of transformative 'intensity', 'where the Church is called into being and where its calling is refreshed' – and where the fulfilment of the kingdom of God is anticipated.[25] Importantly, however, we should not lose sight of the way in which the Eucharist is the 'gathered interval' in the scattered life of the church – an interval where we are measured and reshaped.[26] As Williams notes, the life of the church is 'not exhausted at the Eucharist' even if it is where the church 'may be perfectly the Church'.[27] What I am claiming in this section is that the Eucharist (as with all the gathered life of the church) involves the gathering of the scattered life of the church and all the ways that God is encountered in its scattered life, and that the gathered life of the church must therefore be shaped by, and depend on, what is encountered in its scattered life.

One way in which we can understand the church's gathered life being dependent upon its scattered life can be seen in the way in which the gathered life of the church works to relate the scattered experiences of the church to what has been given in the Christian tradition – to make sense of these findings through the lens of the given. We can see this dynamic at work clearly in Tim Jenkins' description of corporate prayer. Jenkins observes that:

> The business of recollection in preparation involves a certain assembling of those persons, causes and projects for whom one has to pray, by each of the small number of people present. In this way, they represent a community. At the same time, each of the persons, causes and so forth is itself tied to larger groupings: the local church as part of the church in that place, and outward in the rings of the Communion of Saints; the institutions as part of wider economic, political and so forth systems, and so on. There is therefore a set, loosely ordered in a hierarchical fashion, of human groupings brought together and represented by the congregation.[28]

In the gathering of corporate prayer, Jenkins pictures everyday life as passing through a transformative 'sieve'.[29] He makes the case that the Anglican offices of morning and evening prayer are intervals that facilitate a confrontation of 'all one's passions, desires, burdens, tasks, responsibilities, relationships with Scripture: not therefore with reflections of the human will and understanding and point of view, but with God's'. In the time of reflection that is provided by the office, the participant is 'read by Scripture'.[30] This confrontation then 'issues in the intercessions, which deal not only with local projects and persons, but also with matters of Church and State, and current affairs ... So, there is a quite complex process of construing everyday life, consisting of recollection, representation, meditation and intercession, all conceived in terms of entering into the mind of God, or being read by the mind of God'.[31]

From this account of the offices, we get a sense of gathering in which the contingency of that which is gathered up is affirmed as significant, even as these scattered experiences are transformed through the process. In relating the 'findings' of life in the world to the 'givens' of Scripture, the desires of the participants are re-formed (as is expressed in the intercessions). However, I want to suggest that, in the gathering of scattered gifts, it is not only that which is gathered that is transformed. Instead, the life and practices of the church as the context in which this gathering occurs can be transformed in the receiving and celebrating of these scattered gifts – the found, as we have seen, can also illuminate the given. This suggests an account of the church in which its gathered and scattered moments have gifts to offer to one another in a dynamic of giving and receiving. As we shall go on to see, this will demand an openness of the church to the life of the world outside it, as this is where the scattered life of the church will encounter the work of the Spirit. This means that the church must be engaged in unending new encounters with the world.

The image of pilgrimage is one that can help us to picture what it means for the church to be engaged in such unending new encounters in the world, in which the church is undertaking a journey of 'careful walking'.[32] We discover things about God on our journey of interaction in the world that we could not discover otherwise. Gittoes helps us to see some of the implications of an ecclesiology based on a practice of careful walking, which 'both recognises and strives for the manifestation of the kingdom in the world through participation in the complexity of its social life'.[33] By this account, rather than being necessarily antithetical, 'the life of the Church and the fabric of modern society are bound relationally and with mutual influence'.[34] Gittoes further argues that, 'Too often our discussion of discipleship focuses on service in the gathered life of the Church, or perhaps on close relationships or specific projects'; yet, 'We do not cease to be the Church when we are offering legal advice or on duty as a classroom assistant. In those places we are caught up in the energetic of attraction – seeking the flourishing of human beings.'[35]

So, ongoing encounters with realities outside the church calls the church to see and understand itself anew. As we saw in Chapter 2, these journeys outward carry with them the expectation that what one encounters out in creation will drive one back into what one has already been given. For while there are, as Hardy highlights, distracting and corrosive forms of engagement with the world around us, there are also those forms of extensity through which Christians encounter out in the world new dimensions of the God that they meet in the church. We should expect both of these forms of extensity to be part of the day-to-day formation of the church.

This picture of the church being called to 'careful walking' through its gathering and scattering is in keeping with a sense of the church's proper confidence and humility. As Gittoes, Green and Heard argue, 'To think of our ecclesiology as "moving" develops the idea of the Church as a pilgrim people on the way. It enables us to speak of healing and provisionality; discipleship and humility.'[36] The church is called to be on the move both through the movement between its gathered and scattered life, and through the openness to change that comes through an attentiveness to God's ways with the world.

Conclusion

Having argued that the life of the church will always depend on ongoing fundamental formation, in this chapter I have indicated the directions of this ongoing formation. I have suggested that the church is (or should be be) a *polis* that is also an *oikos* (and vice versa); that it should be marked by humble confidence and confident humility; and that its life takes place in gathering and scattering. If the church is to be ethically and politically formative in a way that responds both to its own and the world's complexity, then it will be so through the ways in which it inhabits these twin callings.

I take my lead from Hardy in exploring the ways in which the church navigates this complexity. He argues that the church 'claims neither completeness nor infallibility, but – in the provenance of God – the capacity to bring free, moral agents together by their common consent in a fashion which mediates the character of God and God's saving grace in human society. The visible means by which it achieves these purposes are not so much theoretical as liturgical and practical-political.'[37] On this basis, Hardy argues for greater attention to be paid to the practices of liturgy and governance in the church. In Chapters 4 and 5 I will seek to do precisely this – to attend to the practices that take place when members of the church are gathered in worship and in the church's practical political life. Gittoes writes of the need to take both liturgy and the world more seriously, and I will go on to argue in the following chapters that this is a mutually reinforcing attention: that is, taking the world seriously will change the way one attends to and understands liturgical practice, and vice versa.

Notes

1 I am using 'polity' as a way of speaking of the corporate social and political identity of the church, and in a way that lends itself later on to discussion of other forms of polity. However, I readily acknowledge that this is not a neutral way of speaking of how the life of the church is enacted and regulated, and risks downplaying the kinship/*oikos* shape of ecclesial identity. Nonetheless, my use of the term 'polity' is intended to include both of these, and other, descriptions of the community of the church.

2 Anglican polity is, of course, deeply entwined with every dimension of the relationship between the church and the wider civic community in the formation of Christian political identity, and in Part III I will discuss how this plays out in civil society and in relation to the state. However, for now, my concern is with describing and analysing how conceptualizations of polity shape the church's corporate identity and relations of belonging, and with suggesting how this could and should work better. At times, when talking about polity that is specific to the Church of England, I use the term 'Anglican polity'. This is done for the sake of brevity, not to imply that Anglican polity is reducible to the polity of the Church of England, or that the polity of the Church of England is the same as the polity of all the churches of the Anglican Communion, separately and combined.

3 Bernd Wannenwetsch, *Political Worship* (Oxford: Oxford University Press, 2009), p. 143. In drawing on Wannenwetsch's work, I am mindful of his personal ethical history. This becomes particularly relevant in later discussions of power and status within the church.

4 Wannenwetsch, *Political Worship*, p. 144, referencing Ephesians 2.19. See also Luke Bretherton, *Christ and the Common Life: Political Theology and the Case for Democracy* (Grand Rapids, MI: Eerdmans, 2019), p. 409.

5 Dorothea H. Bertschmann, '"But *Our* Constitution Is in Heaven": New Testament Sketches on the People of God between Divine Law and Earthly Rulers' in Nick Aroney and Ian Leigh, eds, *Christianity and Constitutionalism* (Oxford: Oxford University Press 2022), pp. 58–74, 58.

6 Rowan Williams, 'Rethinking the Church: Lesslie Newbigin and the Household of God' (Lecture, 2017), https://newbiginhouse.org/rt-revd-dr-rowan-williams-lnsi-talk/, accessed 04.08.2022. William Cavanaugh likewise argues that the church as *ekklesia* is not an 'association ... gathered around particular interests', but 'an assembly of the whole', where 'those who are by definition excluded from being citizens of the *polis* and consigned to the *oikos* – women, children, slaves – are

given full membership through baptism'. William Cavanaugh, *Theopolitical Imagination: Christian Practices of Space and Time* (London: T&T Clark, 2001), pp. 117–18.

7 Bretherton, *Christ and the Common Life*, whereas, 'Noncommunion means one is subject to a realm of spiritual and moral chaos' (p. 406).

8 Williams, 'Rethinking the Church'.
9 Williams, 'Rethinking the Church'.
10 Williams, 'Rethinking the Church'.
11 Rowan Williams, 'Trinity and Revelation', *Modern Theology* 2:3 (1986): pp. 197–212, p. 137.
12 Julie Gittoes, 'Where Is the Kingdom?' in *Generous Ecclesiology: Church, World and the Kingdom of God*, eds Brutus Green, James Heard and Julie Gittoes (London: SCM Press, 2013), pp. 98–119, 98–9.
13 Williams, 'Rethinking the Church'.
14 Williams, 'Rethinking the Church'.
15 Williams, 'Rethinking the Church'.
16 Williams, 'Rethinking the Church'.
17 Gittoes, 'Where is the Kingdom?', p. 116. Gittoes goes on: 'A theology of careful walking celebrates the Church's calling as provisional. We live and worship and work between the now and the not yet. We are called to make real the divine transformation. We continue to seek mercy in our own relationships, we work out our disappointments and mistrust in the public sphere.'
18 Williams, 'Rethinking the Church'. Peter Sedgwick, 'On Anglican Polity' in *Essentials of Christian Community*, eds David Ford and Dennis Stamps (Edinburgh: T&T Clark, 1996), pp. 196–212, 196.
19 Rowan Williams, 'The Church as Sacrament', *International Journal for the Study of the Christian Church*, 10:1 (2010): 6–12 (p. 9).
20 Williams, 'Rethinking the Church'.
21 Daniel Hardy, *Finding the Church: The Dynamic Truth of Anglicanism* (London: SCM Press, 2001), pp. 158–9.
22 O'Donovan, *The Ways of Judgement: The Bampton Lectures, 2003* (Grand Rapids, MI: Eerdmans, 2005), pp. 268–9.
23 Gittoes, Green and Heard, 'Introduction', *Generous Ecclesiology*, p. 4.
24 Gittoes, Green and Heard, 'Introduction', pp. 12–13. Gittoes, Green and Heard go on: 'Working out the implications of the Eucharist in this way is vital for parishes. It demands the empowerment of the laity, rather than relying on a single parish priest. It blurs the boundary between Church and world in a way that generously accommodates the spiritually curious or those seeking the Church's blessing in the midst of birth and death and committed relationships' (p. 6).

25 Gittoes, Green and Heard, 'Introduction', p. 5.
26 Gittoes, 'Where is the Kingdom?', p. 118.
27 Rowan Williams, *Anglican Identities* (London: Darton, Longman and Todd, 2014), pp. 99–100. This is so because, as Mike Higton puts it, the church is 'the place where the source of [the world's] transformation in God is named, acknowledged and pursued', and therefore it is also 'the place where the particular human being Jesus of Nazareth is named, his unlimited significance explored, and his active and dangerous exceeding of the Church's present understanding acknowledged and awaited'. Mike Higton, 'Rowan Williams' in *The Oxford Handbook of Ecclesiology*, ed. Paul Avis (Oxford: Oxford University Press, 2018), p. 508.
28 Timothy Jenkins, 'An Ethical Account of Ritual: An Anthropological Description of the Anglican Daily Offices', *Studies in Christian Ethics* 15, no. 1 (2002), 1–10 (p. 8).
29 Jenkins, 'An Ethical Account of Ritual'.
30 Jenkins, 'An Ethical Account of Ritual'.
31 Jenkins, 'An Ethical Account of Ritual'.
32 Gittoes, 'Where is the Kingdom?', p. 109, referencing Daniel W. Hardy, *Wording a Radiance: Parting Conversations on God and the Church* (London: SCM Press, 2010).
33 Gittoes, 'Where is the Kingdom?', p. 114.
34 Gittoes, 'Where is the Kingdom?', p. 113. Gittoes goes on: 'To describe this in terms of abduction and *sociopoiesis* reveals that the movement and energy involved have their source in the divine life.'
35 Gittoes, 'Where is the Kingdom?', p. 114. This emphasis on the church and its members being always contingently 'placed' is particularly pertinent to certain ways of talking about the Church of England's polity – as we will return to in later chapters.
36 Gittoes, Green and Heard, 'Introduction', *Generous Ecclesiology*, pp. 12–13.
37 Gittoes, Green and Heard, 'Introduction', *Generous Ecclesiology*, pp. 12–13.

4

Formation through Conviction of Sin

We have seen that the church needs to be subject to ongoing formation in part because of the ongoing struggle within it with sin. This chapter is, therefore, an attempt to advance an ecclesiology in which it is impossible to account for the nature of the church without an account of the pervasive presence of sin within its life. This attempt is rooted in my sense that the failures of the church actually tell us something about what the church is called to be, and how it is to become what it is called to be. We need to pay close attention to the way sin shapes the life of the church if we are to learn to also attend to the way the Spirit is at work in forming the church. So, I am arguing, there is a particular Spirit-led ecclesiology that can only emerge when we attend to sin as an ongoing and pervasive presence in the life of the church, not just an occasional blip. I realize that an ecclesiology that begins with sin may not sound like a very promising contribution to a constructive theology of political formation. Yet I hope to show that, underneath it all, this account of the malformed church rests upon and makes possible an ultimately hopeful account of how God is at work in the world.

I get to this conclusion by working with the pneumatology outlined in Chapter 2, by which the work of the Spirit in grace can be understood as bringing us to new findings of truth. Bringing this understanding of the work of the Spirit into conversation with a deepening recognition of sin in the church leads us to a picture of the church in which openness to the Spirit means that we will always be coming to see anew our complicity in structural injustices. I will demonstrate this dynamic of circling into increasing awareness through offering a deepening account of the levels at which sin is operative in forming ecclesial polity.

Limited theological attention has been paid to the possibility of liturgical practices to malform, and this has to do with the tendency of those who commend the formative potential of these practices to speak of them in quite a high level of abstraction – to speak of how they are *supposed* to be enacted and what they are *meant* to do to participants, rather than what they in fact do. As Don Saliers argues: 'Liturgical theology suffers when it fails to acknowledge "hidden" power issues and the malformative histories of practice.' This inattention to malformation fosters a sense that sin is not really an endemic force shaping the church – rather, sin becomes a kind of add-on to the essential life of the church, an aberration from the church's usual enactment of its vocation. As Saliers continues, 'The point of normative questions, that is, what moral dispositions and ethical intention-action behaviours ought to be formed in us by liturgical celebrations of the teaching, death, and resurrection of Christ, can only be discerned when we gain an adequate description of what actually takes place.'[1] In this chapter, then, I will draw on more granular accounts of liturgical practices out of the conviction that when we start to look at how Christian practices are enacted and the kinds of formation that follow, we come to a profounder engagement with the fact of ethical and political malformation in the church. In this chapter and the next I will keep on returning to the Church of England as an extended case study, offering snapshots of current and historic practice. These examples are not, therefore, intended to be representative of the full gamut of Anglican practice and this approach is balanced by a concern for the church's provisionality, which leads me to seek to avoid being rigidly prescriptive about what should be done within the Church of England today.[2]

I set out three levels of ecclesial malformation: first, the church's mirroring and compounding of the oppressive systems of the world; second, the church's creation of its own matrices of power; and, third, the church's instigation of wider forms of social oppression and/or provision of a theological narrative by which to justify these. I explore these levels through the examples of white supremacy and class-based hierarchy. There are many other areas in which the church's complicity in oppression and injustice has come to light in recent years, but these two forms of hegemony are especially pertinent for a work that has a particular concern with the Church of England, given its position as the established church of a nation with an imperial past. This chapter is set against the backdrop of renewed global conversations about race and racism that were precipitated by the murders of George Floyd, Breonna Taylor and Rayshard Brooks in the US in the summer of 2020. These conversations have extended to the church and theological discourse and have demanded a grappling with the presence of racism – and white supremacy, in particular – in the church, including reflection on the kind of practices we need to resist racism in the church. There has also been, albeit in a less urgent fashion, a renewed concern with questions of class-based marginalization in the Church of England over the past several years. I think we can get a better handle on what kinds of changes are needed in relation to both of these (overlapping) matrices of oppression if we step back for a moment and ask how we might make sense of these revelations of sin as part of a wider ecclesiology.

Deepening recognitions of ecclesial sin

We begin by paying attention the way sin shapes the life of the church. I think we can identify three depths at which the sins of classism and white supremacy are operative in the church, and so also three levels of recognition of complicity in oppression.

The church as replicator of oppression

First, white and middle-class Christians (including theologians) are coming to recognize that the church is not a 'pure' bubble separate from the surrounding structurally racist and classist social context.[3] This means recognizing the ways in which the church often commits the sin of failing to resist and so replicating forms of marginalization and exclusion, present in the surrounding society, in its own life. We describe this as recognizing the centripetal malformation of the polity and its members.

In Mathew Guest's exploration of the social functions of worship within a community, and of the way in which worship shapes how we relate to one another (which he thinks it does to a significant extent), he argues that 'Worship events are often key contexts in which relations of power are negotiated, as they bring church communities together in a public space. At such events, norms of authority and hierarchy are often implicit in the very structure of devotional practice.'[4] These norms of authority and hierarchy shape how participation takes place in the church – both in devotional contexts and in decision-making (or 'practical-political') processes.[5] And, importantly, these ecclesial norms of authority and hierarchy can take on the shape of oppressive power relations in surrounding society.[6]

As part of this, recent years have seen an increased recognition by predominantly white churches and theological institutions in the UK of the need to name racism as a sin, in which white Christians are complicit at both an individual and a structural level.[7] This widening awareness of racism as a structural problem takes the form of a recognition that the way power is structured in the church replicates the prevailing racial hierarchy in our society – and that this protection and preservation of white supremacy is corporately sinful.[8] This matrix of oppression shapes how members participate in the life of the church, with Black and Brown members all too often being sidelined and excluded from certain roles and shoehorned into others – both in contexts of being gathered for worship and in decision-making (or 'practical–political') contexts.[9]

FORMATION THROUGH CONVICTION OF SIN

In turning to consider how Church of England practices reflect and compound the social hierarchies of class, we begin with Gustavo Gutiérrez's remark that 'the Church (and its worship) perpetuates the dominance of elite groups and reinforces social divisions if it fails to confront the injustices of the class system'.[10] In the Church of England (and the UK church more widely), an increased awareness of the way class divisions shape ecclesiology has come to the surface in recent years, particularly through discussions around mission. This has been spurred on by the findings of surveys such as one conducted by YouGov in 2015 which reported that 38 per cent of respondents who identified as regular churchgoers also identified as working-class, as against the findings of the 2015 British Social Attitudes Survey, in which 60 per cent of those surveyed defined themselves as working-class.[11] Meanwhile, the 2015 *Talking Jesus* survey estimated that 81 per cent of practising Christians had a university degree.[12] Probably the most visible response at a national level in the Church of England has been the establishment of the National Estates Churches Network. Philip North, the Bishop of Burnley and chair of the Network, has voiced this growing recognition among senior church leaders that, 'Our language, culture, resources, literature, and structures alienate many from poorer backgrounds.'[13]

This alienation can take place through many seemingly neutral features of gathered worship – as Bretherton observes, 'the form, timing, language, and aesthetic of worship are often determined in unacknowledged ways by class'. While there is scope for liturgy to constitute 'an alternative mode of production to that which dominates contemporary forms of social order', middle- and upper-class Christians need to be brought to recognize the real tendency of their churches to reproduce and reinforce the separation of the social classes, and so too to preserve and compound class conflict.[14] All too often this fractures the communion of the church: as Bretherton argues, 'with whom we do or don't gather on a Sunday' shapes 'what kind of peace we bear witness to in our worship'.[15]

Even well-meaning attempts to address the Church of

England's exclusion of the working class have at times ended up reinforcing the problem. Attempts to bridge this problem by middle-class Christians 'reaching out' to those who are working-class contains within it a sense that, as North puts it, 'the onus is on middle-class people to be more astute and clever in sharing the gospel with the poor, as if we "have it" and "they" don't'.[16] This runs alongside an expectation implicit in such 'reaching out' that working-class members of the church will 'convert' to its middle-class norms as part of their integration into membership of the church.[17]

Systems of power and oppression distinctive to the church

There is a growing recognition that, as Stephen Sykes puts it, the church – along with the rest of human existence – is located 'in a deeply ambiguous context, a world of overlapping and intersecting powers in which we are [all] enmeshed'.[18] Forms of marginalization out in the world have an impact on the life of the church and are not only not sufficiently resisted but are, in fact, often reproduced and reinforced within the life of the church. The kinds of roles and activities in which members of particular groups can participate is shaped by church polity replicating and compounding the way power structures and identity markers operate in the surrounding society.[19]

Further, white and middle-class Christians are being brought to recognize that racism and classism in the church is not just something that happens as the church mirrors wider societal structures and practices. Rather, racism and classism mutate into new and virulent strains in the church as they combine with other strains of exclusion and oppression distinctive to the church.[20] In this exchange there is not just replication taking place, but also a compounding of oppression through the church's iteration of it.

One obvious example of a matrix of power distinctive to the church (and other faith communities) is clericalism: the tendency for ecclesial hierarchies to be created which privilege the role of clergy in liturgical contexts and decision-making processes. Bretherton writes of clericalism as 'a characteristic deformation of all forms of ecclesial polity, which is for them to be shot through with the patriarchal form of the classical *oikos*'. This is, then, part of what can go wrong when the church's calling to be a household can be separated from, or emphasized over, the twin calling to be a *polis*, whose life depends on and is shaped by the active participation of each citizen. As Bretherton goes on to identify, this tendency can take the form of priests and bishops (or, indeed, popes) making 'absolute claims ... to be the *patresfamilias* of the people and thereby [to] exercise absolute and centralized sovereignty marked by the attempt to determine the life of the polity without reference to the consent of the people/commoners/laity'.[21]

We can get one snapshot of what this assertion of sovereignty can look like from Siobhán Garrigan, in her analysis of the liturgical rites of a Roman Catholic church in Ireland.[22] Garrigan's analysis of one particular enactment of the Eucharist yields painful insights into the way priestly liturgical practices can result in what she calls 'systematically distorted communication'.[23] This distortion can be seen most starkly in her description of the over-amplification of the presiding priest's microphone which, coupled with a failure to give sufficient time for congregational responses, meant that a single voice dominated proceedings. Moreover, consent to the validity of that voice, and the claims made by it, was never truly established through clearly audible congregational responses. Garrigan goes on to interpret the generally muted or absent linguistic congregational participation – for example, only approximately 10 per cent of the congregation joining in with the prayer of confession – as connoting a sense of alienation from, and even hesitancy regarding the validity of, the service.[24] This attention to just one aspect of a service – sound – illuminates how reifying the role of the priest can alienate the rest of the people of God from participating fully in the *leitourgia* – the ministry or work of the people.

Clericalism, classism and white supremacy

This emphasis on the status of the priest intersects with white supremacy and class-based hierarchies and creates an expectation that those who take on this (supposedly) most important role will be those who have the greatest social value – that is, those who are white and middle or upper class. So, when these forms of oppression are overlaid, the result is often a failure to foster a call to ordained ministry in those who are not white or middle class, and to fail to appoint Black and minority ethnic and working-class clergy in powerful decision-making roles in the church. In the Church of England, Azariah France-Williams and Augustine Tanner-Ihm are among those who have spoken of their experience of being marginalized as those who do not fit the mould of what clergy are expected to look like.[25]

This expanding discussion of the ways these dynamics of classism and clericalism are misshaping the life of the Church of England has led to particular attention to the selection and training of church leaders (with clergy currently overwhelmingly drawn from middle and upper classes).[26] North, for instance, has spoken of the current selection procedures for ordained ministry as having created an 'executive class', which 'hugely favour eloquence and education and confidence, over authenticity and evangelistic gifts and genuine vocation', and 'reward those who have done professional jobs and have led teams'. This overemphasis on certain types of lived experience has a clear class dimension, in that 'Candidates from less affluent backgrounds are far less likely to have had the kind of life chances that enable them to evidence, for example, leadership skills', against the white-collar metrics currently used for assessing these. North further highlights how 'expectations that candidates should have experience of the Church of England in a variety of contexts are often completely unrealistic for those who have not moved away from their home towns to go to university or for work'.[27]

North's remarks point to a growing realization of the forms taken by the sin of classism in the Church of England, and the ways this shapes the selection and training of ordained ministers. This is beginning to be true too in relation to white supremacy in the church – for example, as spotlighted through the BBC *Panorama* programme, 'Is the Church Racist?' in 2021, which was followed just a couple of days later by the report of The Archbishops' Anti-Racism Taskforce, *From Lament to Action*.[28] Their report offers (or, more accurately, often reiterates) recommendations and revisions to procedures surrounding the selection, training and promotion of ordained ministers. However, the focus of discussion around these responses continues to centre ordained ministry as the most important form of ministry. This way of seeking to address the malformations of classism and racism unfortunately largely ends up reinforcing clericalism by perpetuating the sense that if we can just ensure equal access to the priesthood, the ethical and political problems of the church will be solved.[29]

Overall, this tendency to centre the life of the church around the priest denies the necessity, and giftedness, of the voices of each member of the body. Each member is not, in practice, made essential to the church's political life. Part of the problem here is the assertion of the church's gathered life as more constitutive to its polity than its scattered life. Such a polity will necessarily fail to recognize the gifts and challenges brought by *all* of its members and will exclude many from full participation in liturgical and practical-political structures.[30]

The church as instigator and/or narrator of oppression

At these first two levels, already extant forms of oppression are actively reproduced, strengthened and passed on in new and virulent ways by the structures and practices of the church. At this point, however, we could still labour under the impression that we can fully address the church's power to be ethically and politically malformative simply by stopping doing certain things as the church and doing others more seriously.[31]

However, my claim is not just that the church mirrors the

prevalent power relations of a given social context, or that it is only its own members who are malformed by distortions of polity. We must also confront the fact that the church has also been, and continues to be, an *instigator and theological narrator* of oppression. We might describe this third level as centrifugal malformation, coming *from* the church *to* wider society. We can see this clearly at play in relation to white supremacy, in which the church's role as an instigator of racism has been highlighted by a growing number of theologians – including Willie Jennings' *The Christian Imagination*, in which he offers a powerfully persuasive account of how, in the colonial moment, the church created 'whiteness'.[32]

When it comes to the Church of England's role as an instigator and narrator of racial oppression, we have to consider the way Anglican theology and practice intertwined with the British imperial project. I will touch on how this played out in just two areas: the role of Anglican theologies of providence in enabling possession of colonies; and the role of baptismal practices in enabling slavery.

Colonial possession by providence

First, the belief in colonial possession by providence. A theology of providence strongly shaped attitudes to the British Empire. It was widely held that colonies were given to England by God for its possession – and the growing wealth that came through this possession was proof of God's favour.[33] The ascription of colonial expansion to divine providence was also reflected in missionary activity, as an arena in which Empire and Anglicanism intertwined particularly closely.

Rowan Strong's historical study of the Society for the Propagation of the Gospel (hereafter SPG), an Anglican missionary organization founded in 1701, helps to illustrate this relationship.[34] Strong argues that 'one of the most obvious ingredients of the Anglican perspective of the SPG, right from its inception, was to see the empire as the opening up of territories of missionary opportunity'.[35] It was God who had granted

FORMATION THROUGH CONVICTION OF SIN

overseas territories to the English, which had brought wealth to England, and the SPG Anglicans affirmed that the divinely providential purpose in so doing was principally to bring about the saving spread of the Christian gospel to non-Christians.[36] We can see this thinking in the report of Revd Zachary Pearce to SPG in 1729, in which Pearce argued that the expansion of Christianity within North America since the continent's 'discovery' was 'no obscure indication that the Designs of Providence and of this Society go together, and that in the Decrees of Heaven this new Way was ... for the Spiritual Advantage which its Inhabitants *may* make of it'.[37]

This sense of providence incorporated a belief in what we might call Anglican exceptionalism: for, not only was it English Christianity, but more specifically the Christianity of the Church of England that had been providentially chosen by God for this task.[38] This exceptionalism can be seen in a 1713 sermon by George Stanhope, Dean of Canterbury, which made the case that Anglicanism was territorially blessed by God in order that it might in turn spread abroad the best of all possible religions:

> This moves me to intreat, that you would seriously reflect, how deeply you are indebted to God as English Christians. Our happy island was probably by the preaching of St Paul, but undoubtedly in the time of the Apostles themselves, bless'd with the early knowledge of the Gospel; The first profession of the Truth countenanced and enjoined by Laws and publick Authority; The Birth of the first Christian Emperor; To Us, the shining of this glorious Light, never totally extinguished among us. And, when eclipsed with those Corruptions and Superstitions, which God, in his Judgement, permitted to overspread the face of this *Western* World; We are again among the first, and far the best, Reformed; ... But, Are such signal Favours remembered as they ought to be, unless our Gratitude express itself, in as uncommon Measures of Piety, and Charity, and Holy Labour, to plant this excellent religion, where it is not yet ... shall not We,

who have all the Advantages of truly Primitive Doctrine, lay the Good of Souls, and the Enlargement of the Lord's Territories to heart?[39]

Having themselves been (repeatedly) brought out of pagan darkness and religious corruption, so the logic went, Anglicans must now bring their faith to the indigenous people of the Americas.

This way of construing providence also directly shaped Anglican attitudes to slave-owning. In a sermon given in 1705, Bishop John Williams of Chichester affirmed the humanity of slaves, while also giving thanks for the opportunities that the captive and subordinate condition of the slaves provided for conversion by Anglican missionaries. He believed that, 'Here we may reasonably expect a greater Success in the Conversion of such, than of natives, because they are wholly in the Power of their Masters, and not in a Condition to refuse whatever they demand of them.'[40]

The SPG itself became a slave owner in 1710, following the bequest of the Barbadian slave estates of Christopher Codrington, a former governor, captain general and commander-in-chief and plantation owner. Codrington's will expresses his desire:

> ... to have the Plantations Continued Intire and three hundred negros at Least Kept always thereon, and A Convenient number of Professors and Scholars Maintained there, all of them to be under the vows of Chastity and obedience, who shall be oblidged to Studdy and Practice Physick and Chyrurgery as well as divinity, that by the apparent usefulness of the former to all mankind, they may Both indear themselves to the People and have better oppertunitys of doeing good To mens Souls whilst Takeing Care of their Bodys.[41]

The terms of the will make clear Codrington's belief that it was in service of Christendom that 300 Black slaves should be kept on the plantation: that their highest welfare consisted in being

Christianized, not in being freed, and that this Christianization was properly part of the missionary work of the seminary in Barbados that he provided for.[42]

Baptism and civil status

Undertaking this task of evangelization, however, required overcoming the opposition of slaveowners, who believed that their slaves' conversion could result in them becoming emancipated. This fear was based on a successful lawsuit brought in 1656 by the daughter of a slave in Virginia, who had successfully argued for her freedom on the grounds of her baptism.[43]

The response of the SPG and other Anglicans was to disconnect freedom in Christ from civil freedom, repudiating any idea that baptism meant liberty for slaves. The Bishop of Chichester stated in 1705 that he knew 'nothing as to Christianity that alters men's Rights for the sake of it; but such as they were, so they remain till alter'd by a humane law'. Likewise, in 1727 Bishop Gibson of London claimed that 'Christianity and the embracing of the Gospel, does not make the least alteration in Civil Property ... but in all these Respects, it continues persons just in the same State as it found them'. Gibson and others argued that the freedom Christianity brought to converts was purely a spiritual freedom without any connotations whatsoever for a person's 'outward Condition'. It was further argued that the spiritual welfare of slaves actually depended upon their remaining under the oversight of a wise and benign owner.[44]

In this way, the meaning of baptism shifted: spiritual freedom was firmly detached from the conditions of social and political life and the fundamental social hierarchy between slave and free was retained. Moreover, the social and economic hierarchy between the races was strengthened through theological undergirding. While one could be Black and a Christian, an altered doctrine of baptism allowed slave owners to feel no necessary discomfort about owning fellow Christians as property and so necessarily to exclude them from the conditions understood to be necessary for the flourishing of white Christians.

Looking at this period in the history of the SPG can help us to see the role played by Anglican theology and practice in providing support and legitimization for the British imperial project – shaping an understanding of territory as given by God to be possessed by one ethnic people group, under a single nation's sovereignty. The Church of England therefore shares in responsibility for the ethnonationalist visions that this history continues to feed.[45] The 'Christian-colonial' imagination can be discerned today in the Church of England in, for example, military language in hymns and liturgy: seen in the light of Anglican history, this language risks feeding a sense of dissonance between the glorious might of the past and the present 'diminished' state of the nation (and so also feeding a sense of dissatisfaction with the current state of affairs – that imperial status is something to be sought to regained).[46]

Here, the church does not just act as the carrier of an infection, but rather *generates* racism by deep practices of Christian thinking. I have spent a bit more time on this third level, because I think it helps us to see the difficulties of recognizing sin in the church when it is fed by dearly held doctrines and practices. As I have noted, at the first two levels we could still hold on to the hope that ecclesial malformation can be undone through ceasing certain practices and intentionally fostering others.[47] At this third level, however, the very practices that we think are positively formative are themselves malforming. So, we cannot just advocate throwing ourselves more fully into the processes and forms of life to which we are already committed. We cannot say, 'at least we know where to stand', for what the church needs to be is not something that is already known.

This is a very brief overview of (some of) the depths at which the sins of white supremacy and classism are operative in the church and the ways these feed into, and are fed by, deep-rooted theological commitments and ecclesial practices. The reason I have spent some time unearthing these deepening levels of sinfulness is not as an exercise in self-flagellation (with the effect of making racial and classist oppression really about the experience of white middle-class guilt) or as a call to despair of the church. The point is not to impute the colonial history of the Church of England with wholly sinister motives. I am not saying that the church, deep down, has only ever been a damaging institution and there is nothing good to be said of the ethical formation it offers. Rather, my aim is to establish that sin is present in the life of the church in ways that we will never be fully aware of. The SPG's slave owning perhaps displays this best: the very fact that it now seems so obvious to us that slavery is deeply antithetical to freedom in Christ in a way that was not self-evident to Codrington and the SPG tells us something about the doubt it is necessary to exercise about the ability of those with hegemonic privilege to recognize a structure as sinful. The church's tendency to under-recognize the presence of sin in its life is not, therefore, an accidental feature of ecclesial polity: rather, we will never be fully aware of how *unaware* we are of sin.

The troubling gifts of the Spirit

With this in mind, how can we make sense of these deepening recognitions of sin – or, more bluntly, this recognition that we never will fully recognize sin – as part of a wider ecclesiology?

The given and the found

Strange though it may sound, Quash's account of 'found things' as the gift of the Holy Spirit can help us here. As we saw in Chapter 2, in his work on the Spirit and history, Quash distinguishes between the found and the given.[48] The given is understood as that which we receive from the past, that which is part of our inheritance, and which helps us to make sense of the world we encounter. The found, on the other hand, is that which we encounter, which is genuinely new, and that we have to find some way of reckoning with.[49] Through finding, 'God is constantly inviting human beings to relate the given to the found'.⁵⁰

As we have seen, relating the given to the found has two dimensions. First, new findings offered by the Spirit are to be attended to in the light of the gifts already received by God: 'the givens of Christian faith will help to order and illuminate newly ordered experiences or challenges'. And second, found things 'reconfigure, unlock and amplify what is already held true by the Church'.⁵¹ Findings should, therefore, be understood in the light of the 'givens' of faith *and* should also reshape what we have received from the church – including the practices that order its life. Keeping the given and the found in relationship in this way, Quash argues, we receive 'ever more' of the riches of God's gifts.

Findings include our sinfulness

If we put this understanding of the work of the Spirit in leading us deeper into truth together with what we have seen of the dawning and deepening recognition of complicity in sin, then we can come to understand the work of the Spirit to include drawing us into new 'findings' of our sinfulness.

In her engagements with feminist and post-colonial theologies, Jenny Daggers writes of this recognition of sin as a 'troubling gift' of God, given to the church. She draws attention to the way it is given through the witness of those who have experienced oppression, naming those who testify in this way as 'graced persons'. For, she argues, 'If God's grace effects the dismantling of sinful hegemonies, this has implications for what it means to be receptive of grace; not only is grace received as a direct personal gift, but "second-hand" grace reaches out to us through the challenge of graced persons who, when we come close, make visible to us our hegemonic privileges.'⁵²

In this way, then, the gifts of the Spirit are taken to include the 'troubling gifts' of exposure to others' experiences of oppression – through which the Spirit works to convict us of

FORMATION THROUGH CONVICTION OF SIN

sin.[53] Challenges to the malformation of the church are in fact part of the 'gift' given through multiple members of the body. This is part of the way the whole body of Christ is formed by the Spirit, and the Spirit speaks through each member – including in the form of prophecy and conviction of sin (as we see in 1 Corinthians 12—14).

So, part of the work of the Spirit in grace can be understood as bringing us to new findings of truth, in the form of new convictions of sin. I should briefly note here that I am not claiming the *experience of oppression* is itself a gift of the Spirit. Rather, it is the *witness to oppression* that I am claiming can be understood as a way through which the Spirit works to bring conviction of sin.

The found reshaping the given

In understanding the found as a genuinely new thing given by God, we also draw attention to the danger, as we saw in Chapter 2, of constructing theology and practice around an understanding of the given in terms of that which has been already received as representing 'the finished, the fixed' – with the meaning of what has been given understood to have been already fully or sufficiently grasped.[54] Against this tendency to try to seal and fix understandings of the Christian faith, we return to the disruptive pneumatology offered by Hardy and Quash. The central dynamic that characterizes the work of the Spirit here is 'turbulence': an ever-deepening encounter with and participation in God – and in God's purposes for human life. A perpetual arrival and invitation to 'ever more' that can yet feel, in its strangeness, like divine departure.[55]

It follows that Christians should expect their encounters with the Spirit in the world to feel surprising and sometimes discomfiting. Such encounters are to reshape how the 'givens' of faith are understood, and so too re-form the worship of the gathered people of God. Quash's description of stumbling across 'findings' out in the world can also help us to see that our understanding of where the Spirit is at work should not stop at the doors of the church. I do not think it is coincidental that areas in which the sin of the church has been more fully recognized in recent years are those in which the church can be thought of as lagging behind 'secular' institutions. A refusal to receive challenge, correction and resourcing from the world is precisely part of the problem. If the Spirit forms the church through ongoing encounters – 'findings' – amid the messiness of life in the world, then a movement such as Black Lives Matter can be understood as a convicting 'finding' of the church's complicity in white supremacy (as we will return to in Chapters 7 and 8). Fostering this kind of attention to sin opens the church to sources of renewal.[56]

As we respond to the invitation to relate the found to the given, we come to see that the church has all too often calcified its 'givens' into distorted shapes which reflect the image of those who carry hegemonic privilege in ecclesial life. The 'troubling gifts' of testimonies of oppression, we can now say, are given to reshape unjust structures. This is how they mediate grace. In this light, testimonies which challenge and expose racist and classist oppression can be seen as part of the 'gift' given through multiple members of the body. On this side of eternity, we will never cease to need others to challenge and correct us, to call attention to our sin.

Conclusion

I have offered here an account of a deepening recognition of the depths at which sin is operative in the church. We have seen that we must expect the ongoing and disruptive presence of sin in the church. Indeed, we need to be aware that we will never be sufficiently aware of the presence of sin. If we begin with a model of the church as basically a source of good formation and then try to add sin onto this picture later, we end up blinding ourselves – and so also cutting ourselves off from the Spirit's work through each member and from the ongoing formation to which the Spirit is ever inviting the church. If we are to make ourselves open to receiving the convicting work of the Spirit it is, therefore, necessary for us to recognize that sin is a pervasive feature of the life of the church – the extent of which we will never fully recognize – and that, as a result, the church needs ongoing challenge and correction.

This is not a call to despair of the church. As Faith Spotted Eagle says of talking about the losses and traumas of First Nation tribes in North America, the point is not to 'impart a sense of guilt, it's to impart a freedom from denial'.[57] Recognizing the pervasiveness of sin is, therefore, a necessary part of an ecclesiology based on the Spirit working through each member. The concept of 'finding' has helped us here, as a dynamic of always being driven to see with new eyes what one has already received; it is the way the Spirit works to reveal truth. And the work of the Spirit in bringing us to new findings of truth involves being brought to new convictions of sin. These findings are to reshape the 'given': to trouble unjust structures and so mediate grace. This is part of a wider pattern of ongoing ecclesial formation by the Spirit: the life of the church lies in the unfolding of the 'ever more' that happens through relating the given to the found.[58] Offering and receiving these troubling gifts is therefore part of making room for the strange act of trust on which ongoing formation of the life of the church depends.

So, how does the church make itself receptive to the Spirit's 'troubling gifts'? What are the kinds of practices the church needs to cultivate? It is to these questions that we turn in the next chapter.

Notes

1 Don Saliers, 'Afterword: Liturgy and Ethics Revisited' in *Liturgy and the Moral Self: Humanity at Full Stretch Before God*, ed. E. Byron Andreson and Bruce T. Morrill (Collegeville, MN: Liturgical Press, 1998), pp. 209–224, 214–15.

2 I should note too, that while there is certainly overlap between the tendencies of the Church of England and those of other churches in the minority world, this focus is certainly not intended to suggest that the Church of England can stand in for every church.

3 For example, James K. A. Smith has discussed how the church has often been 'captured' by worldly liturgies, assimilating to the often prejudicial and oppressive practices of rival kingdoms. James K. A. Smith, *Awaiting the King*, Cultural Liturgies volume 3 (Grand Rapids, MI: Baker Academic, 2017), pp. 170–9, 181–6.

4 Mathew Guest, 'Sociological Strand – Worship and Action' in Helen Cameron et al., eds, *Studying Local Churches: Perspectives on the Local Church* (London: SCM Press, 2005), pp. 98–109, 100.

5 Luke Bretherton, for example, notes that while the form of polity to which the church is called is one in which differences of role entail 'no essential conflict of interests between ... roles', in actuality the 'distribution of roles may be unjustly determined by false criteria based on gender, ethnicity, or class'. Luke Bretherton, 'Sharing Peace: Class, Hierarchy, and Christian Social Order' in *The Blackwell Companion to Christian Ethics*, 2nd edn (Oxford: Blackwell, 2011), pp. 329–43, 337.

6 Analyses of race, class, gender and colonization have helped to display the matrices of power and oppression across which liturgical practices and social context feed into one another. See, for example, Siobhán Garrigan, *The Real Peace Process: Worship, Politics and the End of Sectarianism* (Abingdon: Routledge, 2014), p. 189.

7 This is part of a wider social trend, moving away from a reductive tendency to understand racism as being about what is in a person's heart – the kind of tendency that allows people to deny that they are racist because they do not consciously hate Black and Brown people. Instead, racism is increasingly understood as participation in social structures that privilege the welfare of white people, to the detriment of other races.

8 There are, of course, notable exceptions to this widening recognition: see, for example, the Statement on Social Justice and the Gospel, https://statementonsocialjustice.com/, accessed 04.08.2022.

9 We might think here of Black Anglican women being expected to enjoy providing food for church events (and to do so more lavishly than white women, for example), or there being an expectation that Black church members will be particularly musically gifted or will preach in a particularly rousing and charismatic style.

10 Gustavo Gutiérrez, *A Theology of Liberation*, trans. Caridad Inda and John Eagleson (London: SCM Press, 1988), pp. 145–8.

11 Quoted in Madeleine Davies, 'Class Divide at Church Must Be Addressed, New Study Suggests', *The Church Times*, 4 August

2017, https://www.churchtimes.co.uk/articles/2017/4-august/news/uk/class-divide-at-Church-must-be-addressed-suggests-new-study, accessed 04.08.2022; and in 'Church Attendance Dominated by Middle Class', *Premier Christian News*, 29 January 2015, https://premierchristian.news/en/news/article/church-attendance-dominated-by-middle-class, accessed 04.08.2022.

12 'Talking Jesus: 2015 Research', https://talkingjesus.org/2015-research/, accessed 04.08.2022.

13 Quoted in Davies, 'Class Divide at Church Must Be Addressed, New Study Suggests'.

14 Bretherton, 'Sharing Peace', p. 337.

15 Bretherton, 'Sharing Peace', p. 331. This segregation for gathered worship obviously also takes place along lines of race too.

16 Quoted in Davies, 'Class Divide at Church Must Be Addressed, New Study Suggests'.

17 As Martin Charlesworth and Natalie Williams argue in *A Church For the Poor: Transforming the Church to Reach the Poor in Britain Today* (Eastbourne: David C. Cook, 2017). The church's response to a recognition of the majority middle-class nature of its membership can also end up in an attempt to appeal to white working-class people as a way of trying to build up the church's power and relevance in a post-Brexit context. There is also the danger that focusing on inclusion of the working class in the church (and so also the use of the language of classism) becoming a distraction from the economic struggle to improve the working conditions of the working class.

18 Stephen Sykes, *Power and Christian Theology* (London: Continuum, 2006), p. 152.

19 In this exchange, there is in fact not just replication going on but also a compounding of oppression through the church's iteration of it, for replication in an ecclesial context often involves a kind of sacralization.

20 As Sykes notes, analyses of race, class, gender and colonization in recent decades have helped to display the matrices of power and oppression across which liturgical practices and social context feed into one another. Sykes, *Power and Christian Theology*, p. 152.

21 Luke Bretherton, *Christ and the Common Life: Political Theology and the Case for Democracy* (Grand Rapids, MI: Wm B. Eerdmans, 2019), p. 414.

22 Siobhán Garrigan, *Beyond Ritual: Sacramental Theology after Habermas* (Aldershot: Ashgate, 2004).

23 Garrigan, *Beyond Ritual*, pp. 135–7.

24 Garrigan, *Beyond Ritual*, pp. 125–33. Garrigan does also note moments in which assent is expressed – for example, pp. 133–4.

25 A. D. A France-Williams, *Ghost Ship: Institutional Racism and*

the *Church of England* (London: SCM Press, 2020); 'Black Durham trainee vicar denied job at "white" church', BBC *News*, 17 June 2020, https://www.bbc.co.uk/news/uk-england-tyne-53064929, accessed 04.08.2022.

26 It is obviously not class and race alone that need to be considered here – gender, sexuality and disability are all facets of identity that, whether consciously or not, also play into who is allowed to participate in ordained ministry.

27 Madeleine Davies, 'Selection Procedures "Favour Middle Class"', *The Church Times*, 27 April 2018, https://www.churchtimes.co.uk/articles/2018/27-april/news/uk/selection-procedures-favour-middle-class, accessed 04.08.2022.

28 *Panorama*, 'Is the Church Racist?' (2021), BBC, originally available at https://www.bbc.co.uk/iplayer/episode/m000vc34/panorama-is-the-church-racist, accessed 04.08.2022. The Archbishops' Anti-Racism Taskforce, *From Lament to Action* (2021), https://www.churchofengland.org/sites/default/files/2021-04/FromLamentToAction-report.pdf, accessed 04.08.2022. This report is not, of course, a bolt from the blue, but builds on many decades of work by the Council for Minority Ethnic Anglican Concerns, among other bodies.

29 Sykes also notes the need to recognize the power that is held by Anglican clergy, partly in order to acknowledge and protect against the temptations that accompany power. Sykes, *Power and Christian Theology*, p. 138; pp. 150–1. This propensity for the Anglican priest to be unaware of their power exists within a broader tendency of the Church of England, as an established church, to fail to recognize (and also to presume upon) the social power and status to which it has become accustomed over the centuries. This power and an insider status has often fostered an implicit and unreflective expectation that Anglicans will be included in the conversation. With the questioning of this insider status in recent decades, the failure of the Church of England to recognize its own continuing power not only plays into corrosive power relations, but can also feed a narrative of the erosion of the Church's power. Dan Hardy identifies Peter Sedgwick's 'On Anglican Polity' as displaying this kind of preoccupation with the Church of England's loss of power. David Ford and Dennis Stamps, *Essentials of Christian Community: For Daniel W. Hardy on His 65th Birthday* (Edinburgh: T&T Clark, 1996), p. 339. In this vein, it is plausible that understandable anxieties about the future reduction of stipendiary posts also plays into this assertion of the importance of ordained ministry in the life of the church.

30 While there are notable recent attempts to offer a richer account of lay vocation, this is still far from evident in the predominant modes

FORMATION THROUGH CONVICTION OF SIN

of Anglican thought and praxis. See for example: Archbishops' Council report, 'Setting God's People Free' (February 2017), https://www.churchofengland.org/sites/default/files/2017-11/GS%20Misc%20 2056%20Setting%20God%27s%20People%20Free.pdf, accessed 04.08.2022.

31 Smith, for example, tends towards this emphasis in *Awaiting the King*. Yet Smith's response, which is to highlight that the church's liturgies are too weakly embodied, is not quite sufficient. It is also important to recognize how the church can not only mirror the oppression of its societal context but also instigate it.

32 Jennings clearly sees the colonial logic of slavery as drawing its power from theology, rather than simply being a political agenda that was provided with a post hoc theological justification, contending that: 'It would be a mistake to see the church and its ecclesiastics as entering the secular workings of the state in the New World. No, the church entered with the conquistadors, establishing camp in and with the conquering camps of the Spanish. The reordering of Indian worlds was born of Christian formation itself.' Willie James Jennings, *The Christian Imagination: Theology and the Origins of Race* (New Haven, CT: Yale University Press, 2010), p. 81. Jennings records how, as part of this theological imagining, liturgical forms were extended to incorporate the new practices of slavery of the fifteenth century, focusing particularly on the account of Gomes Eanes de Zurara, chronicler for Prince Henry of Portugal. Jennings renarrates Zurara's account of the unloading of a slave ship on 8 August 1444, during which, 'Prince Henry, following his deepest Christian instincts, ordered a tithe to be given God through the Church. Two black boys were given, one to the principal Church in Lagos and another to the Franciscan convent on Cape Saint Vincent.' Jennings draws the conclusion that this ritual places the slave auction which followed 'inside Christian society, as part of the *communitas fidelium* ... [and so allowed the auction to] draw ritual power from Christianity itself while mangling the narratives it evokes'. *The Christian Imagination*, pp. 16, 22.

33 Rowan Strong, *Anglicanism and the British Empire, c.1700–1850* (Oxford: Oxford University Press, 2007), p. 60. By focusing on this example, I am not suggesting that this period in the SPG's history represents the entirety of colonial missionary movements, nor the entire relationship between Christian mission and empire.

34 SPG is today renamed as USPG (United Society Partners in the Gospel).

35 Strong, *Anglicanism and the British Empire*, p. 43.

36 Strong, *Anglicanism and the British Empire*, p. 60. In 1707, Revd William Beveridge was among the first of the SPG's preachers

to express the belief that there was a providential purpose behind England's territorial acquisition overseas, arguing: 'Now, that we have so many Factories settled in *Asia* and *Africa*, and so many Colonies in *America*, all among the Infidels and Heathens, whereby we may have the fairest Opportunity that ever can be offered, to open *their Eyes, and turn them from Darkness to Light, from the power of Satan to God.*' Strong notes that Beveridge 'backdated this providential acquisition of territory by the English to the geographical discoveries of the previous two centuries, by which the guidance of God had provided the English with the opportunity to preach the gospel to all the world'. Strong, *Anglicanism and the British Empire*, p. 60.

37 SPG, *Proceedings* (1729), pp. 26–7, referenced in Strong, p. 63. We should note that this sense of God's provision of access, through empire, to these as yet unevangelized peoples was not confined to eighteenth-century Anglican thought. Future archbishop William Temple wrote in 1926: in the British Empire 'we cannot doubt that we have found something fashioned in the providence of God for the fulfilment of his purpose'. 'Christianity and the Empire', *The Pilgrim*, 1926, 6: 447–57.

38 This theology of providence also included a belief in God's particular protection of England, 'which had been so recently demonstrated in the Glorious Revolution, and before in England's Protestant history.' Strong, *Anglicanism and the British Empire*, pp. 109–10.

39 Strong, *Anglicanism and the British Empire*, p. 62.

40 Strong, *Anglicanism and the British Empire*, p. 90.

41 Bodleian Library, 'Extracts from the Will of Christopher Codrington', http://emlo-portal.bodleian.ox.ac.uk/exhibition/uspg/items/show/33, accessed 04.08.2022. See also Carlton Turner, 'Christopher Codrington's Will: A Personal Reflection on Anglican Theological Education in the Caribbean', *Academia*, https://glos.academia.edu/CarltonTurner, accessed 04.08.2022.

42 Bishop William Fleetwood was among those who argued that this was the line of action the SPG ought to follow. Strong, *Anglicanism and the British Empire*, p. 91.

43 Following this, the Virginia Assembly ruled in 1667 that 'the conferring of baptism does not alter the condition of a person as to his bondage or freedom'. Strong, *Anglicanism and the British Empire*, pp. 92–3. There is a long lineage here, of course, with debates about baptism and civil freedoms going on in New Testament texts such as Philemon.

44 Strong, *Anglicanism and the British Empire*, p. 94. In 1754, Gibson still maintained it was a 'vulgar error, that Christianity makes them free', which had been so often 'obviated by the Plantation-laws, by the justest meanings upon the laws of the Realm, and the laws of the

Gospel'. Indeed, as Strong argues, 'the Society's push for the evangelism of slaves was not just about eliminating the negative objections to Christianization; it was also keen to accentuate the positive outcomes of conversion. Far from being a threat to a slave society, Christianity should prove a boon to it. John Williams in 1706 had proclaimed that conversion was an added security in a slave-owning society because Christianity facilitated control of slaves by increasing their respect and obedience for those set over them in the Lord. The Christianity that was proclaimed by the SPG was one holding no threat of slave freedom, or to the commerce in slaves, but rather a religion that facilitated the status quo by making slaves more economically obedient.' (Strong, *Anglicanism and the British Empire*, p. 111.)

This distortion of baptism chimes with recent American scholarship on the mangling of the meaning of sacramental practices in support of enslavement. Katie Walker Grimes speaks of the use of the sacrament of baptism within the Catholic Church to control African slaves in the Americas, as part of stripping them of their sense of belonging to their native country and binding them to their new white masters. Before they boarded ships to the Americas, captives kidnapped from across Africa were forcibly baptised at ports by Catholic priests, sprinkled with holy water while shackled, and then assigned a European name. As Walker Grimes writes, 'Performed *en masse*, baptism stripped Africans of their social identities as well as their individuality, helping to consolidate them into a single racial type.' In this way, baptism, perversely, 'ushered slaves not out of bondage and into freedom, but from freedom and into bondage. It brought slaves not out of death and into life, but from life and into death, both social and physical.' Katie Walker Grimes, *Christ Divided: Antiblackness as Corporate Vice* (Minneapolis, MN: Fortress, 2017), pp. 190–1, 195.

45 See, for example, Anthony G. Reddie, *Theologising Brexit: A Liberationist and Postcolonial Critique* (Abingdon, Oxon: Routledge, 2019) and Robert Beckford, *Documentary as Exorcism: Resisting the Bewitchment of Colonial Christianity* (London: Bloomsbury, 2014). This history also continues to shape the Church of England's relationship with the wider Anglican Communion. For example, the Bishop of Exeter and three business colleagues were paid nearly £13,000 to compensate them for the loss of 665 slaves in 1833. The organizations that received compensation, including the SPG, thus continue to benefit from the legacy of slavery. Mark Oliver, 'Archbishop urges church to consider slavery reparations', *The Guardian*, 26 March 2007, https://www.theguardian.com/world/2007/mar/26/religion.race, accessed 04.08.2022.

46 See, for example, Michael N. Jagessar and Stephen Burns,

'Hymns Old and New: Towards a Postcolonial Gaze' in *The Edge of God: New Liturgical Texts and Contexts in Conversation* (London: Epworth, 2008), pp. 50–66.

For Jennings, this baptism continues to be part of the way race distorts Christians' ability to imagine belonging in the church: '[Baptism into racial existence] has stolen from the Church its revolutionary power of belonging in Christ. People from vastly different regions, histories, and ways of life through the optic of race imagine themselves or imagine others as part of a white race, or a black race, or something in-between. The point here is not how they designate themselves. The point is the power to imagine connection, belonging. In almost all cases such racial imagining is always stronger, more enduring, and more decisive than ecclesial belonging. Moreover ... the Church, crippled by its colonialist-born disease, is utterly impotent in the face of ethnic strife, becoming in many cases simply the church of a particular people and not a place for the radical belonging of all people.' Jennings, 'Being Baptized: Race' in *The Blackwell Companion to Christian Ethics*, 2nd edn, p. 284. Whereas baptism should properly disrupt our allegiances and priorities and draw us closer to one another, this is also not always reflected in contemporary Anglican practice. Robert Beckford has described how the privatization of the rite of baptism occurred as whites moved the celebration away from Black presence in the parish church to domestic spaces, and there are ways in which this still happens today. See *Documentary as Exorcism*, pp. 84–6. For example, as Alison Walker argues, the practice of holding designated baptismal services after the Sunday morning service can show an unwillingness to disrupt the regular pattern of worship, and to acknowledge the disruption that joins members of the church to the newly baptized. Alison Mary Walker, 'A Place for Joining? The Theology of Willie James Jennings and the Anglican Parish' (PhD Thesis, University of Aberdeen, 2021), pp. 144–8. This resonates with Winner's discussion of *fin de siècle* American Christening parties, in which the biological family usurps the place of the ecclesial *oikos*. Lauren F. Winner, *The Dangers of Christian Practice: On Wayward Gifts, Characteristic Damage, and Sin* (New Haven, CT: Yale University Press, 2018), pp. 116–27.

Another example at this level of malformation concerns the sense of the sacred particular to the church, and the way language of black and white, darkness and purity is used in liturgical texts. There are many implications to be considered here, but to mention just one: Anthony Reddie has drawn attention to the white supremacist undertones in the insistence on a white cloth covering the eucharistic host in Methodist liturgical rubric. This sense of the sacred can also overlap with the intertwining of white supremacy and clericalism: the priest's proximity to the sacred has the potential to feed into UK minority ethnic/global majority heritage Anglicans being discouraged from pursuing ordained ministry.

47 James K. A. Smith, for example, tends towards this emphasis in *Awaiting the King: Reforming Public Theology* (Grand Rapids, MI: Baker Academic, 2017). Yet, Smith's response, which is to highlight that the church's liturgies are too weakly embodied, is not quite sufficient. It is also important to recognize how the church can, and often has, not only mirrored the oppression of its societal context, but also instigated it.

48 Ben Quash, *Found Theology: History, Imagination and the Holy Spirit* (London: Bloomsbury, 2013), p. xiv.

49 Quash, *Found Theology*, p. 17.

50 Quash, *Found Theology*, p. xiv.

51 Quash, *Found Theology*, p. xiv.

52 Jenny Daggers, 'Troubling Gifts of Second-Hand Grace: A Feminist and Postcolonial Reimagining', plenary paper given at the annual conference of the Society for the Study of Theology, April 2019, p. 2. While I am arguing that this circling into new findings of brokenness is one of the ways that, as Daggers puts it, 'God's grace effects the dismantling of sinful hegemonies', this is not to deny the agency of those 'graced persons' who bring challenge: 'If God's grace effects the dismantling of sinful hegemonies, this has implications for what it means to be receptive of grace; not only is grace received as a direct personal gift, but "second-hand" grace reaches out to us through the challenge of graced persons who, when we come close, make visible to us our hegemonic privileges.' Daggers, 'Troubling Gifts', p. 2. So, to speak of grace in this way is not to deny the agency of graced persons: non-contrastive relations between humans and the divine mean that second-hand grace is not just the effect of grace rubbing off on one another, so to speak, but is the ongoing work of the Holy Spirit through us (and so is our ongoing participation in grace).

53 Jenny Daggers, 'A Theological Anthropology for Human Flourishing: Postcolonial and Feminist Reflections for These Troubled Times', *Louvain Studies* 41, no. 2 (2018), 152–72. Therefore, we need to cultivate practices and disciplines in the church which open us up to receiving the Spirit in what Daggers terms 'graced persons'.

54 Rowan Williams, 'Trinity and Revelation' in *On Christian Theology* (Oxford: Blackwell, 2000), p. 132. Quash, *Found Theology*, p. 1.

55 Quash, *Found Theology*, p. xvii.

56 In fostering attentiveness to the presence of unjust social attitudes and practices in the church, social scientific accounts of ecclesial prac-

tices can be of particular value. As Sykes notes, 'Experience of the life of the Church suggests to me that there is a good deal for theology to learn about how the Church works as an organisation, including ways of penetrating the disguises which theology sometimes throws up when powers are being exercised.' Sykes, *Power and Christian Theology*, p. 83. Sykes goes on (partly in response to Milbank's denunciation of the parasitic nature of social scientific disciplines): 'To be on one's guard against the abuses of power, and at least to that extent to welcome the development of "suspicion", is by no means to capitulate to a quasi-theological scheme of "original violence".' He concludes that, 'To neglect the analytic opportunity of sociology is wasteful, though (as Milbank justly contends) one must resist the imperialistic suggestion that sociological observation provides a complete explanation of the phenomena it describes, replacing the need for theological interpretation.' Sykes, *Power and Christian Theology*, pp. 83–4.

57 Faith Spotted Eagle, interviewed as part of The WoLakota Project, a collaborative effort between Technology and Innovation in Education and the South Dakota Department of Education: Wo Lakota, 'Faith Spotted Eagle pt 3 Trauma & Resiliency', *Youtube*, 4 September 2013, https://www.youtube.com/watch?v=bqd_gYAhBII&t=13s, accessed 04.08.2022. See also Winner on the need to recognize the deformations of Christian practice as an exercise that is undertaken in hope. Winner, *The Dangers of Christian Practice*, pp. 16–17.

58 Quash, *Found Theology*, p. xiv.

5

Formation through Each Member

In the last chapter, I explored ways in which the church replicates, compounds and instigates forms of oppression and sinfulness. I suggested that conviction of the church's complicity in these is a 'troubling gift' of the Spirit, a gift that is received through attention to the experiences of those who are and have been oppressed. Indeed, I argued that the ongoing formation of the church rests on learning to receive these troubling gifts and that the challenges that others bring can be understood as part of what it is to circle into deeper participation in the life of God. In this chapter, I explore the kind of ecclesial postures and practices that keep the church open to receiving the gifts of the Spirit through each member of the body, in ways that continually re-form church polity.

In the first half of the chapter, I outline the kinds of ecclesial practices which foster the recognition and repentance of the ongoing, disruptive and structural presence of sin in the polity of the church, and which allow for the reception of gifts from unexpected people and places. Specifically, I explore how practices of confession, lament and reconciliation within the liturgy of the church can be the means of receiving troubling gifts. The second half of the chapter offers some pictures of what it might look like for the scattered lives of its members to be received as gifts in ways that reshape its gathered life. In particular, I will explore how the scattered lives of those at the margins can be received as gifts.

This posture of being attentively open to the gifts of the Spirit in every member in ways that continually shape the life of the church requires an insistence that we do not know yet what it will look like (and *cannot* in advance of the contribution of specific participants), because the future of the church is contingent on each member shaping and forming it in as yet unimagined ways. What follows is not, therefore, offered as paradigmatic vision of how any particular church should be, and is certainly not offered as a blueprint for Anglican polity.[1] Such a prescription would run against the contingency of these practices upon the particularity of members and social context, and also contrary to the extent to which they are always provisional and revisable. As I mentioned at the start of the previous chapter, the practices I highlight are not offered as exemplary examples of the self-critical stance this book advocates – I am not presenting them as already sufficiently embodying it. Rather, they are intended to illustrate the kinds of practices that can draw the church into this posture, but without an expectation that the posture can ever be fully achieved. For no practice should be thought of as complete and closed to further revision and alteration by the Spirit moving through the members of the body.

Recognizing and repairing ecclesial malformation

We have seen by now that we must expect the ongoing and disruptive presence of sin in the church. Indeed, we need to know that we will never be sufficiently aware of the extent of sin. Recognizing that sin is a pervasive feature of the life of the church and that we are in need of ongoing challenge and correction is necessary if we are to make ourselves open to receiving the convicting work of the Spirit. There is therefore an urgent need for arrangements that force the church, as the form of the corporate Christian life, to acknowledge pervasive patterns of sin – for practices that force ecclesial communities to continually confront and challenge the presence of sin, and for practices that could reveal blind spots and structure the life of the church away from abuses of power.[2] This entails an emphasis on the fundamental humility of the church, as we noted in Chapter 3: that we will keep on seeing how we are complicit in sin and that that will shape the corporate life of the church.

We have seen that Daggers' conception of 'troubling gifts' helps us to avoid the risk of talking about members' gifts as something separate from their whole being (with all their experiences of life) as itself the gift. So, the every-member pneumatological vision of the church we have been working with *also* matters because that kind of participation allows the prophetic voices of participants to challenge it in particular ways. We see that challenges to the malformation of the church are in fact part of the 'gift' given through multiple members of the body. This is part of the way the whole body of Christ is formed by the Spirit, for the Spirit speaks through all of them – including in the form of prophecy and conviction of sin (as we see in 1 Corinthians 12—14).

So, how does the church – and the Church of England in particular – 'make itself' receptive to the Spirit's 'troubling gifts'? What are the kinds of practices the church needs to cultivate? Fundamental here is the practice of receptivity towards perspectives that highlight the church's accretions of hegemonic privilege – particularly, in this instance, white and middle-class dominance.

Recognizing and repenting of sin

We begin by considering practices which foster ongoing recognition of the structures of sin in which the church is mired and which it upholds. I am beginning with practices that enable recognition of sin, as it is sin that gets in the way of receiving gifts from each member.[3]

To avoid giving the impression that 'pristine' practices can be attained, we open our discussion of penitent praxis by noting that the ability of church members to recognize sin can be masked through practices of confession. Garrigan, for example, demonstrates how practices of confession often end up compounding the 'cold peace' of sectarian Ireland. She identifies a tendency to confess sin at either a very abstract level ('sin as the basic human condition of having fallen away from God') or as something very personal ('the little ways we each individually fail in our relationships').[4] In this way, Garrigan argues, both Catholic and Protestant practices of confession display failures to recognize sin as something that is structural and corporate, and in which each person present is implicated. Instead, the practices of confession observed actually obscure sin, failing to equip Christians to recognize the systems and practices in which they are implicated and for which they share responsibility.[5]

When it comes to recognition of complicity in oppression, there are times when penitence should properly be corporate – at both a congregational and/or denomination level.[6] In the context of the Church of England, there are a number of levels at which it is pressing for the church to repent through corporate confession, particularly in relation to loyalty to prevailing power structures. This is particularly important when we consider the way that structures of accountability and justice have failed in relation to sexual abuse in the church. The use of episcopal powers to protect clergy who have perpetrated sexual abuse, along with failures to support and seek justice for victims, shows that the kind of practices of confession described above are sorely needed.[7] The role that the Church of England has played in providing theological justification for the British imperial project is another such area. For the Church of England, this will mean listening particularly hard to those elsewhere in the Anglican Communion whose accounts of their experiences of the legacy of imperialism are vital if those of us of colonizer heritage are to become conscious of 'our continuing benefits from historical colonial power relations, and of our greater propensity to repeat colonising behaviours'.[8]

While this public confession is necessary, malformation can nonetheless follow in the wake of repentance. The characteristic damages which follow repentance can include the attempt to regain control and to assume that one can know how to rectify the wrong one has caused. Winner remarks on the tendency of the penitent not to see 'that she will, in fact, repeat the act of which she repents'.[9] So, while forms of public corporate penitence have an important role to play in drawing the church into a fuller recognition and repentance of sin, repentance needs to be 'tinctured by [the penitent's] relative certainty that she will again be an agent of or again be complicit in the act of which she is repenting, even if she intends the opposite'. This kind of repentance 'carries within it the recognition of its own incompleteness and thereby opens out onto lament'.[10]

Lament

I want to suggest that it is lament that allows us to 'receive the inevitability of [the church's] gifts sometimes carrying damage in their train'.[11] However, despite its crucial role, lament, with all its angularity and tension, all too often tends to be muffled in Christian liturgy, as Nicholas Wolterstorff points out.[12] Léon van Ommen also notes the lack of space for lament and expression of suffering in formal ecclesial contexts, arguing that 'The language and deportment of Sunday liturgy largely silences the cries of human suffering' – and that this can create a dissonance, whereby participants who feel that the liturgy does not generally address suffering also feel that they cannot express their own particular suffering in the community.[13]

Deryn Guest finds a deep connection between what is expressed with such rawness in psalms of lament (characterizing them as psalms that 'declare dissatisfaction with the status quo and demand change') and experiences of LGBTQ+ Christians in the church.[14] She emphasizes the importance of spending time with 'the weeping, the shame, the alienation' expressed in psalms of lament, rather than skipping too quickly to the praise and thanksgiving with which the psalms close.[15] Moreover, she argues for the need for this to form part of liturgy, with its 'healing properties', rather than remaining a private practice: 'For liturgy to reach these congregants before they are driven away, it needs to be comfortable with lamenting before God, with complaint and protest, with images of the neglectful and abandoning God'.[16] This corporate attention to suffering can also require a 'self-silencing that makes it possible for others to speak'.[17]

Guest's account of lament helps us to see that when the suffering being lamented is one in which the church is complicit, space for lament in liturgy can bring the church to a new recognition of sin. Emmanuel Katongole and Anthony Reddie are among those who have written from a liberationist perspective about the importance of expressing experiences of racial and colonial injustice in liturgical lament.[18] There is a need, therefore, for the liturgy of the church to create space for the admission of the truth of each member's complicity in structures of oppression. Learning to receive in this way from one another in the church also involves learning to see more clearly how one is involved in holding others back from participative flourishing: nurturing the skill of seeing what stands in the way of a richer vision of corporate life.[19] Nurturing this skill will involve allowing the gathered life of the church to be disrupted by the witnessing to experiences of suffering oppression.

However, lament also 'expands to include the damages of the cosmos for which I am not remotely responsible – the sinfulness of the world, the brokenness that we are born into and inherit, the principalities and powers by which we are trapped'. Understood in this way, lament involves the recognition that we cannot wholly repair the world.[20] Lament can thus be a form of the shared attention we noted in Chapter 2: the whole congregation entering into the attention the one suffering is paying to their own pain. As we saw from Stuart Jesson, in the sharing of attention, consolation can be generated and the troubling situation can be seen in a subtly different light, refracted through the other's attention to it. Through shared attention to the suffering of oppression in a liturgical context, the situation, the sufferer and the relationship with the ecclesial community can be reframed in such a way that all of those involved in this attention are changed.[21] In this way, being able to express suffering in the gathered worship of the church can be part of the development of solidarity in the ecclesial community.

Reconciliation

While we should not be too quick to move from recognizing injustice to reconciliation (as we can fail to acknowledge the full extent of the injustice, and so too risk evading questions of what justice demands), and affirming that it is not for the oppressor to dictate when/if they are to be forgiven, we can nonetheless see that there is a base necessity of forgiveness for life together in the church: cycles of revenge and death can only be disrupted by forgiveness, so we truly do need and live by one another's forgiveness.[22] A community marked by passing on this gift is a community of reconciliation.

However, rituals of reconciliation can mask deep structural divisions, and so get in the way of just peace-making.[23] Garrigan describes how, in the context of the Irish congregations she observed, 'while human beings are ostensibly reconciled to God, any requirement for human beings to be reconciled to human beings is circumvented', highlighting in particular the frequent omission of peace-passing from services.[24] All of this plays into the way that 'peace' can be 'adopted, and embraced, but it is not wrought: the things ... that made up the "un-peace" remain'.[25] As Léon van Ommen puts it, 'While stories and rituals are potentially powerful agents of reconciliation, they may be in need of reconciliation themselves as well.'[26] So how should we structure rituals of reconciliation, such that deep divisions within congregations are genuinely disrupted and transformed? There are a few different ways of approaching this.

One way of imagining this process of transformative reconciliation is rooted in the idea that offering the sign of peace to one another enacts a new egalitarian social order. Bretherton offers this kind of account, arguing that reconciliation is a way of reasserting the fundamental equality of all members of the church. For Bretherton, the sign of peace normatively constitutes 'an alternative form of social order to those based on class and its largely economic determination'. However, 'The performance of this alternative social order is enacted within and through a local and catholic body that is simultaneously conflicted and cankered around issues of gender, ethnicity, sexuality, and class.'[27] The sign of peace is, therefore, precisely oriented towards addressing the perennial problem of 'The reproduction of inequitable and unjust social divisions in worship.' For Bretherton, this problem begins to be addressed through the sign of peace unveiling 'the reality of ongoing and unjust inequalities and thence the need to become enemies reconciled'. Having recognized this need, we then 'ritually enact and conform to one's primary identity as those who are brothers and sisters in Christ, and thereby relativize class or other earthly divisions'.[28] This does not mean the straightforward overlooking or abolition of social divisions in the church, but instead 'that in Christ we become enemies reconciled'.[29]

This is a vision of reconciliation in which a radical equality is re-inscribed through participating in the ritual, where belonging to the church depends on receiving one's identity as a forgiven sinner. Sykes writes of this equality which springs from recognition of our common sinful nature as that which ought to so bridge the 'The social gulf separating "rulers" from their subjects' that it is received as a compliment 'to the humility of those who rule if a subject feels able to address to them words of admonition'.[30] This equality of status is enacted through practices of confession, forgiveness and reconciliation – for, as Bretherton argues, 'we cannot know ourselves as sinful members of the world and its systems of idolatry and domination until we gather as the Church and therein encounter each other as members of God's covenantal order'.[31] Taken together, Sykes and Bretherton underline the way in which practices of confession and reconciliation depend on being brought together with other members of the church – that it is this gathering together that allows each to see their position in relation to systems of oppression. Wannenwetsch likewise underscores the importance of the bringing together of these *particular* people to practise reconciliation, arguing that 'Worship is political when the "peace" before communion is not merely practised as a non-committal sign of general solidarity', but is also taken seriously as an act of reconciliation between people 'who may have something against each other'.[32] Core to what is transformative about reconciliation by this account is the gathering of particular people with particular griefs against one another.

In this kind of account, practices of repentance and reconciliation are seen to enact transformation by bringing the life of the church and its members up against a standard of equality that is already known but which is fallen short of. These practices are important because of the way they cut through the kyriarchal structures in which we are all enmeshed and do so by recasting everyone as equal. The Spirit draws all these people together and also speaks and works through all of them, and so the church in its very participative nature overcomes the divisions of class, gender, race, elitism and so forth. This is an egalitarian vision that we can imagine already, although we know it is a vision that will involve learning and negotiation. In this process of learning and negotiation, repentance and reconciliation occurs where members of the body are challenged by the specific people that are there – and are therefore brought up against the specific hurts for which they are responsible.

An importantly different account of what should be taking place in the rituals of reconciliation is offered by Garrigan, who argues that 'a deep part of reconciliation is recognising that there was never a conciliation for us to return to. We must make something new.'[33] In a way that resonates with my insistence throughout this book that there are no pristine practices that can guarantee good formation, Garrigan's account offers a challenge to the very way members practise the peace – born of a recognition that it can bring with it and perpetuate various exclusions. This differs from the account outlined above, because it does not assume that there is prefigured form of the peace which members are trying to reach. Rather, every time the members of the church are brought up against the specific wrongs they have committed against these specific people, a new form of conciliation has to be wrought. Here again we see the importance of the Spirit working through each member. This new conciliation to be wrought is radically dependent upon those members who are present: it flows from and is contingent upon each member involved in making peace.

This acknowledgement that there is not and never has been a paradigmatic form of harmonious church polity for which we should be aiming has far-reaching implications. Conciliation, by this account, involves marginalized groups describing for themselves what their own flourishing looks like. It is part of a wider recognition that we do not have an example to look to, in any realized institutional form, of all the things the church should be, and thus nor do we even yet *know* the form of our common flourishing. We glimpse again here the Spirit working through each member to lead the church to a future that could not be anticipated in advance.

The life of the church, by this account, depends on reshaping ecclesial structures towards the ongoing recognition of (often surprising) sin, through the participation of each member. This humility leads into practices of reconciliation in which a new peace is wrought through each member. This expresses a deep confidence that the Spirit will be at work, drawing the church forward – based in a recognition that the life of the church depends on this ongoing formation by the Spirit.

Receiving gifts of the people

In the first half of this chapter I have argued that practices that enable us to be drawn deeper into recognition of sinfulness lie at the heart of the church's ability to be led by the Spirit to attend to the gifts of its members. Indeed, I have been arguing that being brought into recognition of sinfulness is itself a gift (what I have called a 'troubling' gift). In this second half, I am building on this by exploring what a church might look like that is committed to being shaped by the dynamics of gathering and scattering. I argue that there are gifts to be received from the margins of the church and from outside the church and that these gifts need to be forming the church in constitutive ways. This takes seriously the idea that the gathered life of the church should be fundamentally shaped by gathering up the scattered experiences of its members. There are some particular implications here for the role of the laity.

Hardy argues that clericalism is intertwined with a tendency not to be alert to 'the effects of God's work in non-religious situations', with the result being 'a centripetal notion of the Church'.[34] A commitment to receiving the distinctive contribution of each member will lead, therefore, to looking for the Spirit's work outside the usual centres of religious life. As noted in Chapter 2, a posture of anticipation and attention is necessary in seeking to notice and receive the work of the Spirit in this way.

Receiving gifts from the edges

Forming assemblies where 'God and the people speak and hear each other' requires attending to how voices can speak and be heard that have historically been silenced.[35] Attending to gifts from the margins of the congregation will mean 'hearing to speech' those have not tended to be heard or valued by the church, and freeing them to participate in ways that re-form the church.[36] This new participation will often rest on having been affirmed by communities outside the church.

We have seen that, in the context of the Church of England, there is a particular need to attend to the voices of those who have been excluded from leadership roles and decision-making processes on the basis of race and class. This means UK minority-ethnic and working-class Anglicans moulding the structures and institutions of the church, as well as the content of its message.[37] We can get one small snapshot of what this might look like from Al Barrett, who describes how, in his congregation in Hodge Hill, Birmingham, some of the African-Caribbean congregation members 'have found a space to speak out of their painful (and until recently unacknowledged) historic marginalization from active participation in worship and decision-making structures locally – and, for some at least, to begin to create and claim positions of leadership'.[38] In this way, attending to the 'troubling gift' of a church member's witness to their own experience of oppression can unsettle and re-form the way members participate in ecclesial polity.[39] A recognition can be brought of what the church has been missing out on (where the Spirit has not been expected to be at work), and so of the systems of exclusion at play in the church.

This is part of what Daggers identifies as the need for those with power and privilege 'to learn a new receptivity towards the views of human groups that are on the margins, rather than assume entitlement to define for others what their flourishing might entail'.[40] This helps us to see that through and beyond the conviction of sin, there is an invitation being extended here to abundant life. For there are genuinely new possibilities for what the church could be that can only be brought by those who are on the margins describing for themselves what their flourishing might entail.

A further example of what it might look like for the church to be reshaped through receiving the gifts of the Spirit from those at its margins can be found in Frances Young's account of the role of linguistically disabled people in the church. In particular, Young draws out what is given through the presence of her son, Arthur, in worship. Arthur, writes Young, enlarges understandings of what is going on in worship, allowing those around him a 'deep identification with that reality of not being able to put the sacred into words or grasp it'.[41] In this way, he offers to them an opportunity for more fully understanding what is being performed and pointed to through the liturgy: 'Arthur reminds us that we are caught up in something bigger than ourselves – certainly bigger than our words, and bigger than our understanding.'[42] So, he helps his fellow worshippers to remember that 'what we do matters less than being bathed, like him, in the music of voices and the smiles of presences, in a sense of abandonment to the sensations of sounds and sight, even bodily movement, as we receive grace through the mediation of liturgical actions and through one another'. Arthur's worship helps us to see that participation in the life of the church is always about the receiving of gifts: 'Arthur reminds us that often we may well receive grace without being fully aware of the fact and there is much more to receive than we can know.' This allows worship to become more fully what it is meant to be – as Young argues, 'The aim of worship is to generate the kind of participation that takes [worshippers] out of themselves so that they become more fully themselves in the larger whole', and Arthur's participation does just this.[43]

Young's account of Arthur's role in gathered worship also helps to show how the person themselves is the gift to the body – their very presence – not just the types of skills they are identifiably 'good at'. Although in attending to Arthur's presence, those present with him see that there are, of course, things he is good at – such as being lost in enjoyment. From this it follows that even those who are often assumed to be fully participating are in fact experiencing an attenuated participation if there are barriers to them receiving people with linguistic disabilities like Arthur's as a gift (which in turn create possible barriers to Arthur's participation in receiving gifts from God).[44]

Receiving scattering as gift

Seeking to receive each member as a gift will also include paying attention to the parts of life in the world that have not tended to be celebrated or seen as spiritually significant by the church. This requires attention to the activities members are involved in during the week, in their 'scattered' life.

We will delve into this further in Part III, but for now will briefly note some of the ways we might go about recognizing and receiving gifts from the world in liturgical contexts. In a way that echoes Wells, Barrett writes of the practice of gathering at the start of worship and 'hearing to speech the stories people bring of their encounters during the week, the glimpses they have caught of the kingdom of God, the places where they have been challenged, fed and changed'. He understands this practice as 'inviting the "centres" of the church to learn from and be transformed by ... engagement in the abundant, resource-full "edges"'.[45]

Offerings

This delight in the richness of the 'edges' of life can be powerfully expressed in the offertory, as a way of gathering up the scattered gifts of the congregation. As Quash writes, the offertory can help those gathered realize that:

> ... the whole world belongs to God, not as property, but as something intrinsically communicable and communicating: part of the fellowship of all created things which is made visible in the Eucharist. By the power of the Holy Spirit the whole world can 'belong' to Christians in the same communicable and communicating way, so long as they let their practices teach them that they are in common possession of themselves, of one another and of the rest of creation only because all these things are first and last in Christ.[46]

In this, there is a particular significance for the members of the laity who offer up, and are represented through, the gifts of the people. The practice of the offertory associated with the Parish Communion movement powerfully expresses this faith in the 'communicating' potential of all of life. A reportedly common practice was for the offertory procession to include objects produced during the work of the week, which were brought amid God's people and offered on the Lord's table. Stories are told, for example, of lumps of coal being brought up to the altar by miners in County Durham. This practice both underlines the giftedness of the work of the week and reconfigures it: in showing it to be a gift from God, we also see that it should be offered back in praise. In this way, the Parish Communion offertory also reflected local ties of belonging, receiving the gifts encountered in each member's own neighbourhood.[47] This helps us to see how membership of the gathering and scattering church is, or should be, formed through working with the contingent material of our lives, with the everyday work of the laity shaping and being illuminated by ecclesial liturgies.[48] This kind of practice can also shed new light on the forms of work that the church does not tend to celebrate and support as part of an individual's Christian formation, as well as in relation to the church's ongoing formation. There is scope, therefore, for these practices to lead into renewed reception of the troubling gifts of members' accounts of their experiences of marginalization in the church and in society.

Intercessions

Finally, I touch on intercessions as a way of paying attention to the scattered life of the church. There can be a particular space here for receiving the gift of new pictures of God.

We saw in Chapter 2 and again in Chapter 4 how our malformed desires can cause us to try and possess God, often by making God in our own image. While the Christian tradition has developed practices such as wordless prayer, for example, to help strip away the support structures for these false gods, such practices can allow us still to implicitly operate with these false images. Often, we do not even know we have these implicit images of God until we are confronted with a different image. Unexpected, overwhelming images of God are, of course, part of what has been encountered in the tradition of contemplative prayer, but there is also something valuable about receiving *other people's* descriptions of God.

In particular, there is an important role for public positive affirmations of God which explicitly do not reflect those who are dominant or hold most power in our society. This will mean, for example, drawing on feminist and womanist theology in liturgy – naming and addressing God as mother and Christa, among other names. It might also mean using alternative descriptions of the persons and relations of God – such as creator, redeemer and sustainer – to supplement the Trinitarian formula. These alternative ways of naming God will often express the social particularity of members' scattered lives, bringing these into the gathered worship of the church. Layering up positive pictures of God in this disruptive and destabilizing way can help to displace our cosy godlets – the ways we imagine God in our own image, or through the limited lens of our experience of relationships – with an expectation that this dislodging will reshape the practices of Christian tradition. For example, when we return to the 'given' of more traditional language about God, it will be with a renewed awareness of how it does not straightforwardly capture God.[49]

Receiving a new image of God rests on acknowledging that our current vision of God, and what it means therefore to be part of the people of God, is not exhaustive. As Higton puts it, 'No one individual, no one group of Christians already *possesses* Christ, and so does not need to receive him – and to go on receiving him – from others.'[50] As we have seen, Christ's solidarity means that while all belong to him, none of us possess him. There is an incompleteness to what any one voice can say of what it means to love Christ, therefore, and a need for it to be brought into robust conversation with others in order to be challenged and supplemented. We can glimpse here what Turner calls theology 'straining to speak' with as many voices as it can: speaking through as many people's voices as possible, and with anticipatory attention to the distinctive contribution of each.[51]

These forms of disruption can enable new forms of solidarity to be formed with those experiencing structural oppression – for example, when God is identified with a marginalized group. Yet, the eruption of new images of God in the gathered worship of the church may also reveal others' experiences to be very different from our own, and to even be caused by our own way of being in the world. Receiving new ways of naming God can thus expose how we are not in solidarity with one another: exposing the experiences we do not share, and the guilt we share for the suffering of others. In other words, what may be laid bare in this way are the limits of solidarity that currently exist within the congregation between the marginalized and those belonging to hegemonic groups: the forms of belonging that we are implicated in that make solidarity impossible.[52] Being interrupted by one another in this way may bring a new recognition of how one is involved in holding others back from participative flourishing. This develops what might be involved in seeking to exercise joint attention, as what is sought is an attention to the other's suffering in the way they are attending to it, while also bearing responsibility for the pain they are experiencing. We see here again the way receiving gifts from each member may lead into a deeper reckoning with what it is the church has been failing to receive, and so into a deeper spiralling of formation by the Spirit.

Conclusion

We have seen that attending to the gifts of each member is necessary for the ongoing ethical and political formation of the church. As Bretherton puts it, worship is 'something in which the flourishing of each is intertwined with the flourishing of all: if I don't contribute my charism to the proceedings, or am excluded from doing so, then both I and the body are impoverished'.[53] Ecclesial inclusiveness is thus not pursued for its own sake, but out of the conviction that the life of the church depends on the participation of every member.

Also, that an insistence on holding formative practices open to challenge, disruption and reform, is driven by the belief that the ongoing work of God in the life of the Christian is more richly disclosed when the practices are negotiated and worked out in contingent social settings. In this way, we glimpse the abundance of the divine life in which we participate. A strong affirmation of the ongoing need for disruption and challenge imparts, therefore, a different quality also to an account of how ethical formation takes place through participation in ecclesial practices: practices that are understood to be positively formative are so because of the way they are, in their structure, held open to being disturbed by God. There is joy as well as challenge in these surprising disruptions of the Spirit through every member – in the new things being wrought. This includes what Higton calls 'the ordinary delights of ecclesial life: the fun, the tenderness, the pleasure'.[54]

In this ecclesiology, therefore, the church is always unfinished, and what we are straining towards does not yet exist nor has it ever existed. We do not know what the form of church towards which we are being called will look like exactly, but we continue in trust that participating in this life, which has the Spirit of Christ as its centre, will lead us deeper into our calling.

Notes

1 Tim Jenkins insightfully describes Anglican polity as an ongoing social settlement, that we should not expect ever to be perfected. Timothy Jenkins, 'Anglicanism: The Only Answer to Modernity', ed. Duncan J. Dormor, Jack McDonald and Jeremy Caddick, *Anglicanism: The Answer to Modernity* (London: Continuum, 2005), pp. 186–205, 196.

2 In this, I am seeking practices with a recursivity, as Lauren Winner terms it. Lauren Winner, *The Dangers of Christian Practice: On Wayward Gifts, Characteristic Damage, and Sin* (New Haven, CT: Yale University Press, 2018), pp. 17, 48–9. The kind of recursivity I am seeking is what Alasdair MacIntyre envisages a tradition as having – being able to 'question itself and generate principal-referential arguments that expose its own internal incoherence'. A tradition is supposed to carry 'within itself the apparatus of judgement'. However, as Jennings demonstrates, 'the colonialist moment encases this Christian apparatus of judgement in a new worldly power'. Willie James Jennings, *The Christian Imagination: Theology and the Origins of Race* (New Haven, CT: Yale University Press, 2010), pp. 106–7. This recursivity is there-

fore sought without any expectation that good formation can be guaranteed by such practices – that such practices can be sin-proofed.

3 As Jennings argues, 'If Christianity is going to untangle itself from these mangled spaces, it must first see them for what they are: a revolt against creation.' Jennings, *The Christian Imagination*, p. 292.

4 Siobhan Garrigan, *The Real Peace Process: Worship, Politics and the End of Sectarianism* (London: Routledge, 2016), p. 47.

5 As she puts it: 'When, then, people turn their attention to the peace process, it is without having ever interrogated sectarianism as sinful... it is, therefore, not conceived as something to be confessed or forgiven.' Garrigan, *The Real Peace Process*, p. 48. Léon van Ommen also notes that 'people may have a perspective on their life that is concealing rather than revealing, so at the rite of confession they think there is nothing to say sorry for'. Léon van Ommen, *Suffering in Worship: Anglican Liturgy in Relation to Stories of Suffering People* (London: Routledge, 2017), p. 85.

6 As Jeremy Bergen, in particular, has explored in depth. See for example, *Ecclesial Repentance: The Churches Confront Their Sinful Pasts* (London: T&T Clark, 2011).

7 Alexis Jay et al., 'The Anglican Church. Case Studies: Chichester/Peter Ball Investigation Report' (Independent Inquiry into Child Sexual Abuse, May 2019), https://www.iicsa.org.uk/publications/investigation/anglican-chichester-peter-ball, accessed 04.08.2022.

8 Jenny Daggers, 'A Theological Anthropology for Human Flourishing: Postcolonial and Feminist Reflections for These Troubled Times', *Louvain Studies*, 41:2 (2018), 155, 157. Winner draws out that 'The choreography of repentance involves intent to prevent the sinful action's happening again and it involves attempted redress.' Winner, *Dangers of Christian Practice*, p. 156. Both must be present for repentance to be recognizable as such.

9 Winner, *Dangers of Christian Practice*, p. 157.

10 Winner, *Dangers of Christian Practice*, p. 157.

11 Winner, *Dangers of Christian Practice*, p. 158.

12 Wolterstorff, Nicholas, 'Liturgy, Justice, and Tears', *Worship* 62, no. 5 (1988), 386–403.

13 Léon van Ommen, *Suffering in Worship*, pp. vii, 60–1. Clergy can therefore play a significant role in either allowing space for the expression of suffering or compounding it through further alienation (pp. 66–7). Van Ommen highlights, for example, the significant role of clergy in creating spaces that allow for the expression of negative experiences. This requires overcoming disconnections between the story of the liturgy and the stories of the people gathered – a disconnection that van Ommen sees as particularly pronounced in the Anglican con-

text he studied (pp. 73–8). This particularly needs to be remembered in contexts where the priest is likely to have a different class and/or race than many of their congregation and will therefore have very different experiences of suffering.

14 Deryn Guest, 'Liturgy and Loss: A Lesbian Perspective on Using Psalms of Lament in Liturgy' in *The Edge of God: New Liturgical Texts and Contexts in Conversation*, Nicola Slee, Michael N. Jagessar and Stephen Burns, eds (London: Epworth, 2008), pp. 202–16, 213.

15 Guest, 'Liturgy and Loss', p. 207.

16 Guest, 'Liturgy and Loss', p. 213. Van Ommen also argues that 'The antidote to the exclusion of suffering, and therefore to exclusion of suffering people, is remembering suffering before God.' Van Ommen, *Suffering in Worship*, p. 86.

17 Eric Bugyis, 'Preface' in *Desire, Faith, and the Darkness of God: Essays in Honor of Denys Turner* (Notre Dame, IN: Notre Dame University Press, 2015), pp. xiii–xvi, xiii.

18 Anthony Reddie, 'Liturgy for Liberation' in *The Edge of God: New Liturgical Texts and Contexts in Conversation*, eds Stephen Burns, Nicola Slee and Michael N. Jagessar (London: Epworth, 2008), pp. 67–72.

19 Rowan Williams, *Lost Icons: Reflections on Cultural Bereavement* (Edinburgh: T&T Clark, 2000), p. 129.

20 Winner, *The Dangers of Christian Practice*, p. 158. In this way, it differs from repentance, which 'involves recognizing discrete responsibility, and it is limited to the things for which I am responsible (which might include long-past actions of institutions of which I am a part ...)'. Winner also highlights how lament can also become malformed: 'we self-congratulate about our lamenting, or we look past the edge of lament to what lament will accomplish, or we lapse into quietism' (p. 160).

21 This reframing does not, however, diminish responsibility for complicity in the pain. The form of consolation being generated here is the consolation of knowing one's pain to matter to God and, in a lesser way, to those present.

22 Williams, *Being Disciples*, p. 37.

23 Van Ommen, *Suffering in Worship*, p. 86.

24 Garrigan, *The Real Peace Process*, pp. 50, 86–91.

25 Garrigan, *The Real Peace Process*, p. 48.

26 Van Ommen, *Suffering in Worship*, p. 85. Van Ommen describes a 'spirituality of reconciliation' as weaving together divine and human stories, and sees reconciliation as called for 'whenever stories and rituals are not authentic, and often they are not' (p. 85).

27 Bretherton, 'Sharing Peace', p. 335.

28 Bretherton, 'Sharing Peace', p. 338. Bretherton continues: 'The sign of peace makes visible the otherwise hidden divisions ... while simultaneously gesturing towards their transcendence.'

29 Bretherton, 'Sharing Peace', p. 340.

30 Sykes, *Power and Christian Theology*, p. 143.

31 Bretherton, 'Sharing Peace', p. 338.

32 Bernd Wannenwetsch, *Political Worship* (Oxford Studies in Theological Ethics), trans. Margaret Kohl (New York: Oxford University Press, 2004), p. 76.

33 Garrigan, *The Real Peace Process*, p. 61.

34 Daniel Hardy, 'A Magnificent Complexity' in *Essentials of Christian Community*, eds David Ford and Dennis Stamps (Edinburgh: T&T Clark, 1996), p. 343.

35 Bretherton, *Christ and the Common Life*, p. 408.

36 'Hearing to speech' is a phrase used by Al Barrett and Ruth Harley to describe this kind of receptivity in *Being Interrupted: Reimagining the Church's Mission from the Outside, In* (London: SCM Press, 2020).

37 Philip North argues that 'This means equipping Churches in poorer areas to identify and draw out their own leaders and evangelists rather than ship them in from outside. It means taking massive risks with leadership styles that are counter to the Church's accepted culture. And it means having the courage to allow the mainstream Church to allow its structures, its institutions, and, above all, the content of its proclamation to be moulded by these working-class voices.' Quoted in Madeleine Davies, 'Class Divide at Church Must Be Addressed, New Study Suggests', *The Church Times*, 4 August 2017, https://www.Churchtimes.co.uk/articles/2017/4-august/news/uk/class-divide-at-Church-must-be-addressed-suggests-new-study, accessed 04.08.2022.

38 Al Barrett, 'Interrupting the Church's Flow: Hearing "Other" Voices on an Outer Urban Estate', *Practical Theology* 11, no. 1 (2018): 79–92 (p. 90).

39 My focus here is on troubling gifts for the formation of church polity – for a fuller account of an interrupted ecclesiology in the context of mission see Barrett and Harley, *Being Interrupted*.

40 Daggers, 'A Theological Anthropology for Human Flourishing', p. 159: 'This receptivity is sorely needed towards the insights of those who advocate a variety of gendered forms of human flourishing. A theological anthropology for these times needs to embody such receptivity.'

41 Frances Young, 'Songs without Words: Incorporating the Linguistically Marginalized' in Stephen Burns, Nicola Slee and Michael N. Jagessar, eds, *The Edge of God: New Liturgical Texts and Contexts in Conversation* (London: Epworth, 2008), pp. 91–103, 95. So, Arthur does not just make those around him aware of their own finitude and

vulnerability (as the gifts of those with disabilities are sometimes understood), but brings his own distinctive gifts that enrich the body.

42 Young, 'Songs without Words', p. 96.

43 Young, 'Songs without Words', p. 98. This may indeed be through disruption: 'Arthur's contribution is small and potentially disruptive. That may in itself be a gift to the rest of us, jerking us out of habit into new depth' (p.98).

44 Often, we think about participating in liturgy as being about what we do or contribute. Whereas in the Christian metaphysical tradition, participation is primarily about what we receive. So, full and active participation does not have to be primarily about people doing things but about ensuring that the barriers to people receiving are removed, so that we are able to receive one another as gifts – and to receive ourselves as gift. For some people, actively doing something can make it harder to receive and so harder to participate. This adds a further dimension to what it means to pay joint attention. I owe this perspective on participation to Pete Leith.

45 Barrett, 'Interrupting the Church's Flow: Hearing "Other" Voices on an Outer Urban Estate', p. 89.

46 Ben Quash, 'Offering: Treasuring the Creation' in *The Blackwell Companion to Christian Ethics*, eds Stanley Hauerwas and Samuel Wells (Oxford: Blackwell, 2004), p. 318.

47 Andrew Bishop, 'Eucharist Shaping: Church, Mission and Personhood in Gabriel Hebert's Liturgy and Society' (DTh thesis, King's College London, 2013), p.124, https://ethos.bl.uk/OrderDetails.do?uin=uk.bl.ethos.628479, accessed 04.08.2022. I should note that it is hard to substantiate the exact form of the practices of this movement. Nonetheless, it is a tradition that continues today: St Chad's College, one of the colleges of Durham University, has a service each year in the cathedral where each society brings up objects representing their activities. So, my husband, as a badminton club captain, used to bring up his badminton racket and lay it on the altar.

48 As Jenkins contends, 'paying attention to one's context is fundamental to the Anglican vocation. The practice is not a matter of bringing God into a place, but of discerning him in it. It is not just about gathering people together, but discovering their desires; what moves them: "For if God is already present in the world, in particular people and situations, one encounters truth rather than constructing it, and matters of great importance impinge upon one, rather than one's discovering them through any act of will or intention". Part of the Church's vocation is to go to unexpected places. The chaplain and parish priest, the pioneer and the bishop, are charged with this task – but so are the people of God as they are scattered within the world

before and after the sacramental interval of gathering for worship.'
Julie Gittoes, Brutus Green and James Heard, 'Introduction', *Generous Ecclesiology: Church, World and the Kingdom of God* (London: SCM Press, 2013), pp. 7–8, citing Timothy Jenkins, *An Experiment in Providence: How Faith Engages with the World* (London: SPCK, 2006), p. 7.

49 Additionally, taking the relationship between gathering and scattering seriously means when we hear, for example, of an abusive father in our 'scattered lives', it forces us to recalibrate what we mean when we name God as father. This is all part of a striving to say something that is true of God, rather than just trying to destabilize language.

50 Mike Higton, 'Rowan Williams' in *The Oxford Handbook of Ecclesiology*, ed. Paul Avis (Oxford: Oxford University Press, 2018) p. 513.

51 Denys Turner, *The Darkness of God: Negativity in Christian Mysticism* (Cambridge: Cambridge University Press, 1998), p. 20.

52 Nor does it even allow for a form of solidarity with another Christian where we are acting together as siblings in Christ against an injustice we can both perceive. Instead, for those who are part of hegemonic groups, we are acting against our own vested interest and on the basis of partial sight – both one's own partial vision, and also that of the oppressed (who have also been formed in the air of white supremacy and so forth).

53 Bretherton, 'Sharing Peace', p. 336. He goes on: 'there is an asymmetric dynamic of exchange – some give more than others – but it is one where all are dependent on each other'. While there is a hierarchy in the church, Bretherton argues that this must be based on 'covenant, vocation, and gifting', not on social background, wealth or ownership.

54 He is responding here to a danger he sees in Rowan Williams' account of ecclesial life, that it can become so 'focused on the risks, fragility and pain associated with growth in holiness' that it can lead Christians to mentally distance and hold themselves back – 'always mentally standing to one side, trying to see how one's actions might be read' – from the ordinary interactions in which are found the fun, tenderness and pleasure of church life. Mike Higton, 'The Ecclesial Body's Grace: Obedience and Faithfulness in Rowan Williams' Ecclesiology', *Ecclesiology* 7 (2011), 7–28, p. 16 n.21.

PART III

Formation Through Civic Life

We have already begun to think about the Christian and the church receiving formation from the world, as part of ongoing political formation. We now spend some time thinking about how that resourcing and discipling might happen through engagement with civic life, in particular, as a significant site of political engagement, and one with distinct difficulties and joys. So, what kind of engagement is that? That is, in what position does this put Christians and the church vis-à-vis the world? And what conversations and exchanges are they engaged in as they are formed?

We start, in Chapter 6, with a brief discussion of why it is that the idea that Christian and ecclesial formation can and should happen through political engagement in the world is not one that has received much attention in recent political theology. Filling out this lacuna entails exploring the potentially positive relationship between political participation and discipleship: teasing out how Christians are formed *as Christians*, and the church as *the church*, through belonging to and participating in political life beyond the life of the gathered church. Here, I identify resources from theology and political theory for extending these dominant accounts: making theological sense of a church that is continually engaged in civic life, and shaped by this constant participation, and making political sense of political life emerging through such engagement.

Chapter 7 continues this exploration, making it more concrete, by looking at forms of engagement with civil society and the state. I make the argument that Christians are formed (as disciples, as church, as citizens) by their engagement with civil society *and* the democratic state (which has tended to be overlooked in recent theology as an arena for participation), as well as by their ecclesial liturgies and Christian practices: they are formed in the interaction of all these. So, the Christian's political vocation includes participating in the civic community outside the gathered practices of the church, with the expectation that through this civic participation one will be formed *as a* Christian. Civic life is presented here not only as an arena for working out our Christian calling, but also as a site of the Spirit, where we can be formed as disciples.

6

Radical Democratic Discipleship

The limits of ecclesial political formation

As we noted in Chapter 1, some of the most visible work in Anglophone theological ethics and political theology in recent decades focuses on Christian formation that takes place in the church, especially in worship, with this formation flowing out into ethical action in the world. These ecclesial practices are understood to offer counter-formation to the social, cultural, economic and political practices of late modernity. A related but distinct trend has been a growing sense that Christian formation has political implications baked into it: Christian formation includes being formed to belong to the political community of the church, and so being a Christian is an inherently political identity.[1] This sense is bound up with a concern to demonstrate that the political nature of the church cannot be contained within the conceptual categories through which political life is generally understood. Rather, it is argued, the political character of the church (and of theology) disrupts these categories and a flourishing civic life requires that theology resume a position as host or guide of the political conversation.[2]

When it comes to Church of England thought, dominant strands in the past 30 years or so have displayed these trends.[3] A concern to retrieve the theological roots of political life particularly animates the work of John Milbank, whose project in *Theology and Social Theory* centres on identifying and repairing corruptions of the theological concepts underpinning social and political life.[4] Oliver O'Donovan also shares a concern with unearthing the Christian thought underpinning the liberal democratic polity, so that political life might return to a better course.[5]

This is not to say that the good of Christians being politically engaged outside the church has not been affirmed, whether through the institutions of civil society, or through the structures of the democratic state. Going further back in Anglican political thought, William Temple offers a particularly strong affirmation of the importance of each active citizen's contribution to the common good.[6] These forms of political engagement are understood to be part of one's vocation as a Christian, for which one has been formed by the church. However, here again, the political role of the church is one of *giving to* civic life (including through challenging the status quo of the liberal polity). It is the theological resources of the church – including the formation it gives to its members – that make possible democratic life and virtuous citizenship.[7] So, civic citizenship grows out of, but does not shape, discipleship.

This overlaps with a desire for the church to host and guide civic discourse. As we noted in Chapter 1, Ward preserves a privileged vantage point for the church regarding what is needed for social flourishing.[8] In a similar vein, Joshua Hordern argues for the necessity of the church interpreting and, at times, reorienting the desires of the citizenry.[9] Temple's account of the role of the church announcing social principles to public life also displays similar tendencies.[10] In these accounts, the church is deeply engaged in shaping civic life, but the firm ground upon which the church stands to address the world never shifts. All in all, the flow of political formation is from the church to civic life.

Related to this is a tendency to err on the side of a predetermined form of political life (in both the life of the church and in public life), rather than one that is contingent upon wide, diverse participation and common deliberation.[11] Polity and its members are formed through their form and roles flowing *from* what is common to the community *to* the individual members. This often takes on a top-down and static vision of political life, which can be seen in various forms in Anglican theology. So, while O'Donovan, for example, affirms that a people is 'a community constituted by participation in the common good', this community is nonetheless called forth in response to a conception of the common good that is received from the political authorities above (rather than through common deliberation).[12] Even Temple's more participative political theology is underpinned by what has been called a 'Royal Commission' approach to political life. This is a process – beginning with theological social principles, moving to middle axioms, and ending to specific policy recommendations – that works with a narrowly drawn understanding of those who have valuable knowledge of how society works.[13] In all, then, not much theological attention has tended to be given to the kinds of formation – of individuals and communities – that takes place through mass participation.

These discussions have generated deeply significant insights into the inherently political nature of the church, and the ways Christians can be formed politically through belonging to this community. However, an unintended consequence of these trends – sometimes understood under the umbrella term 'ecclesial turn' in ethics, and/or 'ecclesial political theology' – has been the suggestion that God is to be encountered only, or mainly, within established ecclesial and Christian practices.[14] When it comes to civic life, this includes a tendency to speak of Christians being formed *as Christians* exclusively in the church, from which Christians then undertake wider political action.

Moreover, the church has tended to be positioned as ultimately in charge of the ethical and political conversation. There is very little suggestion that the church's ethical and political vision should itself be formed through engagement with the world – or, more fundamentally, that the church and its members might need to receive from the world in order to become what they are called to be. The church's relationship with society has tended to be framed as one in which the church *gives* what is needed for flourishing and does not need to *receive* in return. Altogether, this limits how we understand

God's formative ways with the world, and so too where and how we expect to encounter God.

There are notable exceptions to this tendency in political theology, which I draw on in what follows.[15] Nonetheless, it is fair to say that the possibilities for ecclesial and Christian formation through civic engagement have not received much attention in recent political theology (nor in Anglican social and political thought, in particular).

The activity of the Spirit in the world: recapping the pneumatology of Hardy and Quash

We turn now to fill out an alternative picture of Christian formation, in which the church needs to learn to receive from society as well as give to it. In focus here is how the activity of the Spirit might encourage Christians to expect to be formed outside the church, and the kinds of practices this might require. To get to a richer picture of this engagement, I draw the account I have been developing of the characteristic pattern of the work of the Spirit in formation into dialogue with radical democratic thought.

We have engaged with Hardy's proposal that the work of the Spirit is 'a kind of turbulence which – as they accept their weakness in fear and trembling – pushes human beings ever more deeply into the deeds of God'.[16] As we have seen, Quash likewise speaks in dynamic terms of the Spirit as 'the God who takes us over new horizons', who, in God's complete otherness from us, we paradoxically experience as both departure and arrival.[17] Christians should, therefore, expect to encounter the work of the Spirit bubbling up in the world in surprising and sometimes discomfiting ways. These encounters will reshape our understanding of both God and ourselves. We have talked about this dynamic of stumbling across gifts of the Spirit in the world using Quash's term 'finding', through which God is inviting us to be attentive to the new offerings of the Spirit, in light of the things we have already received from God.[18]

Discipleship involves, then, making oneself open to encounters with the Spirit. But how do we do this? I proposed in Chapter 2 that a posture of anticipation and openness is necessary to notice and receive the work of the Spirit. As Quash argues, the Christian life is one 'in which love is always concretely and particularly taught and learnt – not in universal and abstract principles – and it requires a response to what is found in front of you, under your nose, here and now'.[19] This attentive responsiveness to the particularities of our lives as sites where God is at work, whether or not we recognize the divine presence, is central to Christian formation.[20] These sites will include those who are strangers to us – and those who make us uncomfortable through their strangeness.[21]

Paying attention in this way will lead us to rethink the familiar 'givens' of faith. Rethinking the familiar requires engaging with movements and ideas from beyond the church that help Christians to rethink their own faith community. We should expect that redeveloping faith in response to the demanding issues of life will lead into new convictions of sin. As we saw in Chapter 4, in the Church of England one instance of this discernment and conviction of sin is coming to recognize the role played by theological narratives and ecclesial practices in the Atlantic slave trade and in the ongoing outworking of that legacy. Moreover, the 'findings' through which we are led to renewed convictions of how far we have strayed from the faith we have been given will often lie outside the church.[22]

Having explored some of these dynamics in relation to ecclesial practices in the previous chapter, we now come to ask: what might these kinds of new and surprising encounters with the Spirit in the world look like in civic life? This is where we turn next, taking this pneumatology into political life and so in a new direction. It is, however, an area where a fruitful conversation between theology and political theory has already begun to emerge, particularly in the area of radical democratic thought.[23]

Radical democratic discipleship

Radical democracy is a broad movement, but my interest here is particularly in the direction that Sheldon Wolin and Romand Coles have taken radical democratic thought. Wolin, in particular, has been described as turning political theory away from 'scientific' models which focus on economics, psychology, sociology and the natural sciences, and returning it to a focus on political action.[24] So this strand of radical democracy is theoretical but closely informed by, and oriented towards, practice. This can be seen in Wolin's description of political theory as 'primarily a civic and secondarily an academic activity'.[25]

In making the argument that Christians can be formed *as Christians* through belonging to their wider political community, I am aware that contemporary political life does not, in many ways, look like fertile ground for Christian formation. I am not arguing that the kind of political life sought by Wolin and Coles is that in which we currently live, nor should it be taken to describe a past political age. There is, and always has been, a great deal of political life that is formative in ways that are antithetical to the practices I go on to describe here. Contemporary political discourse is often dominated by stereotyping and demonizing rather than attending to the particular; by increasing alienation from those who think differently, rather than by openness to surprising encounters with strangers; and by a tendency to be cocooned in bubbles of self-assured groupthink, rather than by a willingness to see one's judgements as provisional and in need of reshaping in ways that demand personal change. Both Wolin and Coles acknowledge this too.[26] Yet, as already noted, the work of both is rooted in concrete political praxis – with Coles' work in political organizing and activism particularly informing his academic writing.[27] Consequently, the hopefulness of the vision that is offered grows out of the civic possibilities they have experienced – 'the possibilities of collectivity, common action and shared purposes'.[28]

In brokering this conversation, we begin by identifying some central points of traction between the account I have been developing of formation by the Spirit and radical democracy, which help to frame civic life as a site of the Spirit's presence. This allows us to draw out how radical democratic thought illuminates where and how we might encounter the Spirit in civic life – the practices and postures through which Christians and the church might be discipled. In what follows, I will argue that we should expect the Spirit's work to form us through civic life to involve practices of tending to the local and quotidian, which lead to encounters with those who are strange to us. These encounters shape – including in disruptive ways – the institutions that make up public life, including the church.

Tending and openness to surprise

Wolin and Coles' work is centrally animated by a commitment to a more diffuse and local form of politics. This form of politics is the 'first best hope' because of the way ordinary people, not systems or institutions, are understood as the primary political actors.[29] So, local and contingent settings are where the heart of political life is expected to be unfolding. Accordingly, this democratic project invites us to attend to our own local ways of 'knowing and naming the political', to the politics of the everyday.[30] Indeed, Wolin's project can be characterized as a '"politics of tending" in which citizens attend to a political culture that cares for the habits, dispositions, practices, and forms of life worth sharing and sustaining'.[31] Coles too describes radical democracy as referring to 'political acts of tending to common goods and differences'.[32]

This attention to, and nurturing of, local and quotidian political culture is predictable and stable in certain ways: it will involve voting; serving on school governing bodies; taking part in community organizing and/or development through one's church, mosque, or other member institution; belonging to a union; and so forth. Yet, 'tending' is also profoundly destabilizing, leading to surprising discoveries which must be responded to in ways that shape the individual citizen and the institutions they belong to in ways that could not have been foreseen. Tending to the world involves learning to pay close attention to what is truly going on in the community around us: attending to the messiness and irregularity of community life, rather than just holding on to our prior narrative of how things must be. This attentiveness to differences, even within very localized communities, helps to illuminate what a willingness to rethink the familiar (noted above as part of attending to the Spirit) looks like in civic life.

Coles further argues that 'a discipleship of tending works ... between the preconceptions and the stories of a tradition, on the one hand, and the surprising substantial textures of the world we encounter, on the other'.[33] This strongly chimes with the categories of the given and the found, and the invitation to relate each to the other so as to be led more deeply into the life of God. My concern with the need to attend to the particularities of our present moments, and their often-surprising possibilities, resonates in strikingly similar ways to Wolin and Coles' proposal of a politics of tending.[34]

Attention to the possibilities of the present moment involves the recognition that we are creatures bound by time. Coles argues for the political virtue of patience, which he characterizes as an acceptance of 'the gift of time': 'time for vulnerable witnessing and discerning and participating in the anticipatable breaking forth'. Unpacking this theologically, we can see this attitude of 'wild patience' – expressing love for what is growing, through careful tending to that which needs time to unfurl – echoed in Christ's habitation of a provisional world.[35] This helps us to see why practices that school us in our finitude, teaching us to inhabit and grapple with the world in its difficulties and its joys, can be particular sites for encounter with the Spirit of Christ. Local and everyday politics are one such site.[36]

Encountering the stranger

We have seen that practising a politics of tending involves listening closely to those around us. Coles writes of listening to voices 'that may seem speechless, believing that they have something crucial to say to us'. This kind of listening not only takes time, but also requires the difficult acknowledgement that our life is not under our own control, and that our flourishing depends on others, who we must learn to trust.[37] So, while far from easy, this training in expectancy and receptivity is necessary for common flourishing: this requires responding to that which we are learning to see around us with readiness for growth and change. In this way, learning to pay attention leads into a further dimension of a politics of tending: openness to surprise by the stranger, whom one lives alongside.[38]

Coles argues that, for the Christian, attending to God's gifts involves reaching 'beyond the church body to scrutinise incarnations of God's "providence" in manifestations of foreignness'. This means that outsiders are needed: in order for the church to 'loop back' and discern ethical practice anew, it must 'loop through' engagements with those who believe and reason differently – whose behaviour and thinking is strange or foreign to us. This encompasses both the church learning where it has been unfaithful to Jesus and Scripture, and also learning 'previously unperceived meanings of faith'.[39] This process of looping *back* by looping *through* fits the pattern we have already seen of coming to new findings and relating these to what has been given, where the found can serve to illuminate and enrich what one already knows. Coles particularly draws out the crucial role played by the outsider to a tradition in bringing about new revelations of the meaning of the given. There will be surprise and delight in this disclosing of new riches.

However, we should also acknowledge that engaging with those who are unlike us will often be uncomfortable, and that there is real challenge involved in discerning and responding to God in an unredeemed world. The way in which this difficulty and discomfort can be part of Christian formation is particularly strikingly brought out by Aristotle Papanikolaou in his reading of political life as an ascetic practice. Papanikolaou describes the ascetical tradition as 'one of thinking on how to acquire the virtue of love, which is to grow in deeper communion with God'.[40] Therefore, the central question of the ascetic life is what practices we need to undertake to make ourselves more available to love both ourselves and the other as God does.[41] The ascetical effort to learn how to love, then, is always 'inescapably' in relation to the other, as well as in relation to God.[42] While there is no space in which this struggle does not take place, Papanikolaou sees the encounter with the stranger, in particular, as provoking a challenge and opportunity for the Christian to learn how to love. In this kind of encounter, we are likely to feel a threat to our identities and so to be tempted to respond with hatred and demonization. It is precisely through encounters with those with whom we are unfamiliar, and whose ways are strange to us, who have some part in shaping the life of our wider communities, that we are likely to be brought to recognize how much more we have to learn about how to love.[43] Political life thus provides an opportunity to be led by the Spirit to new findings of our own sinfulness – our tendency to demonize rather than patiently attend to strangers – and so too of our need for re-formation.[44]

We can see, therefore, that political life can be a site in which Christians more closely encounter those who are strange to them – and so be formed both through the gifts of insights received from strangers, and through the struggle to love those who are not like us. At its best, public life involves encountering unfamiliar civic and religious traditions in the process of seeking a good that is identified as common to all members. This process of seeking to discern a common good will, at times, involve the discomfort of coming to see more clearly how we are each involved in holding others back from flourishing. As Coles puts it, 'at the heart of democratic promise is the wisdom to sense the limits of our own vision, even as we vigorously pursue it'. This involves the recognition that there is an inherent risk of damage in our finite efforts, which should lead all citizens (including Christians) to 'infuse their judgement and action with a greater degree of suppleness, receptivity, and open-endedness'.[45]

The fugitive provisionality of institutions

Receptivity, suppleness and open-endedness are also to the fore in the way institutional life is construed by Coles and Wolin. From their thought, we can construct a dialectical relationship between institutions and political life, in which tending to the world will surprise disciples, including in ways through which they are transformed and the church reformed. In this way, radical democracy can help us to recognize the proper provisionality of any concrete form of the church, as well as the provisionality of all other political institutions and structures.

Wolin's sense of the necessary restlessness of political life is central to his thought. Following his diagnosis of the close and complex relationship between the state and capitalism, Wolin's democratic project seeks to decouple liberalism and democracy. He calls for a 'fugitive democracy': a vision of 'unmanaged' democracy, fleeing liberalism's control. The restlessness of Wolin's democracy derives also from the need to perpetually flee from the fallen powers that subjugate people, and so to avoid any political form which would restrict human beings' freedom as political animals.[46] Any political form that collects consent but rejects wide participation fails to allow for the full flourishing of humanity, and politics ought not, therefore, be tamed into a settled, overarching system.[47]

Seen from this perspective, democracy is not defined by a fixed state form, but is rather a political experience in which ordinary people are active political actors. So, more positively, this restlessness means that the political is located in a quality of relationality, not in any fixed institutional structure. Political acts, understood in this way, 'are always dynamically responsive to a world that always exceeds our terms and settled institutional forms'.[48] This sense of excess and ongoing unfolding of new forms of common life resonates with the 'ever more' that we can identify as the grain of creation, which the Spirit continues to generatively unfurl.

This 'ever more' means that institutional forms are never finalized, including the church. Coles illustrates this with reference to the way the civil rights movement changed the people, in particular the Christians, who participated in it. In his consideration of Ella Baker's community building and organizing, Coles sees the church's role in her early education and formation as significant in shaping her 'prophetic Christian discipleship', but not as wholly determinative. Rather, this formation continued on 'through practices of tending to the people, relationships, and goods of the diverse communities in which she found herself'.[49] As Coles writes:

> ... daily activity in and around co-ops functioned as a sort of liturgy: a regularized public practice in which the most crucial work done was the formation of a public in the sense of people capable of tending to each other and the possibility of common goods ... It was during this time that Baker came to understand transformation in terms of the effort to proliferate dialogical practices and spaces in which more hopeful selves and communities might be engendered, supported, and sustained.[50]

In practices of paying attention to shared goods, through sustained dialogue with diverse communities, 'new ideas and ways of being emerge in our engagement with the world', reshaping the things we thought we understood. As Molly Farneth argues, the participation of Christians in The Student Nonviolent Coordinating Committee (one of the major Civil Rights Movement organizations of the 1960s) changed the meaning of the liturgies of the church itself.[51]

Coles fills out this account of ongoing institutional formation in engagement with Rowan Williams' understanding of discipleship, by which, 'Jesus grants us a solid identity, yet refuses us the power to "seal" or finalise it, and obliges us to realise that this identity only exists in an endless responsiveness to new encounters with him in a world of unredeemed relationships'.[52] Williams relates this pattern of encountering and responding to that which is external to our person and so outside our control to the need for the church to be receptive to encountering deep otherness if there is to be what he calls 'civic vitality'.[53] As I have been arguing, it is also for the sake of the vitality of the church itself that a posture of receptivity must be practised.

Seen in this light, then, the church emerges again as a body whose life depends on ongoing formation and re-formation by the Spirit. This is part of the wider pattern of the work of the Spirit in civic life that we have identified, through which practices of tending lead us to encounter strangers with an openness to being reshaped by the gifts of the Spirit that they offer – including for reshaping the institution of the church. Examples of broad social movements which are – to a greater or lesser extent – reshaping the church today include feminism, the environmental movement and Black Lives Matter.[54]

While fruitful, there are also tensions in this conversation between radical democratic theory and theology. These tensions cluster around questions of ultimate teleological orientation. However, we need not see this lack of a shared ultimate orientation and grounding as ultimately paralysing for this conversation. Coles locates 'the strongest wellspring of ethical and political hope in how the tensions themselves might work ... towards greater receptive generosity, toward plurality'.[55] To put this in a more theological key, we could say that it is through bearing with these tensions that the Spirit draws us into hope.[56]

This means that a truly common life is found in living with these tensions, not in their resolution. With respect to the corrosive political trends of the moment, the kind of re-formation that is hoped for primarily relates to the form of the conversation about common life: the way in which individuals, institutions and communities participate in public conversation.

Conclusion

We have therefore identified a tendency in recent theological ethics and political theology to overlook the ways that discipleship could take place through civic participation. The dialogue explored here between pneumatology and radical democracy offers resources to address this lacuna. Learning to attend to the findings to which the Spirit leads us outside the church has emerged as an important part of Christian ethical and political formation. We have also seen the importance of learning to see the church and our Christian identity in the light of these findings, as we relate the given to the found and vice versa.

The work of Wolin and Coles has aided our discernment of the work of the Spirit in civic life, as we relate the findings of political theory and practice to the givens of the church and Christian theology. In particular, we are led to expect to encounter the Spirit's work in formative ways in civic life through practices of tending, which lead to encounters with strangers, encounters that shape, including in disruptive and challenging ways, the church.

With this vision of discipleship through participation in common life in mind, we now turn to consider more concretely what this looks like in relation to civil society and the state. How can participation in these structures form Christians and the church into becoming more fully what they are called to be?

Notes

1 Again, Hauerwas is particularly influential here in understanding the church to be a political body (an alternative *polis*), whose members therefore have a political identity that is distinctive from that of the surrounding culture. See, for example, Stanley Hauerwas and William Willimon, *Resident Aliens: Life in the Christian Colony* (Nashville, TN: Abingdon Press, 1989).

2 For Milbank, in particular, this rests on a critique of the formation fostered by the liberal democratic state. See, for example, John Milbank,

The Future of Love: Essays in Political Theology (Eugene, OR: Cascade Books, 2009), pp. 248, 259. While expressed in a different tenor, we can see a similar concern at play in Graham Ward's emphasis of the need to counter 'depoliticisation' theologically through a 'repoliticisation' of discipleship: 'If [Christians] cannot act politically, then we cannot counter the enemies either of dehumanisation or dematerialisation.' Graham Ward, *The Politics of Discipleship: Becoming Postmaterial Citizens* (Grand Rapids, MI: Baker Academic, 2009), p. 262.

3 For an extended critique of the American political theological scene along similar lines, see Aristotle Papanikolaou's *The Mystical as Political: Democracy and Non-Radical Orthodoxy* (Notre Dame, IN: University of Notre Dame Press, 2012).

4 John Milbank, *Theology and Social Theory: Beyond Secular Reason* (Oxford: Blackwell, 1990). See also *The Future of Love* (London: SCM Press, 2009), pp. 248, 259.

5 See for example, Oliver O'Donovan, *The Desire of the Nations: Rediscovering the Roots of Political Theology* (Cambridge: Cambridge University Press, 1996), p. 20. The central locus of this project is the relationship between freedom and authority. Having laid the foundations of his understanding of this relationship between freedom and authority in *Resurrection and Moral Order: An Outline for Evangelical Ethics* (Leicester: Apollos, 1994), it is expanded with respect to the church in *The Desire of the Nations*, and then to public authority in *The Ways of Judgement*.

6 See, for example, William Temple, *Christianity and Social Order* (Harmondsworth: Penguin, 1942), pp. 98-9.

7 For Milbank too, while hierarchies within liberalism are competitive and utilitarian and therefore destroy the common good, 'spiritual hierarchy' has its *telos* rooted in excellence rather than utility and is not a hierarchy of the privileged but is rather made up of a portion of society that has dedicated life to education and the pursuit of excellence; *The Future of Love*, pp. xii, xiv. See also 'Liberality versus Liberalism' in *The Future of Love*, pp. 242-63, and *Being Reconciled: Ontology and Pardon* (London: Routledge, 2003), pp. 132-3. True democracy requires, Milbank argues, 'sacramental ordination' and citizens formed in virtuous intermediate communities; *The Future of Love*, pp. xii-xiii. This spiritual hierarchy actually, Milbank argues, makes true democracy possible, 'for where there is no public recognition of the primacy of absolute good as grounded in something super-human, then democracy becomes impossible, for it is no longer supposed that one should even *search* for the intrinsically desirable' (p. 259). Democracy, as the rule of the many, can only function without manipulation of opinion if it is balanced by an 'aristocratic' element of the pursuit of

truth and virtue for their own sake on the part of some people whose role is legitimate even if they remain only 'the Few', although they should ideally be themselves the Many. Milbank advocates a central political role for these 'guiding virtuous elite' (who are, he implies, to be supplied by the church); p. 245.

We see this sense of civic life's need of the church also in the work of Ward, for whom 'only a theological or analogical account of bodies', and of the body of Christ most especially, 'safeguards the concreteness' of communities of genuine belonging, genuine participation. Such communities are those 'in which the desire for the good cultivates the virtues of theological citizenship'.

8 Graham Ward, *Cities of God* (Abingdon: Routledge, 2000), p. 70. See also Barrett, *Interrupting the Church's Flow*, p. 73, referencing *Cities of God*, pp. 70, 117–18. As we saw in Chapter 1, Ward's *The Politics of Discipleship* also stresses the need for Christian citizens to be re-formed through the political liturgy of the household of God. We might say that theologians emerge in Ward's model as the legislators for the imagination of the world. This is a different kind of power to setting up theologians as political legislators per se (as Milbank verges on), but it is nonetheless still a position of power.

9 Joshua Hordern, *Political Affections: Civic Participation and Moral Theology* (Oxford: Oxford University Press, 2013), pp. 13–14, 10. O'Donovan likewise highlights the church's position in the social order on which the political order depends: *The Ways of Judgement: The Bampton Lectures, 2003* (Grand Rapids, MI: Eerdmans, 2005), p. 156.

10 Temple, *Christianity and Social Order*. Temple's account of the world as offering only the expertise necessary for the *application of* the social principles also means that Christian formation ultimately remains located in the church. Participation in the world gives Christians knowledge which they then 'Christianly' apply to the world's problems, using the principles they have already received from the church. The principles themselves do not undergo any transformation as a result of their being collaboratively enacted. William Temple, *Religious Experience and Other Essays and Addresses* (London: James Clarke, 1958), p. 244.

11 One prominent example is John Milbank's sense of the role of the theologian in the church. Amid what Milbank characterizes as the uncertainty over where to 'locate true Christian practice', he argues that 'the theologian feels almost that the entire ecclesial task falls on his own head'. John Milbank, *The Word Made Strange: Theology, Language and Culture* (Oxford: Blackwell, 1997), p. 1.

12 The chief role of the Christian citizen is ultimately as a subject *or* as one exercising judgement (but not, either way, as one engaged in

robust, quotidian civic deliberation). Related to this is O'Donovan's account of ethical and civic formation taking place at the 'pre-political' level of social life, within associations such as the church and the family. Citizens chiefly influence their community, O'Donovan argues, 'by exercising the pre-political social virtue on which any good community is founded'. There is a separation of the architecture of political processes and political ethics, whereby when citizens do participate politically it is primarily with an acceptance of existing power structures. O'Donovan, *The Ways of Judgement*, p. 138.

13 Alan Suggate, 'The Temple Tradition', ed. Malcolm Brown, *Anglican Social Theology: Renewing the Vision Today* (London: Church House Publishing, 2014), pp. 28–73, 47. See also Wannenwetsch, *Political Worship*, pp. 98–100: If the primary political task of the church is to provide and announce social and moral principles, which individual believers are then to put into practice in society, then 'the collaboration of the many' ('The really political thing'), 'comes into play ... only at the application stage, with the implementation of the principles in a local situation', p. 99. So, there is no real scope in Temple's account of civic action for one to be formed *as a citizen* (to be made capable of political action) through deliberative processes of contestation and negotiation. Rather, Temple seems to understand political life as consisting in the application of self-contained expertise: the picture is of political decisions being made by those who sit on boards and committees: Suggate, 'The Temple Tradition', p. 57. Elaine Graham, Laurie Green, Christopher Baker and Malcolm Brown are among those seeking to extend and deepen the Temple tradition in the light of this challenge – to connect it more closely to the life of local communities and the contribution of these to public life. Suggate, 'The Temple Tradition', pp. 49–54.

14 Barrett proposes the category of 'ecclesial political theology' in *Interrupting the Church's Flow* (London: SCM Press, 2020), pp. 58–72.

15 Particularly the work of Charles Mathewes, Aristotle Papanikolaou, Luke Bretherton and Anna Rowlands.

16 Daniel Hardy, *Finding the Church: The Dynamic Truth of Anglicanism* (London: SCM Press, 2001), p. 233.

17 Ben Quash, *Found Theology: History, Imagination and the Holy Spirit* (London: Bloomsbury, 2013), p. xvii.

18 Quash, *Found Theology*, pp. xvi; xiv.

19 Quash, *Found Theology*, p. 24.

20 Hardy, *Finding the Church*, p. 282.

21 We began to explore in Chapter 5 what this receptivity to strangeness might yield in the life of the church. This is a theme discussed by Rowan Williams in his lecture on 'Encountering the Other'

and by Charles Mathewes in *A Theology of Public Life* (Cambridge: Cambridge University Press, 2007), pp. 71–2.

22 Faithful judgement involves, as Luke Bretherton argues, discernment to see 'where the Holy Spirit may be at work within and beyond the church in the life of the people'. Luke Bretherton, *Christ and the Common Life: Political Theology and the Case for Democracy* (Grand Rapids, MI: Wm B. Eerdmans, 2022), pp. 7, 29, 31. Andrew Shanks makes similar arguments about the disclosive role of social movements for the church in *Civil Society, Civil Religion* (Oxford: Blackwell, 1995). See also Ian McFarland's *In Adam's Fall: A Meditation on the Christian Doctrine of Original Sin* (Oxford: Wiley-Blackwell, 2010), pp. 210–12.

23 As we can see, for example, from Coles' engagements with Stanley Hauerwas, John Howard Yoder and Rowan Williams. In the other direction, Chad Pecknold and Luke Bretherton are among those who have found radical democracy fruitful for provoking theological reflection.

24 See, for example, Eugenia Siapera (ed.), *Radical Democracy and the Internet* (London: Palgrave Macmillan, 2007).

25 Sheldon Wolin, *The Presence of the Past: Essays on the State and the Constitution* (Baltimore, MD: Johns Hopkins University Press, 1989), p. 67.

26 See, for example, Romand Coles, *Beyond Gated Politics: Reflections for the Possibility of Democracy* (Minneapolis, MN: University of Minnesota Press, 2005), p. ix.

27 Referenced, for example, in *Beyond Gated Politics*, pp. viii, x, 213–37.

28 Wolin, *The Presence of the Past*, p. 35. As Wolin puts it, this work is centrally concerned with the possibilities and limits of popular democracy. Like Coles, he casts himself and his profession in activist terms, concerned with 'the being and well-being of collectives'.

29 Wolin, *The Presence of the Past*, p. 78.

30 Chad Pecknold, 'Migrations of the Host: Fugitive Democracy and the Corpus Mysticum', *Political Theology* 11:1 (2010): 77–101 (p. 97); Romand Coles and Stanley Hauerwas, 'Introduction' in Romand Coles and Stanley Hauerwas, *Christianity, Democracy, and the Radical Ordinary: Conversations Between a Radical Democrat and a Christian* (Eugene, OR: Wipf and Stock, 2008), p. 4.

31 Molly Farneth, 'A Politics of Tending and Transformation', *Studies in Christian Ethics* 32:1 (2019): 113–18 (p. 114). See Sheldon Wolin, 'Tending and Intending a Constitution' in *The Presence of the Past* and also Coles, *Beyond Gated Politics*.

32 Coles and Hauerwas, 'Introduction', p. 3 n.4.

33 Romand Coles, 'To Make this Tradition Articulate' in Romand

Coles and Stanley Hauerwas, *Christianity, Democracy, and the Radical Ordinary: Conversations Between a Radical Democrat and a Christian* (Eugene, OR: Wipf and Stock, 2008), p. 59.

34 See, for example, Quash, *Found Theology*, p. 282.

35 Coles, *Beyond Gated Politics*, pp. 130–1. It is worth mentioning here power relations and the limits of receptive vulnerability – especially as Coles' writing on trust, vulnerability and receptivity is significantly influenced by the theology of Yoder and Jean Vanier (albeit prior to their abuses becoming widely known). As these men demonstrate, trust can be abused and not all attention is generously oriented towards the other's unfolding and flourishing. So I am not proposing trusting receptivity as a stable virtue, irrespective of context; there is thinking to be done about how we discern what is to be received. Nonetheless, I think a posture of openness to receiving unexpected gifts from others can still be affirmed as central to encountering the Spirit.

36 In a similar vein, Mathewes and Williams describe the Christian's ascetic task of learning to inhabit temporality: Mathewes' *A Theology of Public Life* and Williams' 'Politics and the Soul: A Reading of City of God', *Milltown Studies* 19/20 (1987): 55–72 (pp. 68–9). While sharing this sense of *ascesis*, Mathewes' emphasis is on the way in which learning to endure rightly is part of discipleship – with political life understood as one sphere in which this kind of endurance can be practised. This picture of ascetic formation stays in quite a negative key: Mathewes does not explore the possibility of the Christian encountering unexpected gifts of the Spirit through participation in public life. Likewise, in his account of engagement with strangers, noted above, there is not much suggestion that in encountering those outside their tradition Christians might encounter new riches from God.

37 Coles and Hauerwas, 'Introduction', p. 5.

38 We should note, however, that some local communities contain very little economic, demographic or ideological diversity – whether these are relatively homogenous neighbourhoods or insular cyber-communities. For those living in such communities, 'tending to the local and quotidian' may not lead to many encounters with strangers. In these contexts, rethinking the familiar might mean being more attentive to differences even within local communities.

39 Coles, *Beyond Gated Politics*, pp. 120–1.

40 Aristotle Papanikolaou, *The Mystical as the Political* (Notre Dame, IN: Notre Dame University Press, 2012), p. 197.

41 Papanikolaou, *The Mystical as the Political*.

42 Papanikolaou, *The Mystical as the Political*.

43 Papanikolaou, *The Mystical as the Political*, pp. 198, 84.

44 It should be acknowledged, however, that there are highly local

and participatory movements that inspire people not to attentive and transformative encounters with strangers but to angry opposition to programmes like refugee resettlement.

45 Coles, *Beyond Gated Politics*, p. xii.

46 Chad Pecknold, *Christianity and Politics: A Brief Guide to the History* (Eugene, OR: Cascade, 2010), pp. 133–4; 137, referencing Sheldon Wolin, *Democracy Incorporated: Managed Democracy and the Specter of Inverted Totalitarianism* (Princeton, NJ: Princeton University Press, 2008).

47 Pecknold, 'Migrations of the Host', p. 97.

48 Coles and Hauerwas, 'Introduction', p. 3 n.4.

49 Coles and Hauerwas, 'Introduction', p. 115.

50 Coles, 'To Make this Tradition Articulate', p. 61.

51 Farneth, 'A Politics of Tending and Transformation', pp. 116–17.

52 Rowan Williams, *Resurrection: Interpreting the Easter Gospel* (Harrisburg, PA: Morehouse, 1982), p. 84, referenced in Coles, 'The Pregnant Reticence of Rowan Williams' in *Christianity, Democracy, and the Radical Ordinary*, p. 181.

53 Mike Higton, *Difficult Gospel: The Theology of Rowan Williams* (London: SCM Press, 2004), p. 56.

54 See, for example, the relationship between the involvement of Anglicans in the campaign for women's suffrage in the United Kingdom and the roots of the campaign for women's ordination in the Church of England.

55 Coles, *Beyond Gated Politics*, p. xiii.

56 Quash, *Found Theology*, p. 226.

7

Formation through Civic Participation

So far I have outlined a picture of ongoing formation through encounter with the Spirit in forms of common life. With this in mind, we now turn to consider more concretely what this looks like in relation to participating in civil society and the state. I pay particular attention to these spheres out of a conviction that in politics there are particular difficulties to learning to love and seek the good of those with whom we share civic space: as Papanikolaou puts it, 'In no other field is the temptation to demonize the neighbor more compelling or more seemingly justifiable than in the field of politics; in no other space than in the political, then, is the Christian more challenged to fulfil the commandment to love'.[1] It is not just that democratic life is a further area to consider in relation to Christian formation, but that it has a distinctively rich formational potential in part because of where it is most difficult. Yet, as I have suggested in the previous chapter, while there are particular difficulties to learning to love one's fellow civic members, there are also distinctively joyful surprises of the Spirit to be received in this 'desert'.

How can participation in these political structures be part of how we are formed as Christians? And how might this democratic participation also (positively) reshape the political life of the church? In this chapter, I argue that participating in democratic life – in civil society and in the state – can shape Christians in forms of solidarity they could not fully learn inside the church, but which are needed in both the wider political community and in the life of the church. Engagement in both civil society and the state can, therefore, reshape the always provisional polity of the church, teaching the ecclesial community about what a fuller belonging and participation of its members can and should look like.

Being formed through participation in civil society

We begin by looking at participation in civil society. We have seen from Papanikolaou that politics can be fruitfully understood as the process of strangers learning to relate to one another. Participation in civil society, in particular, involves encountering those one would not otherwise encounter and, more than this, must work together with strangers in pursuit of a common good. For the Christian, this means that the ascetic task in civil society is of learning to love 'the neighbour, who may also be the stranger'.[2]

The Christian tradition has a strong understanding of being called to be good neighbours and Christian engagement in public life – and civil society, in particular – has often been conceptualized in terms of 'neighbourliness'.[3] However, a 'neighbourly' mentality can become controlling and possessive: we see this in the assumption that the vicar of the parish ought by default to chair a local interfaith body, for example, or that their approval must be required for government-funding for interfaith initiatives (such as Near Neighbours). There is also a risk in theological discussions of neighbourliness of implying that Christians already know what it means to relate to someone as a neighbour, and that we need only more seriously exercise this already known vocation.

However, as our experience of distorted neighbourliness shows, we must go further than this and recognize that we know very incompletely what it means to relate to someone as a neighbour, and need to be taught over time in encounter with those around us what it means to exercise this kind of solidarity.[4] As Andrew Draper's reading of the Good Samaritan illuminates, learning to be a neighbour in civil society does not primarily involve being surprised by the extent of our ethical responsibility, but about learning to receive the gifts of our neighbours – in ways that have the potential to continue the church's ongoing ethical and political formation.[5]

Learning to receive from each member through community organizing and development

With this in mind, we turn to consider how involvement in asset-based community development and broad-based community organizing, in particular, can be positively formative of Christians in ways that in turn shape the church.

As we saw in the previous chapters, there is no practice that is a guarantor of good formation. However, we can assume postures that make us more open to receive from the Spirit, and I suggest here that the methodologies of community organizing and development can help us to assume such postures.

Asset Based Community Development (ABCD) is an approach to building community life which begins with seeking to recognize the gifts a community already has. It starts by constructing a map or inventory of the gifts a community has to offer. These gifts – or 'assets' – can fall into a number of different categories: the skills of the members of a community, for example, someone with a skill for cooking for lots of people; the enthusiasms or passions of members, a delight in amateur dramatics, for example; features of the particular place in which that community is situated: this could be an open space where people tend to congregate, or a popular pub; and the relationships that exist between members.

On the basis of these gifts, connections are then built between members of the local community. The identified assets of an individual, group or place are matched with other people or groups who have an interest in or need for those strengths. The key is beginning to use what is already in the community, and then working together to build on the identified assets of all involved. In this way, the direction and strategy for the development of the community is fundamentally shaped by the gifts of its members. Building community in this way will often involve removing obstacles that are blocking community members using their gifts together: for example, not having a space in which to rehearse a play.

From the start an asset-based approach spends time identifying the gifts of individuals, associations and institutions that form the community. When applying ABCD principles, communities are not thought of as complex masses of needs and problems, but rather diverse and capable webs of gifts and assets. Each community has a unique set of skills and capacities it can channel for community development. This makes it different to a deficit-based approach that focuses on identifying and meeting needs: a system that divides people into providers and recipients, and in which people are pressured to identify themselves by their needs in order for space to be made for them in the community.

While not an explicitly theological model of community building, ABCD's core values and methods resonate deeply with an ecclesial commitment to receiving the gifts of each member. In places of apparently overwhelming need and a critical lack of resources, we are encouraged to discover what turns out, in the end, to be more than enough. Christians are well-practised at rehearsing what Walter Brueggemann calls this 'liturgy of abundance', a song of praise for God's creative generosity, in relation to the earth's flora and fauna (at harvest time, for example).[6] In ABCD, this kind of attention to abundance is exercised in a new way, in relation to one's neighbourhood. Barrett puts it this way:

> ABCD begins with a shift in vision: from seeing the world around us, our neighbours and our neighbourhoods, for what they are lacking, to seeing them for what they have ... ABCD invites us to practise the same liturgy of abundance in our own neighbourhoods: to open our eyes to the ways God has blessed *this* place and *this* people with goodness, vitality

and fruitfulness. It may be in the place itself, in the stories that it contains or in the webs of relationships that knit it together. It certainly begins by recognising the wealth of gifts of the people who inhabit it and the marks of the 'image of God' that define each and every one of them.[7]

So, there is an expectation that through encounters in this community one will also encounter the work of the Spirit, just as Christians expect to encounter the Spirit at work within the gathered practices of the church. We can see, then, how community organizing might help us to be attentive to opportunities for the church to receive from those outside its membership – to see the people we encounter in our neighbourhoods as bringing gifts to be received, not primarily problems to be solved.[8]

Implications for inclusion in the church

How might practising this attention to gifts through ABCD also change the 'inner' life of the church – and of the Church of England in particular? The logic of this approach means that those who are currently excluded and marginalized from church life can be reimagined and attended to not as a problem to be solved but a gift to the church to be all the more fully received. This reimagining has a particular potential to help the church to encourage lay participation and leadership in ministry. As we have seen, the Church of England's imagination can often be marked by a tendency towards clericalism. Too often, the priest is seen as the paradigmatic Christian figure in the life and ministry of the church.

In contrast to this, an asset-based approach offers what we might call an 'Encanto' model of thinking about congregational life, and of ministerial leadership in that setting. The 2021 Walt Disney film *Encanto* is a story about the magical Madrigal family. Through a miraculous gift in a time of peril, they have come as a family to each possess a magical gift of their own. Sister Luisa is super strong; uncle Bruno can prophesy the future; aunt Pepa can control the weather; mother Julieta's cooking contains healing properties; nephew Antonio can talk to animals, and so forth. All except for Mirabel, the heroine, who has no magical gift. Except, of course, it turns out that she does. In the course of the film, we (and Mirabel's family) come to recognize Mirabel's gift as that of keeping her family's gifts alive and helping them flourish – of preserving the miracle of their community life.

This is not, of course, to imply that those in ministry leadership positions do not have any particular gifts of their own to offer! But I do think that *Encanto* can usefully illuminate something of what is involved in taking an asset-based approached to leadership in ministry. This approach means that, rather than trying to run every area of the church's ministry, the priest or lay leader plays Mirabel's role of attending to the gifts of those around them, nurturing these and connecting them to one another.[9] This approach expresses a confidence that there are abundant and surprising gifts of God to be discovered in each local church and neighbourhood, through which all members can be drawn ever more deeply into participation in the mission of God.

Seen from this perspective, ABCD resonates with and illuminates the 'every-member' vision of church we are given in in 1 Corinthians 12—14. Yet, as we have seen, sometimes the gifts that we need to receive more fully in the church will be uncomfortable and troubling. We should expect this because 'conviction of sin' and 'prophecy' are named among the gifts of the Spirit. In this way, challenges to oppression in the church will be part of the 'gift' given through multiple members of the body. We saw in Chapter 5 how, in Barrett's congregation in Hodge Hill, Birmingham, some of the African-Caribbean congregation members have begun to publicly name their experience of marginalization 'from active participation in worship and decision-making structures locally – and, for some at least, to begin to create and claim positions of leadership'.[10] Barrett credits these members' involvement in community development in their neighbourhood as the formation driving this unsettling of dominant power relations, and reshaping of membership relations in the church. Receiving from each member in ministry will change the very form and structures of the church, not just the content.

It is, however, worth noting the way this kind of language of abundance can be used punitively, creating the impression that people who are struggling already have what they need and just need to pull their socks up and try harder. This is especially pertinent on the back of a decade of welfare cuts and local government funding cuts.[11] It is important, therefore, that ABCD is always kept in relationship with the levers of state decision-making at a local and national level (as we will come to in the next section).

Organized ecclesial communities

Second, and more briefly, there are also ways in which participation in broad-based community organizing (BBCO) might enable fuller belonging and participation in the church.

In BBCO, leaders are defined as those who have a following. This is a challenge to understandings of leadership based on position or qualifications and expertise, as this kind of 'relational leadership' is not limited to particular roles (such as priest or church warden). This form of leadership also involves a willingness and ability to turn followers into leaders themselves. In this way, community organizing, as well as community development, challenges the ways leadership tends to be understood in the church.

Approaches to leadership can also be reframed and re-formed through engaging in power analysis, a central practice in BBCO. In a power analysis, the institutions that are gathered to organize map out which people and institutions have the power to effect change within the networks of relationships in which they are interested. In the context of the church, this practice has the benefit of bringing power into the open, for power must be acknowledged if it is not to be aggregated and abused. During a symposium on community organizing in the Church of England held in 2018, several lay leaders reflected on how their community organizing training in power analysis and meeting for one-to-ones had equipped them to build power with others and make change – and to use the structures of their church to do so. One church warden spoke of her parochial church council using the tools of community organizing to coordinate a listening campaign during an interregnum, as part of the process of putting together a parish profile in such a way that they were able to open the church up to appointing a female priest for the first time.[12] We can see, then, that drawing on community organizing thinking can allow lay members to more fully participate in the life of the church and so to significantly shape ecclesial polity.

However, we should also recognize the potential for organizing methodologies to reinforce the problems of church polity – for example, through shoring up ecclesial hierarchies. As we have seen, leadership, in BBCO, is defined in terms of having followers. Leaders are those who have 'relationships of trust and loyalty with a number of others in their locality or institution', and who have relationships with power: 'they are taken seriously and listened to by those in positions of authority, whether within the hierarchy of their church, union, or school or by local officials and business leaders'. While this will ideally honour the slow accretion of trust and respect over time, relationships of trust, loyalty and power are always formed against the backdrop of a kyriarchal matrix, and so are often not earned at all but simply bestowed (by those who are like them).[13] There is also the danger of power shifting only in short term or tokenistic ways, and so simply collapsing back into the priest's role following an interregnum, for example. Alternatively, power can end up being wielded in obstructive or domineering ways by a small number of lay people. It is out of an awareness of such dangers that community organizing methodology describes an ongoing cycle of organizing, disorganizing and reorganizing. This is important if power is not to end up concentrated in the hands of just a few, whether lay or ordained. As we noted at the beginning of this chapter, there is no practice – whether ecclesial of civic – that is a guarantor of good formation.

While mindful of these dangers, there is still demonstrable scope for community organizing and development to be part of the ongoing formation of the church, through focusing attention on the gifts that can be received from each member and on the power relations present in the church. This is one way in which participation in civil society can help the church to become more fully what it is called to be. We have also seen that the Christian calling to be good neighbours is a vocation that requires participation in civil society, with the opportunities this brings for living alongside and receiving from those who are strange to us (that is, those whom we first encounter as strangers). This conversation is not, therefore, undertaken with the aim of offering community organizing or development as a technique or strategy through which the church can regain its social dominance. Rather, the concern is with the opportunities offered by the church's membership of civil society to encounter the work of God outside the church, in order for the church to become more fully a political community shaped by the gifts of each member, in which common flourishing is possible.

Being formed through participation in the democratic state

We have seen how discipleship can and should involve receiving from one's neighbours in civil society. We now turn to consider how discipleship can be more fully understood and grown into through participation in the democratic state. In speaking of participation in the structures of the state, the kind of practices I have in view include the basic democratic activities of voting in local and national elections and serving as an elected representative at local and national levels. However, what is included in the state apparatus often goes beyond what we narrowly think of as the government. Therefore, these kinds of participative practices also include working as a member of the civil service and, at the other end of the spectrum, involvement in party politics.

The question of how Christians should understand the formative implications of their interactions with the state have not received much attention in recent political theology, and this is also true of the work of Anglican theologians. Where the state has been theorized in recent Anglican thought, it has tended to be as a legal broker between the interests of different groups in a culturally plural setting (as expressed by Rowan Williams, for example), or as a mediating institution between voluntary associations in civil society (as cast by Luke Bretherton).[14] Either way, the theological focus has tended to be on the political character, and formative implications, of participation in civil society associations. Rich though their accounts of associational democracy are, both fail to fully extend that account of participation in pursuit of the common good to the structures of the state. Both see government as necessary for community flourishing, yet suggest that the practices of government in state structures simply provide the framework for this flourishing. There is an ambivalence around the practices that express and constitute the moral purpose of the state, and little suggestion that participation in state structures could be part of individual and social flourishing.[15] While disruption and confrontational negotiation, for example, are necessary aspects of the citizen's relationship with the nation state, I do not think the full relationship is captured by these practices. An account of relations of participation is also needed.

I offer this account of the ways in which political participation in the structures of state shapes us as disciples through consideration of Dietrich Bonhoeffer's understanding of solidarity. Through this engagement, I come to argue that participation in the structures of a representative democracy can, in fact, illuminate Christian solidarity. This is not just in the sense of it being a duty of discipleship (that is, something our Christian formation has taught us to do), but also as something that teaches us what our discipleship can be. In the state, acting in solidarity with fellow members of the state can form one to more fully receive the solidarity offered in Christ.

Bonhoeffer on solidarity

In accounting for Christian responsibility, Bonhoeffer set out three modes of solidarity in community: *Miteinander* – being 'with-each-other as appointed by God' (including in sin); *Füreinander* – being 'for-each-other'; and *Stellvertretung* – the principle of vicarious representation, which brings these together and 'becomes the lived meaning of responsibility'.[16]

We will consider first the notion of *Füreinander* – of 'being for' the other. This form of solidarity is rooted in Christ's self-abandonment for us. For Bonhoeffer, there is nothing in Christ of defended, isolated self-regard: Christ has no anxiety that being in solidarity with others will destroy his own identity. Therefore, to be in Christ means seeing the full extent of one's solidarity with others in the light of the solidarity of Christ with us. In such solidarity, *Füreinander* is thus closely related to *Miteinander* – 'being with' each other. Bonhoeffer urges us to recognize that we can and ought to be aligned with the life of God – with God's solidarity with us – in the ordinary forms of human sociality. Bonhoeffer calls these forms of human sociality 'mandates', and they are formulated as: church; family; work and culture; and politics (or government).[17] As these routine, prosaic forms of human life are arenas in which we can align with the life of God, Bonhoeffer argues, they can be for us the life of grace.

Bonhoeffer extends this account of responsible solidarity to argue that the mandates also display a form of *Stellvertretung*. In explaining how vicarious representation is basic to the life of the mandates, Bonhoeffer gives the example of the father in the family: by working, providing, interceding, struggling, suffering for them, he stands in the place of the family.[18] In this way, the father takes on some of the risks involved in creating together a stable and flourishing family life – for example, economic risks, which he shoulders on behalf of the family. It is clear from the language Bonhoeffer uses (particularly that of struggling and suffering) that *Stellvertretung* should not be used to excuse relationships of dominance and subjugation, but rather requires that we are to be vulnerable to what the other is vulnerable to and to risk what the other risks. There is also a note here of being vulnerable so that the other need not be and risking so that the other need not risk. For Bonhoeffer, this solidarity with others in our representation of, our being for, others also involves a responsibility to liberate others into their own responsibility: I represent their need in order to make them more free to participate in decision-making themselves. Therefore, Bonhoeffer understood representation as *not necessarily* entailing a denial of agency on the part of the person being represented.[19]

Political resistance as solidarity

So, what does this mean for the way we understand Christian solidarity in relation to the structures of the state? Bringing all of this together, we can say that because Bonhoeffer sees social life as a context for alignment with the life of God, and because for Bonhoeffer representation and responsibility should characterize our participation in social life, he views this mutuality of representation and responsibility in mandated social forms, including in the state, as the normal state of affairs. Yet, famously, we also have the fact of his resistance to the mandate of the state. So how are we to hold these together?

We can answer this in terms of appropriate authority claims: if, for Bonhoeffer, the authority of the state lies in its position alongside other mandated forms of human sociality, then any move by the state to undermine the authority of these other social forms calls into question the legitimacy of the state. In these conditions, with one social form claiming the authority to disrupt the other mandates, the possibility of breaking the law for the sake of preserving the law must be confronted.[20]

Yet Bonhoeffer is clear that, in the nature of the case, you can never turn this into a new generalization, a new law, by which you can be sure that you were right.[21]

As one can never be sure that one acted rightly, the readiness to accept guilt is required, and it belongs equally to the person who decides to abide by the law and the person who decides actively to resist.[22] In the extreme situation, there is no human possibility of absolution. Bonhoeffer's own political biography illuminates what is meant by this: the final years of his life were marked by precisely the incurring of guilt of which he writes. In addition to his affirmation of government authority, Bonhoeffer's pacifism also cast his involvement in an attempt to assassinate Hitler as a sin.[23] This is expressed in his poem on Jonah (written a couple of days before being transferred to the Gestapo cells) which, as Stephen Plant argues, communicates Bonhoeffer's sense that he has incurred guilt on behalf of the German people, is under the judgement of God, and as such has been thrown into the water. He made no attempts to justify his actions as a means to a greater good that has been secured through acting in this way, and which somehow therefore absolves the ethical agent of guilt. The poem on Jonah makes this clear, ending as it does with the waters becoming still, rather than with rescue by the great fish.[24]

In this, Bonhoeffer is facing the possibility that the mandates (the normal order of things) could become so distorted that extreme action must be taken to restore the balance of mandated life. Such action is undertaken so that mandated life can become once again free to be what it is meant to be: 'the arena of God's involvement in all aspects of human solidarity'.[25] The guiding concern is for what will ground a restored society (not assent to abstract democratic principle). So we could say that active resistance, for Bonhoeffer, is a disruption of the normal order of things undertaken in response to a disruption of the normal order of things (that is, a response to a disordering of the state).[26]

Participation in representative democratic institutions

From this we see that, far from connoting a low view of political authority, it was Bonhoeffer's affirmation of the legitimacy of government that led him to see his resistance as rendering him parlously guilty. Bonhoeffer's view of the state along these lines is centrally shaped by Augustine and Luther.[27] Bonhoeffer's mandates can be read in continuity with Luther's three estates of family, economy/work and government, with the third estate of government therefore understood to be one of the means by which God acts within the penultimate to preserve creation.[28] Under normal circumstances, therefore, we owe obedience. Government is 'an institution of God', and an 'ethical failure' on the part of government does not therefore automatically strip it of 'its divine dignity'.[29]

From his reading of Luther and Augustine, Bonhoeffer not only affirmed the legitimacy of governing authorities but also discerned a possible Christian duty to participate in governance (for example as judge or magistrate) for the restraint of evil. As Plant notes, Bonhoeffer's attention to both Old and New Testaments meant that his political theology was concerned with situations where God's people are called to make governing decisions, rather than simply seeing political power as something exercised by those outside the community of faith (whether legitimately or for persecution).[30] In a democratic context, this work to make government more just for the sake of a common peace will include participation in the structures and institutions of the state (yet without ruling out actions such as whistleblowing from within state institutions).[31]

As we saw earlier, for Bonhoeffer, all of human sociality, not just the act by which one incurs guilt vicariously (the *ultima ratio*), requires responsible action on one another's behalf. As Williams explains, living faithfully under mandate means, 'prosaically living out the obvious duties and obligations of the relations in which we stand even before we choose'.[32] Living according to Bonhoeffer's ethics means practical labour in service of the security and wellbeing of the other, seeking 'the conditions for living and living well so that they can grow into responsibility'.[33] It is worth noting that the solidarity we are called to express is also transgenerational. Bonhoeffer famously considered 'The ultimate question for a responsible man to ask' to be 'not how he is to extricate himself heroically from the affair, but how the coming generation is to live'. As such, solidarity requires institutions that will perdure and support common life in years to come. Strengthening these institutions is therefore also part of faithful living under mandate.[34] Strengthening institutions for the sake of future flourishing might at times involve visibly disruptive action, such as participating in a trade union strike. Yet we can also see how this practical labour for the wellbeing of the other (both in the present and for generations to come) could be performed at the ballot-box, in the local government chamber, or even in the committee rooms of parliament.

While these civic actions, like voting and so on, will often be quotidian to the point of being almost automatic, the particular call of each person must be received and worked out in this area of life as in every other sphere. This is drawn out in Bonhoeffer's sermon on Gideon, which makes clear that while political authority comes from God each person is also responsible for their own actions.[35] Further, in seeking to describe this mode of political agency, it is worth recalling again that responsible and representative action is undertaken without certainty of virtue. As Plant makes clear in his presentation of Bonhoeffer's political theology, there are no easy answers about what we must render, to whom, and under what circumstances.[36] For Bonhoeffer, creating an ethical system that allows one to pin down one's obligations in advance and to be sure of the righteousness of one's decisions is the very opposite of faith.

Nonetheless, we are called to continue in the attempt to try and 'make sense', as Williams puts it; that is, to keep on speaking and acting for the good of the other, while suspending any narration of our actions in terms of ultimate meaning.[37] Such 'making sense' implies a radical loss of security, and means making judgements that are, necessarily, provisional and risky.[38] Yet, as Quash also affirms, 'The provisionality and risk of error that attends this process [of imaginatively engaging with the world and seeking to 'find' the Spirit] is part of life in the Spirit; part of the call to human responsibility that marks human vocation.'[39]

This vocation to responsibility can be more fully understood and inhabited, then, through participative political practices, such as voting. Voting for your preferred party – or even for the least worst option – in an election is an action in which you risk your fallible ability to 'make sense' of what will best allow for common flourishing and stake yourself on that choice, despite being unable to foresee how it will play out. Voting almost inevitably means, then, implicating oneself in a party or politician who will go on to take actions that are ethically questionable, whether in government or opposition.

Yet we have also seen in Bonhoeffer's account of solidarity a deeper level of loss, which we might name as loss of moral integrity. This more active kind of moral complicity can be more fully understood through considering the kind of decisions made by elected representatives. So it might take the form of following the party line over personal conviction on a legislative vote, out of a commitment to the importance of political parties in enabling distinctive forms of solidarity and dissent in democratic life. Or sitting on a Select Committee which produces a report whose recommendations do not fully express the personal convictions of any of its individual members. In these and other scenarios we can see how the parliamentarian who seeks to represent faithfully an opinion they themselves view as damaging to common flourishing will bear deep tension and guilt within themselves.

I do not mean to present these as the only ways in which public representatives could ethically act in such situations. However, I hope this helps to illustrate the kinds of loss of self that are involved in belonging to, and therefore participating in, a democratic polity. For the Christian disciple in particular, it requires a willingness to let go of certain forms personal sovereignty; for the same uncertainty which characterizes the *ultima ratio* act of political resistance runs through all political action (indeed, through all ethical action).

The ground of participation in the democratic state

In considering these forms of loss of self, it is also important to hold in mind Bonhoeffer's sense of our unified eschatological identity. This sense of ultimate personal unity is brought out by Williams in his reading of Bonhoeffer, for whom understanding oneself as finite and incomplete should drive one to depend more deeply upon God for one's sense of wholeness.[40] For Bonhoeffer, our ultimate worth as a child of God is beyond doubt because the fact of our Christian identity is not something that falls within our purview of responsibility. Therefore, we can risk disunion with God without achieving it, as this is not something that humans *can* achieve. This can perhaps help us to make sense of Bonhoeffer's suggestion that becoming compromised yields a paradoxical deepening of communion with God through renunciation. To risk ultimate disunion in this ethically agonized way, can be to express and strengthen one's trust in God.

With this in mind, we can return to the poem on Jonah with new eyes, seeing that being under the judgement of God is, yes, total loss, but also the beginning of life. It was this assurance of an ultimate identity held by God that enabled Bonhoeffer to face both worldly and spiritual diminishment this side of eternity. Recognizing this has the potential to free the Christian to act politically in a way that takes personal responsibility seriously, but without making an idolatry of the individual conscience.

Bringing all of this together, we see that solidarity in pursuit of common flourishing, which all are called to exercise, cannot be reduced to any single template of political action.[41] The call to solidarity and shared risk (both bearing risk on behalf of others, and the risk of staking oneself on a provisional and fallible way of making sense of what our life together demands) cannot be predetermined and made comfortable. Yet, while following this call to responsibility will mean we can never justify with certainty the virtue of our actions, we can still be assured of the necessity of action.

Discovering the shape of ecclesial solidarity from the state

We can see how, in this way, Christian formation can take place through participation in the structures of the state, as well as in civil society. In particular, participation in the structures of a representative democracy can enable us to see dimensions of the solidarity we owe one another that we would otherwise struggle to glimpse.

I am, however, left with some serious concerns over the fostering of neoliberalism and the military industrial complex – among other ills – entailed when one participates in the liberal democratic state today. It is important to be clear that I am not arguing that participation in the state is part of discipleship because the state consistently acts more ethically than the church. Nor am I arguing that all forms of complicity in guilt should be sought out as part of Christian ethical formation.[42] It is for these reasons that I am not commending participation in the state as the totality of Christian political vocation. As we have seen, there are many other forms of political participation – including protest and, at times, resistance – which solidarity may demand of us. Nonetheless, there are also dimensions of ethical responsibility that can be distinctively learned through the kind of participation we have been exploring here.

In this final brief section, I consider what this kind of participation in a democratic state might mean for the reshaping of the institution of the church. In *A Brutal Unity: The Spiritual Politics of the Christian Church*, Ephraim Radner discusses the church's indebtedness and responsibility to the state (as well as liberal democracy's indebtedness to the church). In line with the types of participative democracy we have been thinking about so far, Radner argues for a liberal and pluralistically ordered civil space, protected by the state.[43] He grounds this account with reference to the failure of the church in Rwanda to fulfil its 'moral responsibility to form individuals capable of ordering a liberal state'.[44] Following this, he contends that 'churches must orient their practice more fully, not less so, to the needs of a stable and accountable liberal democracy', and as such has a role (in certain ways) as 'servant' of the state.[45]

Radner understands this inhabiting of pluralist settings 'As a providential shadow of true self-giving', by which 'liberal political engagement presses the Church towards its true vocation'. From this, it follows that 'To reject this engagement in practical terms robs the Church of her internal and external prods and thereby obscures the true nature of the Church.' So the church's ability to be the church, when situated in the context of a liberal democratic polity, requires engagement with that polity.[46] It is not enough simply for the church to not actively seek a culturally or politically privileged status for Christianity in their national polity. Rather, 'the churches have a moral responsibility to further their own liberalising polities and to support and engage those forms of liberal civic polities in which they either already live or might potentially live'.[47]

This is not just in order to ensure universal freedom of religion but, more profoundly, so that the church, through its practical engagement in democratic life, might receive the 'prods' of external scrutiny and accountability. Radner explicitly urges a two-way dynamic of formation between church and state, arguing that the church needs the liberal state, 'not so much to protect it from itself ... as to provide a framework for self-accountability'.[48] He contends that the moral accountability of religions is enhanced rather than injured 'by their being embedded within liberal political institutions'.[49] Of Rwanda, Radner argues that 'the dynamics of order and accountability undergirding the liberal state ought to have also informed the shape of the Church's own life'.[50] So Radner is clear that what is needed for the ongoing formation of ecclesial polity cannot be fully learned within the church. The church does not only have a responsibility 'to encourage within her own sphere a kind of "civil society" of Christian interaction', but also to learn the meaning of its responsibility to its members from the world outside its own sphere.[51] As we noted in Part II, there is a profound sense in which we do not yet know the particular ecclesial practices required for common flourishing. These must be learned through encounter with the Spirit, both within the gathered life of the church and outside. From Radner, then, we see how state structures can also contribute to the shaping of church polity in ways that reveal and correct blind spots.

Therefore, the Christian response to secularization within 'modern economically diversified societies' cannot simply be that 'we must try harder to do what we have already said we should do, that we should get back to basics'. Rather,

> Christian ecclesiology should not fear looking at these secular 'civil' alternatives to the Church but also should positively learn from them as perhaps examples of things that the Church has simply been unable to fulfil in herself ... The lesson for the Church, at any rate, is this: let us look at ... the secular world, and ... gain a glimpse of our better self.[52]

There is, then, an important sense here in which the church is not just regaining an identity it once knew but forgot, but also that the church comes to see and to more fully become what it is called to through these engagements.

Conclusion

A touchstone of political theology from Augustine onwards has been the affirmation that 'a person nurtured in the Church and in the ordered *caritas* it inculcates is uniquely qualified to take responsibility for wielding political power'.[53] Yet here we have seen how we must also consider how our ability to become who we are called to be *as Christians* can be shaped by discerning and taking on our political responsibilities. There is, therefore, a two-way dynamic involved in Christian civic formation: being formed in the church to participate in civic life, and being formed as Christians and the church through participation in civic life (in ways that we could not have anticipated in advance).

I have highlighted learning to attend to the findings to which the Spirit leads us in the world as an important part of Christian and ecclesial political formation. So too is learning to see the church and our Christian identity in the light of these findings, as we relate the given to the found and vice versa. This is all part of seeking to discern how the Spirit is at work in the wider political community (of which we are members) and the possibilities offered there for redemption.[54]

Notes

1 Aristotle Papanikolaou, *The Mystical as Political* (Notre Dame, IN: Notre Dame University Press, 2012), p. 4.

2 Papanikolaou, *The Mystical as Political*, p. 4.

3 Stephen Backhouse, for example, argues that we should understand the Christian vocation to neighbourliness as foundational to discipleship because of the way the incarnation fundamentally disrupts all prior relations and loyalties: Stephen Backhouse, *Kierkegaard's Critique of Christian Nationalism* (Oxford: Oxford University Press, 2011). See also the Church of England's Near Neighbours programme and 'Who is My Neighbour? A Letter from the House of Bishops to the People and Parishes of the Church of England for the General Election 2015'. Nick Spencer's account of political readings of the Good Samaritan parable draws out further invocations of neighbourliness: *The Political Samaritan: How Power Hijacked a Parable* (London: Bloomsbury, 2017). Luke Bretherton likewise frames the relationship between congregation and *demos* in a consociational democracy as one of neighbourliness: a mutually disciplining partnership in which the congregation has to 'listen to and learn from its neighbours'. In return, the congregation's cosmic vision of the good 'brings a wider horizon of reference and relationship to bear on the immediate needs and demands of the demos. Through this exchange, neighbours are formed': Luke Bretherton, *Resurrecting Democracy: Faith, Citizenship, and the Politics of a Common Life* (Cambridge: Cambridge University Press, 2015), pp. 97, 99, 116.

4 As Andrew Rumsey puts it, the Christian's calling to love the 'other' is 'a universal command that only becomes particular when placed within a "neighbourhood" of proximate relations that allow for peaceable encounter with those who differ from us': Andrew Rumsey, *Parish: An Anglican Theology of Place* (London: SCM Press, 2017), p. 85. Wannenwetsch also argues that Christian ethical identity '*comes into being* through identification, in the course of which one person becomes the other's neighbour'. He goes on to argue that neighbourliness does not exist as a prior known category, for while we 'may *be* people who act more or less in solidarity with others ... as "neighbours" we are always still becoming': Bernd Wannenwetsch, *Political Worship*, trans. Margaret Kohl (New York, Oxford University Press, 2009), p. 232.

5 Andrew Draper, *A Theology of Race and Place: Liberation and Reconciliation in the Works of Jennings and Carter* (Eugene, OR: Pickwick Publications, 2016), p. 277.

6 Walter Brueggemann, 'The Liturgy of Abundance, The Myth of Scarcity', *Christian Century* (24–31 March l999).

7 Al Barrett, 'Asset-Based Community Development: A Theological Reflection', Church Urban Fund, 2013, p. 2, http://www2.cuf.org.uk/sites/default/files/PDFs/Research/ABCD_Theological_Reflection_2013.pdf, accessed 04.08.2022.

8 This is reflected, for example, in the practice of one-to-ones in community development, in which there is an expectation that one will encounter in the other person distinctive experiences and gifts which will enable both to better pursue a common good.

9 This, of course, raises important questions about the types of gifts church leaders are prone to recognize, and how this ability to recognize others' giftedness can be formed – as discussed in Chapters 4 and 5.

10 Al Barrett, 'Interrupting the Church's Flow: Hearing "Other" Voices on an Outer Urban Estate', *Practical Theology* 11:1 (2018): 79–92 (p. 90). This is in the context of practising asset-based community development, which strongly emphasizes attending to the gifts that each member of a community brings.

11 Indeed, the Big Society policy agenda exposed some of these dangers.

12 Jackie Ashmenall, 'Organising Among Anglican Churches in Ealing: A Reflection', Reimagining the Ministry of the Church (Leeds, 23 November 2018).

13 Bretherton recognizes some of the dangers lurking here and argues that 'such interaction needs to be habitual, public, analysed, and evaluated so it can occur more effectively and constructively.' He also draws out how, within BBCO, the sustained authority and legitimacy of leaders

rests on their ability to negotiate both their sustained trusted position within their institution and performing well BBCO political actions: Bretherton, *Resurrecting Democracy*, p. 141. For a fuller discussion of the power relations encoded in theological accounts of community organizing see Bretherton, *Resurrecting Democracy*, pp. 136–7 and Vincent Lloyd, 'Of Puzzles and Idols', *Syndicate* blog (2 March 2016), https://syndicate.network/symposia/theology/resurrecting-democracy/#vincent-lloyd, accessed 04.08.2022.

14 The thinking of both Williams and Bretherton on the character of the democratic state is strongly influenced by the early twentieth-century strand of 'political pluralism' associated with F. W. Maitland, Harold Laski and J. N. Figgis (and their more contemporary follower David Nicholls). This group of theorists emphasized that persons are not primarily, and certainly not exclusively, members of the single comprehensive community of the state, but rather first of all belong to what Williams terms 'first-level associations'. These associations are larger than the individual but smaller than the state. These are the primary locations in which people learn to act corporately to govern their own internal affairs, and so are also the primary locations in which they are formed as persons and from which position they negotiate their social identity. For the Pluralists the state is not, as Williams puts it, 'the all-powerful source of legitimate community life and action' but, rather, 'the structure needed to organise and mediate within a "community of communities"'. He goes on: 'State authority simply means that, in an association of such associations ... power is delegated to the unifying structure in order to balance the claims and order the relations of the smaller units.' See, for example, Rowan Williams, *Faith in the Public Square* (London: Bloomsbury, 2012), pp. 50, 81, 126.

This retrieval of the Pluralists is also undertaken in the context of Britain becoming an increasingly multicultural society, as a resource for seeking to maintain conversations about national goods in common amid deep difference. In Williams' thought, this takes the form of 'interactive pluralism', which he differentiates from the 'static pluralism' produced by 'Balkanizing' versions of multiculturalism, which offer only the 'juxtaposition of mutually non-communicating groups'. In contrast, interactive pluralism requires a public framework in which groups are prompted to cooperate with each other in action and to engage with each other in civil but critical dialogue. This requires a body capable of initiating 'brokerage' (or 'mediation') between communities where conflict arises or when groups become withdrawn into themselves and, more positively, where facilitation is necessary for mutual cooperation. This body is the state, which through law 'provides the stable climate for all first-level communities to flourish and the means for settling, and enforcing, "boundary disputes" between them'. Williams, *Faith in the Public Square*, pp. 50, 61, 81, 58.

Bretherton, meanwhile, bases his understanding of the relationship between the citizen and the state on consociationalism, which he defines as a system of 'mutual fellowship between distinct institutions or groups who are federated together for a common purpose'. This account of associational life strongly emphasizes the need for groups to be protected from the power of the state, and to have their own power. This is important to Bretherton because associations are, for him, where the heart of politics beats. Fullness of citizenship is understood to be realized in associational life, with being embedded in an intermediate association understood to be central to the citizen's formation. Bretherton, *Resurrecting Democracy*, pp. 219–84.

15 What Jonathan Chaplin calls Williams' 'rich and dynamic account of persons' is not quite consistently worked through in relation to state institutions. Jonathan Chaplin, 'Person, Society and State in the Thought of Rowan Williams' (Lecture, 23 November 2012), pp. 7–8, https://www.vhi.st-edmunds.cam.ac.uk/system/files/documents/paper%20chaplin.pdf, accessed 04.08.2022. Chaplin notes a similar area of oversight in Bretherton's concern with upholding the priority of social relations over economic and political ones, as this leads to a failure to account fully for political life – including the scope for citizenship to involve participation in the full gamut of democratic structures, as well as in their disruption and reform ('Person, Society and State in the Thought of Rowan Williams', pp. 7–8). See also Jonathan Chaplin, 'Book Review: Luke Bretherton, Resurrecting Democracy: Faith, Citizenship, and the Politics of a Common Life', *Studies in Christian Ethics* 30:2 (2017): 228–32.

16 Dietrich Bonhoeffer, *Ethics* (London: SCM Press, 1955), p. 261; Dietrich Bonhoeffer, *Sanctorum Communio*, Dietrich Bonhoeffer Works vol. 1 (Minneapolis, MN: Fortress Press, 1998), p. 178. See also: Esther Reed, *The Limit of Responsibility: Dietrich Bonhoeffer's Ethics for a Globalizing Era* (London: T&T Clark, 2020), p. 122.

17 Bonhoeffer, *Ethics*, pp. 73–138, 252–9. Bonhoeffer's mandates theology continued to be a work in progress throughout his life. So, while he names four mandates, these should not be taken as an exhaustive list, but rather as examples. For more, see Stephen Plant, *Bonhoeffer* (London: Continuum, 2004).

18 Bonhoeffer, *Ethics*, p.194.

19 Bonhoeffer, *Ethics*, p. 204. Nonetheless, we cannot fully escape the paternalism that is present in this advocacy of acting on others' behalf. However benignly this is intended, his writings still display a failure to deeply interrogate how this vision of exercising responsibil-

ity within mandated social structures might shore up oppressive power relations

For instance, Bonhoeffer's insistence that the divine authority for extant social structures must not be taken advantage of by those above to enforce obedience upon those below is somewhat undercut by the example with which he illustrates his study on truth-telling. In this illustration, it is understood to be right for a son to deny to his teacher that his father is regularly drunk, as this loyalty to his father is what is owed within the mandate of the family. So, we should keep in mind questions raised about the extent to which representative action is open to abuse and really engages the agency of the person being represented.

20 Bonhoeffer, *Ethics*, pp. 312, 315, 316. Yet even in these conditions, Bonhoeffer refuses to say that breaking the law then becomes necessary, let alone necessarily virtuous.

21 Bonhoeffer, *Ethics*, for 'An ethic cannot be a book in which there is set out how everything in the world actually ought to be but unfortunately is not; and an ethicist cannot be a person who always knows better than others what is to be done and how it is to be done' p. 236.

22 The distinction between active and non-active incurral of guilt, as highlighted by Christine Schliesser, is relevant here: *Everyone Who Acts Responsibly Becomes Guilty: Bonhoeffer's Concept of Accepting Guilt* (Louisville, KY: Westminster John Knox Press, 2008). While this chapter is primarily concerned with the active incurral of guilt, the category of non-active incurral also helpfully illuminates the 'always-already' fact of our membership of a political community.

23 We should note that while Bonhoeffer's membership of the *Abwehr* is historically well-established, the extent of his involvement in the Canaris/Dohnanyi conspiracy is slightly less clear.

24 Dietrich Bonhoeffer, *Letters and Papers from Prison*, ed. John de Gruchy (Minneapolis, MN: Fortress Press, 2010), pp. 547–8. See also Stephen Plant, *Taking Stock of Bonhoeffer* (Abingdon: Routledge, 2016), pp. 59–70.

25 Rowan Williams, *Christ the Heart of Creation* (London: Bloomsbury, 2018), p. 206.

26 This framing of active resistance is important to note given that Bonhoeffer's political theology has sometimes been read in a way that emphasizes a call to resistance of all state authority, rather than to participate in state institutions.

From this it follows that attention to the particularity of state institutions and their various purposes and practices, rather than speaking of the state as a monolithic edifice, is important if we are to discern where the state should be acting primarily to facilitate associational life and where it should be more directly fostering the common good.

27 Plant, *Taking Stock of Bonhoeffer*, pp. 74–7.

28 Wheaton College, 'Stephen Plant, The Evangelization of Rulers: Dietrich Bonhoeffer's Political Theology' (12 April 2012), *YouTube*, https://www.youtube.com/watch?v=6--CXvgP5xw, accessed 04.08.2022.

29 Bonhoeffer, *Ethics* (1955), p. 304.

30 Plant, *Taking Stock of Bonhoeffer*, pp. 71–83.

31 However, we should also recognize here Bonhoeffer's insistence upon the limits of the state, even to the extent of arguing that the main role of the church in relation to the state is to remind the state of its limits. The role of the church is thus bound up with a strong affirmation of the importance of associational life (in civil society). A play written by Bonhoeffer in prison diagnoses the cause of Nazi ideology's totalizing sovereignty as its rootlessness, disconnected from the lived realities of civil society and simply asserted from above, which stands in contrast with the rootedness in the ordinariness of the local community life of the character generally taken to represent Bonhoeffer. Bonhoeffer, *Ethics*, pp. 310–15; Dietrich Bonhoeffer, *Fiction from Tegel Prison*, ed. Clifford J. Green (Minneapolis, MN: Fortress, 1999), p. 68. Plant, *Taking Stock of Bonhoeffer*, p. 78. As Plant argues, Bonhoeffer's political milieu looked to the second estate, in the form of German middle-class life, for social stability and continuity, and mistrusted liberal democracy, seeing it as having failed in the form of the Weimar Republic. Plant, 'The Evangelization of Rulers: Dietrich Bonhoeffer's Political Theology'. In using Bonhoeffer to support a stronger ethical account of democratic participation I am, therefore, going beyond the forms of government thought by Bonhoeffer to best reflect the mandated order of society. Nonetheless, I think we can still find considerable resonance in our own times with the underlying questions animating Bonhoeffer's writings on the state around whence power derived, and the proper character of power and authority. We can remain true to this account of staking oneself for the sake of one's political community and find in it resources for political participation in our time, while going beyond what Bonhoeffer saw as socially and politically desirable.

32 Williams, *Christ the Heart of Creation*, p. 211.

33 Rowan Williams, 'Bonhoeffer's Ethics: Representing Humanity in Christ' (2016), DuBose Lecture Series given at Sewanee, University of the South, https://vimeo.com/user6199387/review/185991351/13e707c91d, accessed 04.08.2022. See also Williams, *Christ the Heart of Creation*, p. 204.

34 Bonhoeffer, *Letters and Papers from Prison*, ed. Eberhard Bethge (New York: Macmillan, 1971), p. 7.

35 Plant, *Taking Stock of Bonhoeffer*, p. 75. See also Bonhoeffer, *Ethics*, p. 314.

36 Plant, 'The Evangelization of Rulers'.

37 Bonhoeffer cautions against the search for certain types of meaning. So, we can act out of obedience without having to project forward an assessment of the virtue of the action.

38 M. A. Volpe, *Rethinking Christian Identity: Doctrine and Discipleship* (Oxford: Wiley Blackwell, 2102), p. 58.

39 Quash, *Found Theology*, p. xvi.

40 Rowan Williams, 'The Suspicion of Suspicion: Wittgenstein and Bonhoeffer' in *Wrestling with Angels: Conversations in Modern Theology* (London: SCM Press, 2007), pp. 186–202 (pp. 192–3).

41 While he does not give us a template, we can more fully understand what it might mean to inhabit our political communities more deeply and seek their flourishing through looking to Bonhoeffer's own life. As Plant notes, in our 'cultures of self-justification, blame and excuses', 'a man prepared to accept the consequences of his actions' is to be admired: Plant, *Bonhoeffer*, p. 148.

42 This is not, therefore, an argument for the justifiability of practices such as extraordinary rendition and extrajudicial killings by national security services.

43 Ephraim Radner, *A Brutal Unity: The Spiritual Politics of the Christian Church* (Waco, TX: Baylor University Press, 2012), p. 50.

44 Radner, *A Brutal Unity*, p. 53. Radner continues: 'Had [the church] done so, this would not only have served a corporate good but also saved the Church from the suicidal scandal of her own sins.'

45 Radner, *A Brutal Unity*, pp. 53, 55. Papanikolaou likewise contends that 'Christians who shape their lives toward the realization of communion with the divine will ultimately act in such a way as to work toward a political community that affirms, in a broad sense, the basic axioms of liberal democracy': Papanikolaou, *The Mystical as Political*, p. 80. The approach Papanikolaou advocates (and identifies as that taken by Eric Gregory and Charles Mathewes) is an 'indirect Christian defense of democracy', which 'does not take the form "because Christians believe *this*, political community should look like *that*." The focus is on Christian existence in the world created for divine–human communion; as Christians work toward tapping creation's sacramental potential, the political form of community that such work reinforces is democratic' (p. 156).

46 Radner, *A Brutal Unity*, pp. 461–2. Radner continues: 'antiliberalism leaves the Church in ... the realm of complicity with political failure and violence by declaring her irreformability, on the one hand, and ... denying the essential quality of self-giving to the enemy that the Church's location within pluralist settings necessitates' (p. 461).

47 Radner, *A Brutal Unity*, p. 462.

48 Radner, *A Brutal Unity*. The other side of this is that 'the liberal state needs the churches in order to wrest from her any illusion of holding moral monopoly, or indeed any moral standing of its own apart from the values it is able to receive from her citizens, many of whom will inevitably be religious'.

49 Radner, *A Brutal Unity*, p. 22. For Radner, 'there is also a sense in which the emergence of liberal constitutionalism was a providential chastisement of the failures of the church to live as the alternative *polis* it is called to be' (p. 55).

50 Radner, *A Brutal Unity*, p. 462: 'while the Church herself should have provided the encouragement to the state to transform itself in a parallel fashion'.

51 Radner, *A Brutal Unity*, p. 53. Papanikolaou expresses this in terms of the scope for political life to point forward to ultimate union: 'If the political is a community of dispute, in which civic engagement involves not simply tolerating the other but seeing her as an irreducibly unique creation of God, the political community can be a "proleptic communion"' (p. 156).

52 Radner, *A Brutal Unity*, p. 381 n. 52.

53 Williams, 'Politics and the Soul', p. 68.

54 As Quash puts it, 'the Spirit comes to us from that new world, the world waiting to be born', and so 'yields to us a perspective in which consummation can be hoped for and imagined, even if, at times, the hope seems nearly fantastical'. Yet, being drawn towards this hope depends on remembering that we 'belong less fully to God if our anticipation of the future leads us to belong less fully to the world': Quash, *Found Theology*, p. 278.

Conclusion
Forming Common Civic life

This book has been centred on the question of how Christian political formation takes place, with a particular focus on how this happens for members of the Church of England. In doing so, my focus has been not only on how one is formed by belonging to, and participating in, the polity of the church, *but also* by belonging to, and participating in, the wider civic community. The central argument I have advanced is that Christian and civic formation cannot be disentangled from one another and, moreover, that this is how ethical and political formation *should* happen. That humble but determined Christian participation in practical politics is part of discipleship, and there are transformations that such participation can bring in its wake.

Forming common civic life

In challenging and extending the dominant account of formation, I have nonetheless been clear that formation as Christians is important for living well in the world. Indeed, it is to that end that I have insisted on the importance of taking seriously how we might be most fully formed *as* Christians, which I have suggested takes place through participation in civic and political life. This, I have argued, has implications for church polity in ways that help shape the positive formational potential of church life and practices, such that participation in these practices might better form us as Christians and participants in civic and political life. With this model of exchange and reception in mind, I turn, in this concluding chapter, to the question of where all of this leaves us in thinking about how the church could play a part in forming civic identity and belonging in a national polity.

Continuing with my focus on the Church of England, I look at some of the implications of these conclusions for its relationship with the nation. This concluding chapter considers two possible forms of Anglican contribution to national life, as proposed by Tim Jenkins: namely, the Church of England's 'territorial embeddedness' and a 'conversational mode'.[1] I propose that, in the deepening recognition of sin to which we are led by the Spirit, there are in fact resources the Church of England can offer to national life for constructively forming belonging in a polity.

The first half of this chapter grapples with pressing questions about English national identity and belonging through exploring Anglican polity and its relationship with place. In the context of pressing questions about national identity and belonging, I argue that the Church of England's relationship with place has perhaps unlikely resources to offer to the present turmoil over what it means to belong to a national civic community. In the second half of this chapter, the focus is on the need for richer deliberative conversations amid the deep disagreements raging in church and nation. I argue that there is a kind of self-directed scepticism that can be drawn from Anglican theological resources which has the potential to contribute to the discernment and pursuit of common life.

Anglican territorial embeddedness

Questions of national identity and civic belonging press urgently on all churches in the United Kingdom in this political moment, and perhaps especially so on the Church of England, given its particular relationship with the nation. I explore here the scope for the theology and practice of the Church of England to offer a robust response and an alternative to narrow and corrosive forms of nationalism in the UK. Tim Jenkins sees the distinctiveness of the Church of England's relation to the nation as lived out in the form of its 'territorial embeddedness'.[2] I propose that this 'territorially embedded' Church of England polity has the capacity to help us to better understand and inhabit our identity as members of a national political community.

However, this argument is made with an awareness of the troubled history of Anglicanism's relationship with territory, and the ways it can shore up exclusionary and hierarchical ways of understanding and practising civic belonging. Offering Anglican practices as a response to nationalism requires recognizing the extent to which the Church of England shares in responsibility for this corrosive trend, both at the level of the global Anglican Communion and domestically. Resisting these tendencies will entail articulating a different way of understanding the intertwining of national identity and Anglican polity than has often predominated. I outline what the Church of England can, and in some ways does already, distinctively contribute to understanding and practising belonging to a community that shares a particular place. I explore, first, the potential for theological understandings of Anglican polity to illuminate what it means to belong to a place without possessing it. Second, I offer an account of Anglican polity as one in which one does not choose the community to whom one owes responsibility, and the way this can help illuminate civic responsibility within the national polity.

Identifying a crisis of national identity and belonging

Recent years have seen what has widely come to be recognized as a crisis of national identity and political belonging in the UK. The UK's shifting status internationally, combined with rapidly globalizing economies and the loss of regional industry (and concomitant growth in precarious work in the services industry), have combined in what Paul Gilroy calls 'postcolonial melancholia'.[3] The Brexit referendum gave powerful expression to these undercurrents, bringing them to the surface of national discourse.[4] The 2021 report of the Commission on Race and Ethnic Disparities has further stoked debate over the presence – and recognition – of white supremacy in national life.[5] UK state policies have all too often compounded these growing fractures in the national body politic. Existing understandings of citizenship implicit in government policies tend to reduce it to a binary legal status, and/or an assent to 'shared values'. Such understandings mitigate against the pursuit of the common good, sowing division and mutual distrust, and setting up a hierarchy of citizenship statuses.[6] The Windrush scandal provided a stark example of a two-tier system of citizenship, revealing anew the ongoing legacy of Empire on understandings of national identity and belonging.[7]

Recent examples of political decisions which express a distorted sense of what it is to belong to a national political community include the UK Government's ongoing reluctance to grant prisoners the right to vote (even after a judgement from the European Court of Human Rights), and the decision in February 2019 to strip Shamima Begum of her British citizenship.[8] Both of these decisions express a sense that when a person or group of people has failed to uphold the set of values on which their status as full citizens of the United Kingdom depends (in these cases, through violating the prohibition against threatening the welfare of others in society), that status can justly be diminished or removed from them by the state. Perhaps the most troubling expression of this contractual understanding of national belonging is the deliberate use of the state to create a 'hostile environment' for asylum seekers.[9] Their civic exclusion is expressed through alienation from participation in, for example, employment, the economy (through the Azure Card system) and, crucially, the life of particular localities. This final form of civic alienation is achieved through a range of practices, including through being held apart from society in detention centres and transported long distances at frequent intervals.[10]

CONCLUSION: FORMING COMMON CIVIC LIFE

It is clear that the impacts of these trends are not confined to one particular demographic group but can be seen, for example, in the lives of asylum seekers struggling in the 'hostile environment' *and* in the alienation of workers in post-industrial areas struggling with a rapidly globalizing context. There is, all in all, a pressing need for richer conversations about national identity and belonging.

The Church of England as a placed church

It is against this backdrop that we are considering the Church of England's relationship with forms of national belonging and identity. This is a situation which implicates the Church of England, tied as it is to the national footprint and to its political structures. We are led to ask: how can a 'territorially embedded' church be part of forming a flourishing national life, in which there is space for all to belong and participate in shared places?

In theological literature on place, the incarnation of Christ is often invoked as underscoring the importance of the local. As Andrew Rumsey writes of the disciples' encounter with the risen Christ on the Emmaus Road, 'God's self-disclosure was a local affair, and still is.'[11] Jenkins, too, sees the Anglican priest's responsibility for the cure of souls in their parish as corresponding to the doctrine of the incarnation: 'God is to be found embodied in a particular place, locality, people; the materials of time and history can show him forth (which is why any ministry is an experiment in Providence, finding out how God is present in a place).'[12] In this light, the Church of England's tethering of itself to particular 'placed' footprints – from parish to diocese to nation – can be seen as faithful imitation of Jesus' ministry.

Yet we must also note that not all expressions of commitment to a particular locality are oriented towards the kinds of practices that allow all within that locality to flourish and participate in civic life. The 'turn to place' in human geography in recent decades has highlighted the always provisional and contested nature of place, and the way that place can become a conduit for imposing a particular will or agenda to the exclusion of others.[13] The way in which we shape and inhabit places can express competing visions of who that place is for: of who belongs to it and who does not.

The Church of England's ways of inhabiting and shaping places have all too often expressed a vision of belonging that mirrors and compounds forms of social exclusion and marginalization. There are resources in this placed Church for contributing fruitfully to the conversation about national identity and belonging, but we must first acknowledge that the Church of England has displayed a similarly corrosive vision of national life to those that currently dominate and even, to an extent, shares in responsibility for the current situation. Therefore, we must start by unearthing some of the more troubling enactments of Anglican territory that form part of the Church's history before we move on to look at how the Church of England may offer more constructive understandings and practices for shaping civic life. This unearthing must be undertaken if we are not to replicate these destructive ways of relating to territory today.

Anglicanism's troubling territorial tendencies

We saw in Chapter 4 that the Church of England is going through its own reckoning with race, nationalism and the ongoing legacy of empire. We noted there some of the ways in which Anglican theology and practice intertwined with the British imperial project, shoring up possessive understandings of national identity and reinforcing hierarchies between members of the British Empire. We examined how this played out in two areas: the role of Anglican theologies of providence in enabling possession of colonies, and of the people of those lands; and the role of baptismal practices in enabling slavery, and the civic hierarchies that rested upon slavery. In this way,

CONCLUSION: FORMING COMMON CIVIC LIFE

spiritual freedom was firmly detached from the conditions of social and political life, and the fundamental social hierarchy between slave and free was retained. Moreover, the hierarchy between the races was thus strengthened through theological undergirding. While one could be Black and a Christian, one could still be owned as property by another Christian and excluded from civic belonging and participation.

Looking at the history of the USPG has helped us to examine the role played by Anglican theology in shaping an understanding of territory as given by God to be possessed by one ethnic people group, under a single nation's sovereignty. Anglican understandings of the providential spread of the Church provided support and legitimization for the British imperial project, and the Church of England therefore shares in responsibility for the ethnonationalist visions and practices this history continues to feed. As a number of recent works have highlighted, the 'Christian-colonial' imagination is still operative today in the Church of England and this history continues to shape the Church's relationship with the wider Anglican Communion.[14]

The Church of England's relationship with territory domestically also bears consideration – beginning with the parish. There is, as Rumsey notes, 'a deep moral ambivalence about the parochial record that has to be acknowledged'.[15] Core to this ambivalence is the bounded nature of the parish. The use and abuse of boundary in social structures has been extensively explored by the geographer Doreen Massey, who argues that territorial boundaries are inevitably 'exercises of power', which 'establish outsiders – those who do not belong'.[16] David Fletcher, too, has identified the way the parish boundary in particular has historically been a simultaneous agent of 'territorial threat and social cohesion', such that, paradoxically, social inclusion has tended to be generated in the parish by a measure of social exclusion.[17]

As we saw in Chapter 7, the Church of England's relationship to parishes can become controlling and possessive, and this at times renders the church an agent of social exclusion in the name of cohesion. A historic example of this can be seen in the Poor Laws, which drew on the parish as a unit of local government as well as of ecclesial polity. While these laws were normally administered by civil parish authorities, Anglican clergy sometimes served as Poor Law guardians – acting as a partner in the parochial arrangement of poor relief.[18] Raymond Williams is among those who have argued that poor relief was often, despite seeming to be oriented towards neighbourly care, largely indifferent to the needs of the poor – including their need to be able to move across parish boundaries.[19] Here the problem arose in a particularly potent way because of the way in which one's relationship to the Church of England and one's belonging to a particular geographic territory were overlaid with one another in regulating access to welfare. Belonging to Anglican polity has also shaped civic participation at the geographic level of national territory. The Church of England's mottled history in this respect can perhaps be seen most strikingly in the Test and Corporation Acts, which, from the late seventeenth to early nineteenth century, together served to exclude non-Anglicans from entry to certain public institutions (including barring matriculation to the universities of Oxford and Cambridge) and from holding civil or military office.

So, Anglican polity's relationship with territory has shaped citizens' ability to receive welfare provision and to take part in civic life. In talking of the Church of England's relationship with national civic life, therefore, we need to be aware of the danger of allowing civic identity to be dictated by belonging to a particular faith, denomination, race, ethnicity, social class and even nation state. Such understandings give rise to practices, at both a local and a national level, that civically marginalize those who do not fit the mould.

CONCLUSION: FORMING COMMON CIVIC LIFE

Anglican resources for flourishing national belonging

In light of the above, it is hard to deny that Anglican territorial boundaries have disabled, as well as enabled, the formation of a flourishing civic community. Nonetheless, as Rumsey sums it up, 'despite its significant drawbacks – wistful exceptionalism and reactionary jingoism not least among them – the "England-ness" of the parish must be reckoned with', for the sake of understanding both the Anglican and national vocation.[20] With this in mind, we turn to consider what the Church of England can, and does already, distinctively contribute to understanding and practising belonging to a community that is tied to a particular place.

These resources can help to offer an alternative to narrow forms of nationalism and civic alienation, and I explore this in two directions. First, theological understandings of Anglican polity can help to illuminate what it means to belong to a place without possessing it. Second, understandings of Anglican polity as a community in which one does not choose one's fellow members, to whom responsibility is owed, can help to illuminate civic responsibility within the national polity.

Non-competitive belonging to place

We have seen that there are dangers to the Church of England's territorial embeddedness, as well as temptations to seek to possess the land in a manner counter to the church's calling to this kind of responsibility for the people of the land. Nonetheless, the church is still in need of place. For the dangers of attachment to place are not removed by detachment, but are rather compounded. This is clearly demonstrated by Willie Jennings' work: having exposed the detachment and distortion of human relationship with place that unfolded through the colonial moment, Jennings nonetheless avers that 'Christianity is in need of place to be fully Christian'. He argues this on the basis that, 'The moment the land is removed as a signifier of identity, it is also removed as a site of transformation through relationship'. This kind of transformation is understood by Jennings as 'Christian faith receiving its heretofore undiscovered identities, which are found only through interaction with the social logics of language, landscape and peoples.' Right relationships are understood as 'those that invite new patterns of life woven through and by means of the deep structures of Christian faith slowly opened through ongoing interpretation and struggle'.[21]

It is in this light that we consider the potential for the Church of England's territorial embeddedness to be the site of this kind of transformation for the national civic polity. This involves identifying how the Church of England is able to foster modes of belonging to a territory that resist the impulse to possess or dominate a place, and instead allow it to be genuinely shared. This calling of the church, to be a place free of competition for power and control, is rooted in the person of Christ, described by Jennings as a place that is also a person.[22] Rowan Williams likewise describes Jesus as a place, in which God and humanity can belong and dwell together without fear or rivalry: 'a place where a love abides that is vulnerable and unprotected', and 'from which no one is excluded in advance'. Christians are called to follow this way of being in the world, a way that begins with 'not possessing him in whose name we would move beyond being competitors in this world'.[23]

In this way Jesus offers, as Coles puts it, a new 'socio-political possibility beyond historical and spatial territoriality'.[24] Coles describes the church's task as cultivating 'a community in relation to the memory of Christ's trial, cross, and resurrection such that Christians might gradually conform themselves to his generous and vulnerable cultivation of becoming, at and through the edge of life'.[25] This call to dwell at the 'edges' of life, rather than seeking to control it from the centre, is true both of the gathered practices of the church (for example, in seeking to be receptive to gifts to the body coming from unexpected quarters), and of the church's relationship with particular geographical territories (such as the parish). Williams suggests that the eroded nature of the Church of England's

CONCLUSION: FORMING COMMON CIVIC LIFE

social and constitutional status could have something distinctive to offer here, being peculiarly well-placed to communicate something of the central vision of an 'undefended territory created by God's displacement of divine power from heaven and earth'.[26] This attempt to dwell in a particular place without possessing it chimes with Massey's argument that space is never finished: it too cannot be sealed or finalized, and there is no single definitive account of any space.[27] In like manner, the Church of England's relationship with England cannot be oriented towards sealing or fixing an identity interior to territorial boundaries (whether parochial, diocesan or national). As Hardy argues, to have a homeland is a very different thing from possessing or restricting it.[28]

Federated and negotiated identities

What this way of inhabiting a homeland might look like can be illuminated through a peculiarly Anglican sense of polity (and its placed-ness) as something that is federated and negotiated.

The Church of England (and the wider Anglican Communion) is sometimes described as a federated church. This is a form of collective identity that is formed out of the relationship between individual things, but where something more is created than the collection of individual things. Yet the whole that is produced also does not entirely define or subsume the identity of the individual things. So, the component footprints of Anglican territory (parish, diocese, nation) emerge in this light as networked constituent parts, forming something bigger than themselves through their relationship to one another. The Church of England, in other words, can be understood as something that appears through federating together.[29]

This diffuse character of Anglicanism – as a federal body across the Communion, and through the parish network – offers resources for approaching the tortured question of how we are to understand national identity and belonging. Taking this federating approach, we can say that there might be forms of density and overlap between neighbourhoods, but that a reductive search for an identifiable essential shared set of values that define what it means to be a citizen of a national polity should be resisted. As Rumsey argues, we should attend to local notions of nationhood as 'None of us knows our country (our town, come to that) as a whole; we know the parts of it with which we are familiar, projecting from there our wider senses of belonging. Any idea of England, or Britain, or the world as a whole, is at heart an extension of one's local experience.' Federating means starting with immediate localities rather than with the idea of the nation: 'England, in other words, is what you end up with, not begin with.'[30]

In this way, the Church of England can help to shed light on a how a federated sense of national community can be formed. Anglican polity can also illuminate the extent to which all boundaries of belonging involve ongoing negotiation if they are not to become possessive and restricting. A distinction between boundaries imposed from without versus those formed from within is useful here. The former, such as imperial lines, tend to pull communities apart, while it is through the latter, formed by people associating together, that an enduring sense of community comes to exist. In order for this second type of shared territorial imagination to not become narrowly oriented inwards, ongoing contestation and negotiation of boundaries is required. In the case of the parish, this has taken place, for example, through the practice of 'beating the bounds' at Rogationtide.[31] This ongoing negotiation reflects the conviction that no one person or group owns the territory (be it parish, or nation): it is common ground.

Anglican and civic responsibility as 'always already'

Rather than seeing national belonging in terms of dominance and ownership, we are to see homeland, in Hardy's words, as a 'gifting of responsibility'. The constitutional location of the Church of England creates a particular responsibility to respond to policies and practices that lead to civic marginal-

CONCLUSION: FORMING COMMON CIVIC LIFE

ization and exclusion (creating a divide between those who are deemed not to have a share in the life of the nation, which is properly possessed by others). At a parliamentary level, this involves the Lords Spiritual contesting the vision of civic membership expressed in the kinds of policies outlined earlier in this chapter. This is part of the responsibility to create a richer sense of civic belonging and common life for all in the land (and, in so doing, allowing life in our national polity to reflect more strongly the place of Christ).[32]

The binary logic frequently displayed in state policies (whereby one is either a full legal citizen, or one has no place in civic life and nothing to contribute) can and should also be contested at the level of localized praxis. Church involvement in forming common civic life involves not only collaboration with state structures, but also the subversion of these structures. This subversion can take the form of the church and other civil society groups offering forms of civic belonging to those decitizenized by the state, creating 'underground' modes of participation in their neighbourhood. As Jeremy Morris writes, in order for the Church of England to resist the complacency so often characteristic of a state church, it must have 'open church buildings, welcoming liturgies, sustained public prayer, shelter, truth-seeking, resistance to prejudice, willingness to risk failure and loss'.[33] In this way, there is scope for the parish churches of the Church of England to undercut the state's implicit understanding of civic belonging, while contributing to the creation of alternative forms of civic identity.

Alongside the possibility of fostering particular but non-possessive relations of belonging to place in this way, Anglican polity also holds the potential to illuminate civic identity as something that is 'always already'. That is to say, citizenship can come to be seen as an identity that is not at root something to be granted by the state, but rather as an identity that grows out of a set of already extant social relations in a locality. The Church of England is able to illuminate this characteristic of civic identity through its self-understanding as being a church for all the people of the land. So, wherever one stands in England one is always standing in a parish. As Grace Davie puts it, you were born in a parish whether you like it or not.³⁴ Likewise, one is always already a member of a civic community. We can see the implications of this in relation to the political situation outlined at the beginning: prisoners and asylum seekers, for example, are nonetheless members of our national community, even if they are not legally recognized as such.

This sense of prior belonging has implications for the way responsibility is understood. Understandings of Anglican polity as something in which one does not choose one's fellow members and the community to whom one owes responsibility can help to illuminate civic responsibility within the national polity in two main directions: illuminating the collective nature of responsibility for the actions of a community or institution historically; and illuminating the collective nature of responsibility for the welfare of a shared place.

Sharing in responsibility for the past

The bare fact of belonging to a parish can also help us to understand the kind of collective responsibility that is necessary for the functioning of common life in the nation. Belonging connects us in responsibility not only to those around us in this particular place, but also to those who have gone before us. Anglican identity is, in some ways, a particularly public identity, given the constitutional position of the Church of England. To be a member of the Church of England is to share in responsibility for the Church's mottled history as intertwined with the nation state and in the intertwining of the Anglican Communion and the British Imperial project, as well as for the many other forms of structural injustice both perpetuated and instigated by the church.

So, to be part of the Church of England (or indeed, any church) is to accept that I am part of something that I do not control or define – it is to enter into a story that is already being told, by others present as well as those past. The same structure is true of national belonging: as Kwame Anthony Appiah argues, patriotism involves both shared pride and shame for national action in the world.[35] Precisely because the Church of England shares in responsibility for the Atlantic slave trade, for example, it has an important role to play in helping to form a better conversation about national identity and belonging. Part of this involves telling a less selective and brittle national narrative, where Britain is not always cast as the hero, and where the experiences of minorities are treated as a central part of national history. Archbishop Welby's apology for the Amritsar massacre (in which he spoke of 'the sins of my British colonial history') is one instance of the kind of role that can be played by the Church here, as were Archbishop Williams' comments on the 200th anniversary of the UK's abolition of the slave trade (acknowledging the SPG's involvement and the continuing financial benefit of compensations that were paid for the loss of slaves).[36]

This awareness of the corporate and historical dimensions of one's civic identity is therefore something Anglicanism could offer to the nation.[37] However, this is only something that Anglicanism can offer if the Church of England also learns to recognize these dimensions itself. This recognition is something it does with the help of others, allowing the Church's understanding of itself to be shaped by others. So, the Church can learn to give the gifts it has to give only through engaging with, and receiving from, those who are to be the recipients of this gift.

Sharing in responsibility for a place

This quality of being 'always already' is also true of how we can understand the Church of England's responsibility to particular places and people. Rumsey understands the ubiquity of the parish as preventing 'neighbourly relations being subject to mere arbitrary selection', and Peter Ochs likewise commends the Church's responsibility for the citizens of their particular worldly polity, who are not 'determined *a priori*: they come as history has led them'.³⁸ As Ochs puts it, the Church of England 'attaches itself to a worldly polity and ... shares responsibility for the welfare of all citizens of that polity'.³⁹ This sense of responsibility for all those who share one's locality could fruitfully inform how responsibility for one's fellow citizens is understood by local communities throughout this national polity, as well as by our elected representatives.

Learning to practise responsibility to a particular place in this way also depends on *receiving* from others. As Quash argues, 'If Christians are worried that they cannot do it all themselves, cannot make the whole difference, or solve the whole problem, then that is probably a good lesson for them to learn. For in God's providence, Christians must trust that other agencies than theirs are working together for good ... and that it is not all just down to them.'⁴⁰ This willingness to trust in other agencies is necessary for civic action more widely, if it is to be sustained and not given up in desperation at the seemingly insurmountable task at hand.

So, both a willingness to take responsibility for all who come 'as history has led them' and the concomitant awareness of the need for collaboration in the learning and shouldering of this responsibility are practices which the Church of England can, or could learn to, offer to national life. These illuminate the deeper character of civic membership – as a socially embedded identity that is 'always already', not simply invented by the state. In bringing to light richer understandings of civic belonging, these practices also offer something to the imaginative horizon against which state policies are formed.

We have seen that the national turmoil over what it means to belong to a particular nation, and to be a member of that nation's civic community, is a situation that implicates the Church of England which, in its relationship with territory, has historically displayed possessive and hierarchical tendencies. Yet, as we have explored here, Anglican polity still has resources for fruitfully understanding belonging and responsibility within a community tethered to a particular place

– resources which can help to offer an alternative to narrow forms of nationalism, and to civic alienation. Despite – and, in some ways, even *because of* – its past, there is scope for the Church of England to contribute distinctively to the cultivation of a truly common national life.

Anglicanism's contribution to disagreement and deliberation

We turn now to a second contribution the Church of England has to offer to national polity. Jenkins argues that '[the Anglican priest] has to engage conversationally, rather than authoritatively, or in an exclusive fashion. This is because no one voice, opinion or understanding can hold an exhaustive account of the glory of God, and only through conversation are our blindnesses remedied.'[41]

While Jenkins proposes a 'conversational' mode as a distinctively Anglican form of engagement, I am not claiming that the Church of England by any means perfectly embodies this mode (as is obvious to anyone with even a passing knowledge of disagreements within the Church of England and across the Communion). To the contrary, it is precisely out of sustained Anglican failures to engage conversationally that I believe resources for forming wider political life have come to be articulated. It is by having been so bad at acknowledging the depths of disagreement for so long that members of the Church of England have been forced to let go of the aim of a resolution to the immediate disagreement and take action to pay attention to what is going on in the disagreement itself.[42] It is out of this sustained failure that there are resources developing in Anglican thought that grapple with what it means to live as a community amid deep and enduring disagreement about what it looks like for that community to flourish – without a basic consensus about what flourishing looks like and therefore what kind of future should be hoped for. A grammar is developing for talking about our failure to disagree well, and a posture is suggested which begins with acknowledgement of failure and is oriented towards ongoing reckoning with failure. It is in this way that the Church of England's failures of common life can be a resource – a means of grace – offered to a national discourse which is also characterized by similar dynamics of deep disagreement.

It is worth underlining that, for all that these are insights that have emerged through Anglican theologians grappling with their church's failures, they are resources the Church of England still needs to draw upon in its own practice. A failure to engage conversationally can be seen in the wariness about the motivations of others which is often evident in the internal discourse of the Church of England – particularly so in current debates over human sexuality.[43] The wider political climate in the United Kingdom is also marked by scepticism about others' motives. This is evident both between deeply polarized citizens, and as directed against public authorities in whom trust has been substantially eroded.[44] While a single root cause cannot be pointed to (and to do so would perhaps be to feed into the narrative of there having once been a golden age of public trust and civility), the symptoms are evident.[45]

Such wariness about motivations easily becomes a projected knowledge of the inner life of the other. As such, this kind of cynicism about others can be understood as a form of self-deception, which deadens and muffles our ability to attend to one another and protects against vulnerable encounter. As Higton puts it, 'We are finite, we are mortal, we are weak – and in the absence of any sure foundation, these truths are too bitter for us, and we hide them behind layers and layers of fantasy and illusion.'[46] When I am faced with real disagreement with the claims and actions of others, I assume that the other person's difference from me can only be a matter of bad faith, because that means I do not actually have to attend to their reasons for action or to their perspective. My accusation of bad faith – which is a claim to know their motives and to be able to contrast them with my own – protects me from facing their difference, and so protects me from challenge. The problem of mistrust is bound up, then, with our failure to extend doubt also towards our own ability to see and speak truthfully.[47]

There is a frequent failure in these discussions to take seriously that the 'other side' could also be seeking to be faithful to the call to common flourishing. A failure to recognize that, while we are all operating with mixed and obscured motivations, we cannot claim to know that 'they' are acting in bad faith. As we have seen, this does not mean denying the damage wrought by sincerely held commitments to 'faithful' praxis. However, this must also profoundly destabilize certainty over our own existing grasp of what is necessary for common flourishing.

Proposing self-directed scepticism

If cynical discourse derives from self-protecting delusion, then a common life built on genuine exchange (both within the church and in the wider civic polity) must involve practices that highlight and puncture such delusions. This will mean questioning our own ability to see and speak truthfully. So, the response to this socially corrosive scepticism (which encompasses both mistrust and overconfidence) in fact involves another form of scepticism or doubt, a form necessary to enable the growth of mutuality: namely a scepticism directed towards our capacity for self-delusion. We have seen that the kind of scepticism that becomes mistrust and overconfidence is directed towards the other: it assumes knowledge of the other's motivations and an unimpaired ability to judge. Fruitful scepticism, meanwhile, is directed towards oneself: it acknowledges the opaqueness of ourselves to ourselves; and to others; as well as others to ourselves.

In proposing this scepticism about the grasp of our own motivations and of our knowledge of what is in the common good, I am drawing on the argument made in Chapter 2 for the centrality of doubt in Christian formation. This requires that we begin by considering a scepticism proper to an awareness of our finitude. As we saw there, the limitations of any one person's perspective can be positively assessed as a deeper invitation into the particular web of relations in which we are each located.[48] We are 'our limits', not simply in the sense of having a particular location, but in the sense of being material and historical – shaped by all manner of forces in a specific history, in a tangle far too dense for us to tease out our identity with any completeness. We inevitably see only some of the factors that shape our vision and our desire and make us who we are.

So, our identity and social relations are always inherently obscured and occluded. Yet, as we saw earlier, 'My obscurity to myself, yours to me, and mine to you, are not *puzzles*, waiting for fruitful suspicion to discover the real script ...'[49] Rather, acknowledging both our finitude and our opaqueness to ourselves means recognizing that we can only come to know who we are, and what our good consists in, by encountering those who are not us – who exist beyond our limits. We discover more of the tangle of our own identity not just alone, but by interactions with those who exist beyond our limits. Our obscurity to ourselves and to one another should result in 'taking time' in our social relations, if we are to try to understand the other (and so also ourselves).[50]

However, as we have already seen, our limited understanding of ourselves and one another (and of what our individual and collective good consists in) also stems from our sinful condition, with one of the consequences being our all-too-frequent failure to acknowledge the need for ongoing struggle against self-deception – particularly when it comes to our own desires and motivations. Not only do we not know even the shape of our own desires very well (as finite creatures), but our desires are also frequently disordered and will be misread by us until we are confronted with the desires of others. Our ability to perceive what might be a common good is, therefore, refined through coming up against the awkward presence of others. Others' opaqueness thus also acts as a check on delusions that we can know the other person fully. Realizing our need for others to illuminate ourselves, also leads us to continually renegotiate our sense of who we are and how life together

CONCLUSION: FORMING COMMON CIVIC LIFE

should be conducted. Yet, as we saw earlier, this is not a picture of negotiation that starts from clear and fixed positions; rather, we discover who we are together through negotiation.

The contribution of self-directed scepticism to common life

These forms of doubt and scepticism are fruitful in two ways: first, in revealing the limits of any existing understanding or practice of common life, and second, in gesturing towards the possibilities for shared ongoing discernment of goods.

Revealing the limits of any existing grasp on common life

First, we will address the limits. If, as we have seen, part of creaturely existence is the impossibility of ever being sure that one is not deceived by oneself, this will inevitably generate uncertainty about political goods. The fact that I have only a limited grasp of my own interests, motives and desires, and of your interests, motives and desires, means that I do not know what it would take for my real interests to be met or for your interests to be met. I therefore do not know what we are aiming at; I do not know what flourishing looks like. In both the church and the civic polity, this means exercising an ongoing scepticism about our having achieved an existing and complete grasp of what is in the interests of every member of the polity.

Furthermore, if misrecognition of the common good is inevitable (whether through limitations inherent to our finitude or through the way evil is operative in our lives), then it follows that disagreement is also an inevitable feature of seeking to pursue a common life.[51] Yet, as we have seen, when disagreements arise we should not look to identify final resolutions (that is, looking simply to win an argument, or find a resolution that leaves all sides intact), for to do so would be to deny the limitations of our perspectives. Rather, we will look for ways in which the disagreement may challenge us, changing our perception of what we need and want – and we will leave space and time for that.

Additionally, we have seen that the limitations of our ability to recognize the good render all human judgements risky and provisional. Nonetheless, despite offering this profoundly destabilizing account of human limitation, we are nonetheless called to continue in the radically insecure action of making judgements and attempting to 'make sense' in public (not least because to do so is part and parcel of trying to understand ourselves). Acknowledging the provisionality of human judgements must therefore shape what we hope for in terms of the forms of shared life, and the structures that undergird these.

Each of these three forms of limit – first, refusing the temptation of settling with what we take to be an existing and complete grasp of what is in the interests of every member of the polity; second, engaging in disagreements without hoping for final, stable resolutions; and third, acknowledging that the provisionality of human judgements must therefore shape the forms and structure of the shared life that we hope for – offer challenges to corrosive forms of disagreement and deliberation in public and ecclesial discourse.

These limits also offer a challenge to those modes of political theology that tend to suggest that the church has a certain immunity to what Williams calls 'the challenges of questions and resources which others bring'.[52] Acknowledging the inevitability of the misrecognition of goods in the ecclesial community, as well as in the public square, means that as well as fostering this form of scepticism, the church also needs to be the recipient of critical attention. The practice of this kind of scepticism can therefore help nurture the mutuality highlighted in the last chapter as proper to the relationship between the church and wider civic life.

CONCLUSION: FORMING COMMON CIVIC LIFE

Conversational practices for ongoing discernment of goods

So, while the Church of England itself needs to practise self-directed scepticism (in its internal discussions *and* when it is acting as a body in public life), this is also a stance, or form of attention, that the church can offer to deliberative processes in the national polity. It is through belonging to a church that has so often been riven by failures to pay generous attention that Anglican theologians have been brought to reflection in this direction.

What, then, might all this mean for how we go about discerning the nature of common life? First of all, this suggests that the more voices we hear, the closer we come to discerning the good in common life. As Higton remarks: 'Almost the only thing we can know about the good we are to seek is that it is no-one's possession'.[53] This may sound like bad news. However, for those who feel there is something awry with the current state of democratic discourse and participation, this gives a language to describe what is wrong. It also shows what true conversation depends upon.

For the flipside of acknowledging our opaqueness to ourselves and to one another is the need for any one voice to be challenged and supplemented by others.[54] In this way, doubting the completeness of my own existing voice and perspective reveals the need for it to be brought into robust conversation with others, and so also brings into view the possibility that I might discover my own good as well as the good of others more deeply in the process (and thus hitherto invisible possibilities of mutuality).[55] Acknowledging the opaqueness of both myself and others – and so the limitations of our prior knowledge of what is in mine and the other's good – will also mean that we should look and work for a public discourse that is structured by practices of taking time to 'make sense' together (that is, not simply to come to a tidy explanation of the messiness of the world, which will often involve the demonization of those with whom we disagree).[56]

These practices of attention are all the more necessary and

demanding across deep difference. Williams, while Archbishop of Canterbury, described the need to work at recognizing the other with whom one is in disagreement in the church: 'Having heard what you say, can I recognise the possibility of being called to deeper obedience to the gospel (given what I currently understand that obedience to mean) by what you say, and can I see the possibility (given what you currently understand obedience to mean) of calling you to deeper obedience?' As Higton puts it, 'Can I see that his or her discernment is being offered as a gift to the Church, an attempt to show the Church more of the Church's Lord and the demands that his love makes on our lives?'[57] This hard work of attending to the other's obedience and discernment is to be undertaken in the context of an ecclesial community in which each member has committed to 'a promise to be willing to be converted by each other'.[58]

This willingness to be converted entails being prepared continually to renegotiate our sense of who we are and how life together should be conducted. It entails being challenged – again and again – by those with whom a community is shared to look again at something we thought we already understood. The suggestion here is that, through the discomfort of living in sustained disagreement, we can perhaps learn at a deeper level to recognize others' actions as a gift to the body as a whole. In this way, the discipline of sharing a church with those with whom we disagree can perhaps be a gift to a deeply divided public life.[59] We might take the framing of the Church of England's *Living in Love and Faith* discussions of human sexuality as an (imperfect) example of this – suspending the end goal and thinking about the form of the disagreement itself, and through this trying to see how one another can be received as gifts amid this deeply painful disagreement.[60]

If it is the case that we need the voices of others to discover our own good, then our common life is found most fully not in finding out definitively what the common good *is*, but in participation in the discussion of what comprises the common good. The fruitful forms of scepticism we have explored reveal

CONCLUSION: FORMING COMMON CIVIC LIFE

human flourishing to be radically contingent upon participation in decision-making structures. Drawing on Walter Gallie, we could therefore describe the common good as an 'essentially contested concept': that is, a concept that is impossible to resolve through argument, but is rather sustained by such argument. In this light, a common good is so in part because it is discerned in common.[61] The kinds of practical settlements reached through this kind of deliberation are ones in which there is no single definitive account of what the settlement means, but rather one where those with different theoretical understandings find overlap.

Most hopefully of all, there is scope for the practice of this kind of scepticism to give rise to processes of deliberation in which our moment-by-moment mutual dependence points to a more foundational belonging together. Because we are being called to a common future, we do indeed have a common good whether we learn to recognize it or not. Moreover, as Higton says, 'This belonging-together provides the ground on which our negotiating and arguing can go to work'.[62]

These, then, are some of the ways in which this kind of ecclesially-rooted scepticism can help to form a more profoundly confronting and challenging, but also more hopeful politics in pursuit of common life.[63] Such scepticism exposes our attempts to protect against the vulnerability that accompanies finitude and limitation: our attempts to escape the creaturely limits that cause us to need the perspectives of others to see more truthfully. While we can never fully escape our egotism, it can be brought to our attention through confronting the reality of others, who bring a different perspective to bear on ourselves, the world and our place within it. The ongoing need for this self-directed scepticism is not, therefore, a negative final judgement on our capacity for common life, but a positive attempt both to avoid self-deception, and to learn properly about who we are (and who we might come to be) through being confronted by the other. It is only in this way that we can hope to discern forms of life that enable the flourishing of all.

Conclusion

Throughout this book I have been concerned with the way in which the formation of Christian ethical and political identity involves being drawn into seeing more deeply. In the first half of this chapter, I explored the scope for the Church of England, as embedded in particular 'territories', to learn to better attend with its neighbours. We have seen that this involves practices of inhabiting place that foster attention to the particularity of a given social context; are open to challenge and disruption; and are able to be genuinely shared. I then addressed the possibility for the Church of England to learn to better attend, and to enable others to do so, through public conversations. In relation to the cultivation of an Anglican conversational mode, we have seen that learning to attend means recognizing our inability to ever fully see by ourselves what is in the common good, and so fostering practices which open ecclesial and public deliberative processes to disruption and challenge by the voices of others.

A second central strand that has run through this book is the need to resist accounts of Christian and civic identity in which what has been received is understood as fixed and finalized. In this concluding chapter we have considered how the Church of England can bring to light the always negotiated and revisable dimensions of civic identity. In the first half of the chapter, this involved consideration of the way in which place is something both given *to* us and *by* us. The way in which Anglican territorial embeddedness is 'always already' also offers the opportunity to consider the way in which we are all, and properly should be, engaged in the ongoing negotiation of a received identity. This received identity incorporates both the good and the bad and yet, in grappling with the troubling history and current reality we have received (including through penitential practices), we come to a deeper understanding of what it is to belong to a political community – and to bear responsibility for that community. In the second half of the chapter, we see the way that the ongoing negotiation of the form of common life

CONCLUSION: FORMING COMMON CIVIC LIFE

in which we find ourselves (both civic and ecclesial) requires self-directed scepticism, in order to open us up to receive the particular perspective brought by each individual.

There are further avenues for exploration suggested here for developing a richer theology of citizenship and democratic life through engagement with the negative theological tradition. However, these are questions for another day. For now, I hope I have shown that Christian ethical and political formation must and *should* take place inside *and* outside the church. Recognizing the need to be formed through participation in both ecclesial and civic life follows from a recognition of the ways of the Spirit, bubbling up in each of our lives in unexpected ways to lead us deeper into God's abundance.

This bubbling up takes place in both the church and civic life – and in both civil society *and* the state. All of these are arenas in which the Christian can be formed more fully *as a Christian* through their participation. In each of these locations, individual and institutional formation is ongoing. For we do not yet know what we will be, and we do not yet know what the church or our civic institutions will be, but we are called to trust in the abundance of God, through the guidance of the Spirit. It is this hope of being drawn ever more deeply into the life of God that is at the heart of the Christian political formation.

Notes

1 Timothy Jenkins, 'Anglicanism: The Only Answer to Modernity' in *Anglicanism: The Answer to Modernity*, eds Duncan Dormor, Jack McDonald and Jeremy Caddick (London: Continuum, 2005), pp. 197–8.

2 Jenkins, 'Anglicanism: The Only Answer to Modernity', pp. 197–8.

3 Paul Gilroy, *Postcolonial Melancholia* (New York City: Columbia University Press, 2004).

4 See, for example, David Goodhart's analysis of the referendum in terms of a clash between 'Somewheres' and 'Anywheres', in *The Road to Somewhere: The Populist Revolt and the Future of Politics* (London: C. Hurst & Co., 2017) and Jonathan Freedland's critical response: 'The Road to Somewhere by David Goodhart – a liberal's rightwing

turn on immigration', *The Guardian*, 22 March 2017, https://www.theguardian.com/books/2017/mar/22/the-road-to-somewhere-david-goodhart-populist-revolt-future-politics, accessed 04.08.2022.

5 The Report of the Commission on Race and Ethnic Disparities (March 2021), https://www.gov.uk/government/publications/the-report-of-the-commission-on-race-and-ethnic-disparities, accessed 04.08.2022.

6 Legal scholar Tufyal Choudhury has detailed the programme of 'decitizenizing' that has marked Home Office policies towards immigrants over recent decades. Tufyal Choudhury, 'The Radicalization of Citizenship Deprivation' in *Critical Social Policy*, 37:2 (2017), pp. 225–44. These trends can also be seen in the creation of the category of 'non-violent extremism', by which whole strata of the citizenry become suspected of not truly belonging to the nation unless they can demonstrate their assent to 'British values'.

7 The 2018 scandal saw British citizens and legal immigrants detained, denied legal rights, threatened with deportation and, in at least 83 cases, wrongly deported from the UK by the Home Office. Many of those affected had been born British subjects in the Commonwealth and had arrived in the UK before 1973, as members of the Windrush Generation. For more see, Kevin Rawlinson, *The Guardian*, 12 November 2018, https://www.theguardian.com/uk-news/2018/nov/12/windrush-11-people-wrongly-deported-from-uk-have-died-sajid-javid, accessed 04.08.2022; and Wendy Williams, *Windrush Lessons Learned Review*, https://assets.publishing.service.gov.uk/government/uploads/system/uploads/attachment_data/file/876336/6.5577_HO_Windrush_Lessons_Learned_Review_LoResFinal.pdf, accessed 04.08.2022.

8 'Shamima Begum: IS Teenager to Lose UK Citizenship', BBC News, 20 February 2019, https://www.bbc.co.uk/news/uk-47299907?int link_from_url=https://www.bbc.co.uk/news/topics/cd7klnzkyd3t/syria-schoolgirls-case&link_location=live-reporting-story, accessed 04.08.2022. Owen Bowcott, 'Council of Europe Accepts UK Compromise on Prisoner Voting Rights', *The Guardian*, 7 December 2017, https://www.theguardian.com/politics/2017/dec/07/council-of-europe-accepts-uk-compromise-on-prisoner-voting-rights, accessed 22.07.2022.

9 Russell Taylor, 'Impact of "Hostile Environment" Policy Debate on 14 June 2018', Library Briefing (House of Lords, 11 June 2018), https://researchbriefings.files.parliament.uk/documents/LLN-2018-0064/LLN-2018-0064.pdf, accessed 04.08.2022.

10 Anna Rowlands is among those who have highlighted the state's deliberate alienation of asylum seekers, drawing attention to the particular role played by temporality in this alienation: Anna Rowlands, 'Temporality, Dispossession and the Search for the Good: Interpreting the Book of Jeremiah with the Jesuit Refugee Service', *Political Theology* 19:6 (2018): 517–36.

CONCLUSION: FORMING COMMON CIVIC LIFE

11 Andrew Rumsey, *Parish: An Anglican Theology of Place* (London: SCM Press, 2017), p. 6.

12 Jenkins, 'Anglicanism: The Only Answer to Modernity', p. 200.

13 See, for example, Tim Cresswell, *Place: An Introduction* (Oxford: Wiley Blackwell, 2015) and Henri Lefebvre, *The Production of Space*, trans. Donald Nicholson-Smith (Oxford: Blackwell, 1991).

14 Jarel Robinson-Brown, *Black, Gay, British, Christian, Queer: The Church and the Famine of Grace* (London: SCM Press, 2021) and A. D. A France-Williams, *Ghost Ship: Institutional Racism and the Church of England* (London: SCM Press, 2020). See also Anthony G. Reddie, *Theologising Brexit: A Liberationist and Postcolonial Critique* (Abingdon: Routledge, 2019) and Robert Beckford, *Documentary as Exorcism: Resisting the Bewitchment of Colonial Christianity* (London: Bloomsbury, 2014).

15 Rumsey, *Parish*, p. 143.

16 Doreen Massey, *Spatial Divisions of Labour: Social Structures and the Geography of Production* (London: Palgrave Macmillan, 1995), p. 99.

17 David Fletcher, 'The Parish Boundary: A Social Phenomenon in Hanoverian England', *Rural History* 14:2 (2003): 177–96 (p. 187). Looking beyond the Church of England, Siobhán Garrigan's work likewise draws out the way not all senses of locality expressed by the church tend towards seeking the flourishing of strangers: for example, the way that the language of intercessory prayer for 'our community' can smuggle in an oppositional sense of concern for the welfare of this community over and against those other communities which it was established to protect against. As she puts it, 'In Church, the language of "our community" ... reinforces a sense in which our Church is: a) separate from and b) more worth praying for than that of others.' This sense of 'our community' often runs together with 'sticking together' and looking after our own. Garrigan, *The Real Peace Process: Worship, Politics and the End of Sectarianism* (London: Routledge, 2016), p. 112.

18 Robert Lee, *Rural Society and the Anglican Clergy, 1815–1914: Encountering and Managing the Poor* (Woodbridge: Boydell Press, 2006).

19 Raymond Williams, *The Country and the City* (London: Chatto & Windus, 1973). I am not arguing that is this solely – or even primarily – the church's fault: the patchiness of localized welfare provision in this period is the proper primary object of critique here.

20 Rumsey, *Parish*, p. 111.

21 Willie James Jennings, *The Christian Imagination: Theology and the Origins of Race* (New Haven, CT: Yale University Press, 2011),

pp. 248–9. Jennings explains that such 'relationships involve deep joining, the opening of lives to one another in love and desire' (pp. 264–5).

22 Jennings, *The Christian Imagination*, p. 249.

23 Rowan Williams, 'Epilogue' in *Praying for England: Priestly Presence in Contemporary Culture*, eds Samuel Wells and Sarah Coakley (London: Continuum, 2008), pp, 171–82, 175–9, 186.

24 Romand Coles and Stanley Hauerwas, *Christianity, Democracy, and the Radical Ordinary* (Eugene, OR: Cascade Books, 2008), p. 185.

25 Coles and Hauerwas, *Christianity, Democracy, and the Radical Ordinary*, p. 178.

26 Williams, 'Epilogue', p. 176. That is, if this erosion of status is received without brittle defensiveness.

27 Massey, *Spatial Divisions of Labour*. Referenced in Rumsey, *Parish*, p. 71.

28 Daniel W. Hardy, *Wording a Radiance: Parting Conversations About God and the Church* (London: SCM Press, 2010), p. 30.

29 Assemblage theory helps to illuminate this relationship between the particular and the whole. Manuel DeLanda defines an assemblage as an 'irreducible social whole produced by relations of exteriority, a whole that does not totalize its parts'. Manuel DeLanda, *Assemblage Theory* (Edinburgh: Edinburgh University Press, 2016), p. 11.

I should be clear that I am not making a historical claim here about the process by which the Church of England was formed. Additionally, we should note that there are obviously also centralizing structures and dynamics at play within Anglicanism – particularly in the relationship between the Church of England and the rest of the Communion. Nonetheless, federation has become important for the self-understanding of the churches of the Anglican Communion, as articulated mainly by certain academics and clergy, and this sustained articulation has come to shape a broader self-understanding of what it is to be the Church of England and the Anglican Communion. It has come to be part of how we understand ourselves, and so is partially true of how Anglicanism works: it has come to form polity in certain ways.

30 Rumsey, *Parish*, p. 180. See also pp. 83–4, 96. Rumsey proposes that working with the grain of Anglican localism in this way can offer 'a partial check on the more imperious and damaging aspects of national loyalty' (p. 180).

31 Rumsey, *Parish*, pp. 145–7. Rumsey argues there has been a significant historical understanding of the parish boundary as 'a locally enacted reality, often contested and open to a degree of adjustment'.

32 Hardy, *Wording a Radiance*, pp. 30, 85.

33 Morris, 'The Future of Church and State' in *Anglicanism: The Answer to Modernity*, pp. 161–85, 178. Morris argues that only then

CONCLUSION: FORMING COMMON CIVIC LIFE

can the Church 'claim honestly to be cultivating a spirit of honest attention to the practice of building Christian community'.

34 Grace Davie, 'Debate' in *Praying for England: Priestly Presence in Contemporary Culture*, eds Samuel Wells and Sarah Coakley (London: Continuum, 2008), pp. 147–70.

35 Kwame Anthony Appiah, *Cosmopolitanism: Ethics in a World of Strangers* (London: Penguin, 2007).

36 Harriet Sherwood, 'Justin Welby prostrates himself in apology for British massacre at Amritsar', *The Guardian*, 10 September 2019, https://www.theguardian.com/world/2019/sep/10/justin-welby-apologises-in-name-of-christ-british-massacre-amritsar, accessed 22.07.2022. Mark Oliver, 'Archbishop urges church to consider slavery reparations', *The Guardian*, 26 March 2007, https://www.theguardian.com/world/2007/mar/26/religion.race, accessed 04.08.2022.

37 For while the Church of England's proximity to the powers of government has undoubted dangers, it is also, as Ben Quash argues, a framework capable of 'sustaining responsible attention to the world and to history'. *Found Theology: History, Imagination and the Holy Spirit* (London: Bloomsbury, 2013), pp. 10–11.

38 Rumsey, *Parish*, p. 86; Peter Ochs, *Another Reformation: Postliberal Christianity and the Jews* (Grand Rapids, MI: Baker Academic, 2011), p. 173.

39 Ochs, *Another Reformation*, p. 173.

40 Quash, *Found Theology*, p. 25.

41 Jenkins, 'Anglicanism: The Only Answer to Modernity', p. 200.

42 However, this is not to say the Church of England is any more broken than any other church – we are not distinguished in that faux humble way. See Mike Higton on the Church of England being just 'one more messed up church among others' in *The Life of Christian Doctrine* (London: Bloomsbury, 2020).

43 One recent example of this can be seen in the production, and reception of, the Church of England Evangelical Council's short film *The Beautiful Story*, https://ceec.info/resources/the-beautiful-story, accessed 16.12.2022.

44 See, for example, the consecutive findings of the British Social Attitudes survey. The 2013 findings spell this out particularly starkly: 'Key findings', *British Social Attitudes* 30 (2013), https://www.bsa.natcen.ac.uk/latest-report/british-social-attitudes-30/key-findings/trust-politics-and-institutions.aspx, accessed 04.08.2022.

45 As Williams highlighted back in the aftermath of cash-for-questions: 'What we risk in our current situation is a default assumption that the ideal of "public service" is an illusion: if we take it for granted that people habitually act from individual interest alone, it becomes

unimaginable that anyone charged with representing the interest or long-term good of another will do so consistently or effectively.' John Bingham, 'Expenses Scandal Helped Shatter Faith in "public service" – Rowan Williams', *The Telegraph*, 16 June 2012, https://www.telegraph.co.uk/news/newstopics/mps-expenses/9335001/Expenses-scandal-helped-shatter-faith-in-public-service-Rowan-Williams.html, accessed 04.08.2022.

46 Mike Higton, *Difficult Gospel: The Theology of Rowan Williams* (London: SCM Press, 2004), pp. 17–18.

47 As Williams argues, 'I shall not truthfully see the web of lies in which our public life buzzes away ... until I have recognised where the fissures of the same untruthfulness run across my moral vision.' Rowan Williams, *Open to Judgement* (London: DLT, 2002), p. 128.

48 Jonathan Chaplin, 'Person, Society and State in the Thought of Rowan Williams' (Lecture, 23 November 2012), https://www.vhi.st-edmunds.cam.ac.uk/system/files/documents/paper%20chaplin.pdf, accessed 04.08.2022.

49 Rowan Williams, 'The Suspicion of Suspicion: Wittgenstein and Bonhoeffer' in *Wrestling with Angels: Conversations in Modern Theology* (London: SCM Press, 2007), p. 199.

50 Williams, 'The Suspicion of Suspicion', p. 198.

51 As Williams points out, it is only in situations where one is the oppressor that other people do not seem difficult. Rowan Williams, *Lost Icons: Reflections on Cultural Bereavement* (London: T&T Clark, 2000), p. 113.

52 Such certainty about the church's clear-sighted apprehension of the common good stands in stark contrast to Williams' assertion that the Christian vision 'is worked out only in passionate and argumentative engagement in the uncertainties and limitations of human political action'. Rowan Williams, 'The Ethics of SDI', ed. Richard Bauckham and John Elford, *The Nuclear Weapons Debate: Theological and Ethical Issues* (London: SCM Press, 1989), pp. 162–74.

53 Higton, *Difficult Gospel*, p. 128.

54 See also, for example, Williams on the need to read Scripture in company as discussed in Higton, *Difficult Gospel*, p. 67.

55 If we require processes of deliberation that foster an awareness of the limitations of any single perspective, we therefore also need governance structures which tend in this direction.

56 As Williams argues through a reading of King Lear, patience is required to not seek explanation, but rather to make sense amid the untidy fallenness of the world. Rowan Williams, *The Tragic Imagination* (Oxford: Oxford University Press, 2016). See also: Rowan Williams, 'Resurrection and Peace: More on New Testament Ethics' in *On Christian Theology* (Oxford: Blackwell, 2000), p. 273.

CONCLUSION: FORMING COMMON CIVIC LIFE

57 Mike Higton, 'Rowan Williams' in *The Oxford Handbook of Ecclesiology*, ed. Paul Avis (Oxford: Oxford University Press, 2018), p. 515, referencing Rowan Williams, 'Making Moral Decisions' in *The Cambridge Companion to Christian Ethics*, ed. Robin Gill (Cambridge: Cambridge University Press, 2001), pp. 3–15 (p. 11). The church should, by this account, be 'a community in which not only do I seek your deeper obedience, but in which I also seek your seeking of my deeper obedience'. Higton, 'Rowan Williams', p. 518.

58 Higton, 'Rowan Williams', p. 518, referencing Rowan Williams, 'Debate on a Covenant for the Anglican Communion' (13 February 2008), http://rowanwilliams.archbishopofcanterbury.org/articles.php/1522/debate-on-a-covenant-for-the-anglican-communion.html, accessed 04.08.2022.

59 This is not to say that this is guaranteed to be the case: being adversely affected by the decisions of those you deeply disagree with can also lead to greater demonization.

60 The Church of England, *Living in Love and Faith: Christian teaching and learning about identity, sexuality, relationships and marriage* (London: Church House Publishing, 2020).

61 Walter Gallie, 'Essentially Contested Concepts', *Proceedings of the Aristotelian Society* 56 (1956): 167–98. These are concepts that are impossible to resolve deliberation through argument, but are rather, according to Gallie, sustained by such argument. Religion, art, science, social justice and democracy are identified by Gallie as among such contested concepts.

62 Higton, *Difficult Gospel*, p. 124.

63 Higton, *Difficult Gospel*, pp. 140, 142.

Bibliography

Books and journal articles

Appiah, Kwame Anthony, *Cosmopolitanism: Ethics in a World of Strangers* (London: Penguin, 2007)

Ashmenall, Jackie, 'Organising Among Anglican Churches in Ealing: A Reflection', presented at Reimagining the Ministry of the Church, Leeds, 23 November 2018

Astley, Jeff, Leslie J. Francis and Colin Crowder, *Theological Perspectives on Christian Formation: A Reader on Theology and Christian Education* (Grand Rapids, MI: Wm B. Eerdmans, 1996)

Avis, Paul, ed., *The Oxford Handbook of Ecclesiology* (Oxford: Oxford University Press, 2018)

Backhouse, Stephen, *Kierkegaard's Critique of Christian Nationalism* (Oxford: Oxford University Press, 2011)

Barrett, Al, 'Asset-Based Community Development: A Theological Reflection', Church Urban Fund, 2013, https://cuf.org.uk/resources/a-theological-reflection-on-asset-based-community-development

—— *Interrupting the Church's Flow: A Radically Receptive Political Theology in the Urban Margins* (London: SCM, 2020)

—— 'Interrupting the Church's Flow: Hearing "Other" Voices on an Outer Urban Estate', *Practical Theology* 11, no. 1 (2018): 79–92

Barrett, Al and Ruth Harley, *Being Interrupted: Reimagining the Church's Mission from the Outside, In* (London: SCM Press, 2020)

Beckford, Robert, *Documentary as Exorcism: Resisting the Bewitchment of Colonial Christianity* (London: Bloomsbury, 2014)

Bertschmann, Dorothea, '"But Our Constitution Is in Heaven": New Testament Sketches on the People of God between Divine Law and Earthly Rulers' in *Christianity and Constitutionalism*, eds Nicholas Aroney and Ian Leigh (September 2022)

Bishop, Andrew, 'Eucharist Shaping: Church, Mission and Personhood in Gabriel Hebert's Liturgy and Society', DTh thesis, King's College London, 2013, https://ethos.bl.uk/OrderDetails.do?uin=uk.bl.ethos.628479

BIBLIOGRAPHY

Bonhoeffer, Dietrich, *Creation and Fall*, Dietrich Bonhoeffer Works, Vol. 3 (Minneapolis, MN: Fortress Press, 2001)
—— *Dietrich Bonhoeffer Works / Translated from the German Edition*, 1st English language edn with new supplementary material (Minneapolis, MN: Fortress Press, 1998)
—— *Discipleship*, Dietrich Bonhoeffer Works, Vol. 4 (Minneapolis, MN: Fortress Press, 2001)
—— *Ethics* (London: SCM Press, 1955)
—— *Fiction from Tegel Prison*, Dietrich Bonhoeffer Works, Vol. 7 (Minneapolis, MN: Fortress Press, 2000)
—— *Letters and Papers from Prison*, ed. Eberhard Bethge (New York: Macmillan, 1971)
—— *Letters and Papers from Prison*, ed. John de Gruchy (Minneapolis, MN: Fortress Press, 2010)
—— *Sanctorum Communio: A Theological Study of the Sociology of the Church*, Dietrich Bonhoeffer Works, Vol. 1 (Minneapolis, MN: Fortress Press, 1998)
—— *Life Together: Prayerbook of the Bible*, Dietrich Bonhoeffer Works, Vol. 5 (Minneapolis, MN: Fortress Press, 2005)
—— *Berlin, 1932–1933*, Dietrich Bonhoeffer Works, Vol. 12 (Minneapolis, MN: Fortress Press, 2009)
Bretherton, Luke, 'A New Establishment? Theological Politics and the Emerging Shape of Church–State Relations', *Political Theology* 7, no. 3 (2015): 371–92
—— 'Anglican Political Theology' in *The Wiley Blackwell Companion to Political Theology*, eds William T. Cavanaugh and Peter Scott, 2nd edition (Oxford: Blackwell, 2018), 164–77
—— *Christ and the Common Life: Political Theology and the Case for Democracy* (Grand Rapids, MI: Eerdmans, 2019)
—— *Christianity and Contemporary Politics: The Conditions and Possibilities of Faithful Witness* (Chichester: Wiley-Blackwell, 2010)
—— *Hospitality as Holiness: Christian Witness Amidst Moral Diversity* (London: Routledge, 2010)
—— 'Reflections on Graham Ward's The Politics of Discipleship', presented at the Christian Theological Research Fellowship Annual Meeting of the American Academy of Religion, Montreal, Quebec, 2009, https://theotherjournal.com/2010/01/18/symposium-the-politics-of-discipleship-part-2/
—— *Resurrecting Democracy: Faith, Citizenship, and the Politics of a Common Life* (Cambridge: Cambridge University Press, 2015)
—— 'Sharing Peace: Class, Hierarchy, and Christian Social Order' in *The Blackwell Companion to Christian Ethics*, eds Stanley Hauerwas and Samuel Wells, 2nd edition (Oxford: Blackwell, 2011), pp. 329–43

Brown, Malcolm, 'Politics as the Church's Business: William Temple's Christianity and Social Order Revisited', *Journal of Anglican Studies* 5, no. 2 (2007), 163–85

Brown, Malcolm, ed., *Anglican Social Theology: Renewing the Vision Today* (London: Church House Publishing, 2014)

Brueggemann, Walter, 'The Liturgy of Abundance, The Myth of Scarcity', *Christian Century*, 24–31 March, 1999

Burns, Stephen, Nicola Slee and Michael N. Jagessar, eds, *The Edge of God: New Liturgical Texts and Contexts in Conversation* (London: Epworth, 2008), pp. 91–103

Cavanaugh, William, *Theopolitical Imagination: Christian Practices of Space and Time* (London: T&T Clark, 2001)

Chaplin, Jonathan, 'Book Review: Luke Bretherton, Resurrecting Democracy: Faith, Citizenship, and the Politics of a Common Life', *Studies in Christian Ethics* 30, no. 2 (2017), 228–32

—— 'Person, Society and State in the Thought of Rowan Williams', Lecture presented at Von Hügel Institute, St Edmund's College, 23 November 2012, https://www.vhi.st-edmunds.cam.ac.uk/system/files/documents/paper%20chaplin.pdf

Chapman, Mark, 'Rowan Williams' Political Theology: Multiculturalism and Interactive Pluralism', *Journal of Anglican Studies* 9, no. 1 (2011), 61–79

Charlesworth, Martin and Natalie Williams, *A Church For the Poor: Transforming the Church to Reach the Poor in Britain Today* (Eastbourne: David C. Cook, 2017)

Coakley, Sarah, 'Introduction: Prayer, Place, and the Poor' in *Praying for England: Priestly Presence in Contemporary Culture*, eds Samuel Wells and Sarah Coakley (London: Continuum, 2008), pp. 1–20

Coles, Romand, *Beyond Gated Politics: Reflections for the Possibility of Democracy* (Minneapolis, MN: University of Minnesota Press, 2005)

Coles, Romand and Stanley Hauerwas, *Christianity, Democracy, and the Radical Ordinary: Conversations Between a Radical Democrat and a Christian* (Eugene, OR: Wipf and Stock, 2008)

Collicutt, Joanna, *The Psychology of Christian Character Formation* (London: SCM Press, 2015)

Cresswell, Tim, *Place: An Introduction* (Oxford: Wiley Blackwell, 2015)

Daggers, Jenny, 'A Theological Anthropology for Human Flourishing: Postcolonial and Feminist Reflections for These Troubled Times', *Louvain Studies* 41, no. 2 (2018), 152–72

—— 'Troubling Gifts of Second-Hand Grace: A Feminist and Postcolonial Reimagining', plenary paper given at the annual conference of the Society of the Study of Theology, April 2019

BIBLIOGRAPHY

D'Andrea, Thomas D., *Tradition, Rationality, and Virtue: The Thought of Alasdair MacIntyre* (Abingdon, Oxon: Routledge, 2006)

Davie, Grace, 'Debate' in *Praying for England: Priestly Presence in Contemporary Culture*, eds Samuel Wells and Sarah Coakley (London: Continuum, 2008), pp. 147–70

Davison, Andrew and Alison Milbank, *For the Parish: A Critique of Fresh Expression* (London: SCM Press, 2010)

DeLanda, Manuel, *Assemblage Theory* (Edinburgh: Edinburgh University Press, 2016)

Dormor, Duncan J., Jack McDonald and Jeremy Caddick, eds, *Anglicanism: The Answer to Modernity* (London: Continuum, 2003)

Draper, Andrew, *A Theology of Race and Place: Liberation and Reconciliation in the Works of Jennings and Carter* (Eugene, OR: Pickwick Publications, 2016)

Earey, Mark, Ruth Meyers and Carol Doran, eds, *Worship-Shaped Life: Liturgical Formation and the People of God* (Harrisburg, PA: Morehouse Publishing, 2010)

Eliot, T. S., *Four Quartets* (London: Faber and Faber, 2001)

Farneth, Molly, 'A Politics of Tending and Transformation', *Studies in Christian Ethics* 32, no. 1 (2019), 113–18

Fletcher, David, 'The Parish Boundary: A Social Phenomenon in Hanoverian England', *Rural History* 14, no. 2 (2003), 177–96

Ford, David and Dennis Stamps, eds, *Essentials of Christian Community* (Edinburgh: T&T Clark, 1996)

Gallie, Walter, 'Essentially Contested Concepts', *Proceedings of the Aristotelian Society* 56 (1956), 167–98

Garrigan, Siobhán, *Beyond Ritual: Sacramental Theology after Habermas* (Aldershot: Ashgate, 2004)

—— *The Real Peace Process: Worship, Politics and the End of Sectarianism*, Religion and Violence 7 (Abingdon, Oxon: Routledge, 2014)

Gittoes, Julie, 'Where Is the Kingdom?' in *Generous Ecclesiology: Church, World and the Kingdom of God*, eds Julie Gittoes, Brutus Green and James Heard (London: SCM Press, 2013)

Gittoes, Julie, Brutus Green and James Heard, eds, *Generous Ecclesiology: Church, World and the Kingdom of God* (London: SCM Press, 2013)

—— 'Introduction' in *Generous Ecclesiology: Church, World and the Kingdom of God* (London: SCM Press, 2013)

Goodhart, David, *The Road to Somewhere: The Populist Revolt and the Future of Politics* (London: C. Hurst & Co., 2017)

Graaff, Guido de, 'Intercession as Political Ministry: Re-Interpreting the Priesthood of All Believers', *Modern Theology* 32: 4 (2016), 504–21

Griffiths, Andy, *Refusing to Be Indispensable: Vacating the Centre of Church Life* (Cambridge: Grove Books, 2018)

Groom, Sue, 'The Language of Formation in Official Church of England Documents', *Anglican Theological Review* 99, no. 2 (2017): 233–54

Guest, Deryn, 'Liturgy and Loss: A Lesbian Perspective on Using Psalms of Lament in Liturgy' in *The Edge of God: New Liturgical Texts and Contexts in Conversation*, eds Nicola Slee, Michael N. Jagessar and Stephen Burns (London: Epworth, 2008), 202–16

Guest, Mathew, 'Sociological Strand – Worship and Action' in Helen Cameron, Douglas Davies, Philip Richter and Frances Ward, eds, *Studying Local Churches: Perspectives on the Local Church* (London: SCM Press, 2005), 98–109

Gutiérrez, Gustavo, *A Theology of Liberation*, trans. Caridad Inda and John Eagleson (London: SCM Press, 1988)

—— *The Power of the Poor in History*, trans. Robert Barr (New York: Orbis Books, 1983)

Hardy, Daniel W., 'A Magnificent Complexity' in *Essentials of Christian Community*, eds David Ford and Dennis Stamps (Edinburgh: T&T Clark, 1996)

—— 'Church' in *The Oxford Companion to Christian Thought*, ed. Ed Hastings (Oxford: Oxford University Press, 2009)

—— *Finding the Church: The Dynamic Truth of Anglicanism* (London: SCM Press, 2001)

—— *Wording a Radiance: Parting Conversations on God and the Church* (London: SCM Press, 2010)

Hauerwas, Stanley, *A Community of Character: Toward a Constructive Christian Social Ethic* (Notre Dame, IN: University of Notre Dame Press, 1981)

—— *The State of the University: Academic Knowledges and the Knowledge of God* (Oxford: Blackwell Publishing, 2007)

—— 'The Virtues of Alasdair MacIntyre', *First Things*, October 2007, https://www.firstthings.com/article/2007/10/the-virtues-of-alasdair-macintyre

Hauerwas, Stanley and Samuel Wells, eds, *The Blackwell Companion to Christian Ethics* (Malden, MA: Blackwell, 2004)

Hauerwas, Stanley and William Willimon, *Resident Aliens: Life in the Christian Colony* (Nashville, TN: Abingdon Press, 1989)

Healy, Nicholas M., *Hauerwas: A (Very) Critical Introduction* (Grand Rapids, MI: Eerdmans, 2014)

Higton, Mike, *A Theology of Higher Education* (Oxford: Oxford University Press, 2012)

—— *Difficult Gospel: The Theology of Rowan Williams* (London: SCM Press, 2004)

—— 'Rowan Williams' in *The Oxford Handbook of Ecclesiology*, ed. Paul Avis (Oxford: Oxford University Press, 2018), pp. 505–24

BIBLIOGRAPHY

——— 'The Ecclesial Body's Grace: Obedience and Faithfulness in Rowan Williams' Ecclesiology', *Ecclesiology* 7 (2011), 7–28
——— *The Life of Christian Doctrine* (London: Bloomsbury, 2020)
Hopewell, James, *Congregation: Stories and Structures* (London: SCM Press, 1987)
Hordern, Joshua, *Political Affections: Civic Participation and Moral Theology* (Oxford: Oxford University Press, 2013)
Jenkins, Timothy, 'An Ethical Account of Ritual: An Anthropological Description of the Anglican Daily Offices', *Studies in Christian Ethics* 15, no. 1 (2002), 1–10
——— *An Experiment in Providence: How Faith Engages with the World* (London: SPCK, 2006)
——— 'Anglicanism: The Only Answer to Modernity' in *Anglicanism: The Answer to Modernity*, eds Duncan J. Dormor, Jack McDonald and Jeremy Caddick (London: Continuum, 2003)
——— 'Fieldwork and the Perception of Everyday Life', *Man* 29, no. 2 (1994), 433–55
Jennings, Willie James, *The Christian Imagination: Theology and the Origins of Race* (New Haven, CT: Yale University Press, 2010)
Jesson, Stuart, 'Compassion, Consolation, and the Sharing of Attention' in *Simone Weil and Continental Philosophy*, ed. A. Rebecca Rozelle-Stone (Lanham, MD: Rowman and Littlefield, 2017), pp. 121–42
Kärkkäinen, Veli-Matti, *Pneumatology: The Holy Spirit in Ecumenical, International, and Contextual Perspective* (Grand Rapids, MI: Baker Academic, 2002)
Lee, Robert, *Rural Society and the Anglican Clergy, 1815–1914: Encountering and Managing the Poor* (Woodbridge: Boydell Press, 2006)
Lefebvre, Henri, *The Production of Space*, trans. Donald Nicholson-Smith (Oxford: Blackwell, 1991)
Lloyd, Vincent, 'Of Puzzles and Idols', *Syndicate*, 2 March 2016, https://syndicate.network/symposia/theology/resurrecting-democracy/#vincent-lloyd
MacIntyre, Alasdair, *After Virtue: A Study in Moral Theology*, 3rd edition (London: Duckworth Books, 2007)
Martin, Jessica, 'Attention' in *Praying for England: Priestly Presence in Contemporary Culture*, eds Samuel Wells and Sarah Coakley (London: Continuum, 2008), pp. 107–24
Massey, Doreen, *For Space* (London: Sage, 2005)
——— *Spatial Divisions of Labour: Social Structures and the Geography of Production* (London: Palgrave Macmillan, 1995)
Mathewes, Charles, *A Theology of Public Life* (Cambridge: Cambridge University Press, 2007)

—— *The Republic of Grace: Augustinian Thoughts for Dark Times* (Grand Rapids, MI: Eerdmans, 2010)
McClintock Fulkerson, Mary, 'Receiving from the Other: Theology and Grass-Roots Organising', *International Journal of Public Theology* 6 (2012), 421–34
McFadyen, Donald, 'Towards a Practical Ecclesiology for the Church of England', Doctoral thesis, University of Cambridge, 2005
McFarland, Ian, *In Adam's Fall: A Meditation on the Christian Doctrine of Original Sin* (Oxford: Wiley-Blackwell, 2010)
McIlroy, David, 'Oliver O'Donovan, The Ways of Judgment (Review)', *Political Theology* 8 (2007), 373–80
Meyers, Ruth, 'Liturgy and Justice', *Worship* 90 (November 2016), 492–512
Milbank, John, *Being Reconciled: Ontology and Pardon* (London: Routledge, 2003)
—— *The Future of Love: Essays in Political Theology* (Eugene, OR: Cascade Books, 2009)
—— *The Word Made Strange: Theology, Language and Culture* (Oxford: Blackwell, 1997)
—— *Theology and Social Theory: Beyond Secular Reason* (Oxford: Blackwell, 1990)
Milbank, John and Adrian Pabst, 'The Anglican Polity and the Politics of the Common Good', *Crucible: The Christian Journal of Social Ethics*, no. 1 (2014)
—— *The Politics of Virtue: Post-Liberalism and the Human Future* (Lanham, MD: Rowman & Littlefield International, 2016)
Moore, Gerard, 'Let Justice Find a Voice: Reflections on the Relationship between Worship and Justice', *Worship* 90 (May 2016), 206–24
Morris, Jeremy, 'The Future of Church and State' in *Anglicanism: The Answer to Modernity*, eds Duncan J. Dormor, Jack McDonald and Jeremy Caddick (London: Continuum, 2003)
Myers, Benjamin, *Christ the Stranger: The Theology of Rowan Williams* (London: T&T Clark, 2012)
Newheiser, David, *Hope in a Secular Age: Deconstruction, Negative Theology, and the Future of Faith* (Cambridge: Cambridge University Press, 2019)
—— 'Introduction: The Trials of Desire' in *Desire, Faith, and the Darkness of God: Essays in Honour of Denys Turner*, eds Eric Bugyis and David Newheiser (Notre Dame, IN: University of Notre Dame Press, 2015), pp. 1–9
Norris, Kristopher and Sam Speers, *Kingdom Politics: In Search of a New Political Imagination for Today's Church* (Eugene, OR: Cascade Books, 2015)

BIBLIOGRAPHY

Ochs, Peter, *Another Reformation: Postliberal Christianity and the Jews* (Grand Rapids, MI: Baker Academic, 2011)

O'Donovan, Oliver, *Resurrection and Moral Order: An Outline for Evangelical Ethics*, 2nd edition (Leicester: Apollos, 1994)

────── *The Desire of the Nations: Rediscovering the Roots of Political Theology* (Cambridge: Cambridge University Press, 1996)

────── *The Ways of Judgment: The Bampton Lectures, 2003* (Grand Rapids, MI: Eerdmans, 2005)

Oliver-Dee, Sean, 'Integration, Assimilation and Fundamental British Values: Invested Citizenship and 21st Century "Belonging"', *Cambridge Papers* 26, no. 3 (September 2017)

Papanikolaou, Aristotle, *The Mystical as Political: Democracy and Non-Radical Orthodoxy* (Notre Dame, IN: University of Notre Dame Press, 2012)

Pecknold, Chad, *Christianity and Politics: A Brief Guide to the History* (Eugene, OR: Cascade, 2010)

────── 'Migrations of the Host: Fugitive Democracy and the Corpus Mysticum', *Political Theology* 11, no. 1 (2010), 77–101

Percy, Martyn, *Power and the Church: Ecclesiology in an Age of Transition* (London: Cassell, 1998)

Plant, Stephen, *Bonhoeffer* (London: Continuum, 2004)

────── 'The Evangelization of Rulers: Dietrich Bonhoeffer's Political Theology', Wheaton College, April 2012, https://www.youtube.com/watch?v=6--CXvgP5xw

────── *Taking Stock of Bonhoeffer* (Burlington, VT: Routledge, 2014)

Quash, Ben, *Found Theology: History, Imagination and the Holy Spirit* (London: Bloomsbury T&T Clark, 2013)

────── 'Offering: Treasuring the Creation' in *The Blackwell Companion to Christian Ethics*, eds Stanley Hauerwas and Samuel Wells (Oxford: Blackwell, 2004)

────── 'The Anglican Church as a Polity of Presence' in *Anglicanism: The Answer to Modernity*, eds Duncan J. Dormor, Jack McDonald and Jeremy Caddick (London: Continuum, 2003), pp. 38–59

────── *Theology and the Drama of History* (Cambridge: Cambridge University Press, 2009)

Radner, Ephraim, *A Brutal Unity: The Spiritual Politics of the Christian Church* (Waco, TX: Baylor University Press, 2012)

Rashkover, Randi and C. C. Pecknold, *Liturgy, Time, and the Politics of Redemption* (London: SCM Press, 2006)

Reddie, Anthony, 'Liturgy for Liberation' in *The Edge of God: New Liturgical Texts and Contexts in Conversation*, eds Stephen Burns, Nicola Slee and Michael N. Jagessar (London: Epworth, 2008)

Reed, Esther, *The Limit of Responsibility: Engaging Dietrich Bonhoeffer in a Globalising Era* (London: T&T Clark, 2018)

Rivers, Julian, 'Fundamental British Values and the Virtues of Civic Loyalty', *Ethics in Brief* 21, no. 5 (Summer 2016)

Robinson, Marilynne and Rowan Williams, 'Rowan Williams and Marilynne Robinson in Conversation – 2018 Theology Conference', Wheaton College, 4 June 2018, https://www.youtube.com/watch?v=lB1KftoOprI

Rowlands, Anna, 'Temporality, Dispossession and the Search for the Good: Interpreting the Book of Jeremiah with the Jesuit Refugee Service', *Political Theology* 19, no. 6 (2018), 517–36

Rumsey, Andrew, *Parish: An Anglican Theology of Place* (London: SCM Press, 2017)

Saliers, Don, 'Afterword: Liturgy and Ethics Revisited' in *Liturgy and the Moral Self: Humanity at Full Stretch before God*, eds Byron Anderson and Bruce Morrill (Collegeville, MN: Liturgical Press, 1998), pp. 209–24

Scharen, Christian, 'Baptismal Practices and the Formation of Christians: A Critical Liturgical Ethics', *Worship* 76 (January 2002), 43–66

—— *Fieldwork in Theology: Exploring the Social Context of God's Work in the World* (Grand Rapids, MI: Baker Academic, 2015)

—— *Public Worship and Public Work: Character and Commitment in Local Congregational Life*, Virgil Michel Series (Collegeville, MN: Liturgical Press, 2004)

Schliesser, Christine, *Everyone Who Acts Responsibly Becomes Guilty: Bonhoeffer's Concept of Accepting Guilt* (Louisville, KY: Westminster John Knox Press, 2008)

Scott, Peter and William T. Cavanaugh, eds, *The Blackwell Companion to Political Theology* (Newark: Blackwell, 2003)

Sedgwick, Peter, 'On Anglican Polity' in *Essentials of Christian Community*, eds David Ford and Dennis Stamps (Edinburgh: T&T Clark, 1996), pp. 196–212

Shanks, Andrew, *Civil Society, Civil Religion* (Oxford: Blackwell, 1995)

Siapera, Eugenia, ed., *Radical Democracy and the Internet* (London: Palgrave Macmillan, 2007)

Smith, James K. A., *Awaiting the King: Reforming Public Theology* (Grand Rapids, MI: Baker Academic, 2017)

—— *Desiring the Kingdom: Worship, Worldview, and Cultural Formation* (Grand Rapids, MI: Baker Academic, 2009)

—— *Imagining the Kingdom: How Worship Works* (Grand Rapids, MI: Baker Academic, 2013)

—— *Introducing Radical Orthodoxy: Mapping a Post-Secular Theology* (Grand Rapids, MI: Baker Academic, 2004)

—— *Who's Afraid of Relativism?: Community, Contingency, and Creaturehood* (Grand Rapids, MI: Baker Academic, 2014)

BIBLIOGRAPHY

Soskice, Janet Martin, *The Kindness of God: Metaphor, Gender, and Religious Language* (Oxford: Oxford University Press, 2007)

Spencer, Nick, *The Political Samaritan: How Power Hijacked a Parable* (London: Bloomsbury, 2017)

Suggate, Alan M., 'The Temple Tradition' in *Anglican Social Theology: Renewing the Vision Today*, ed. Malcolm Brown (London: Church House Publishing, 2014), pp. 28–73

Sykes, Stephen, *Power and Christian Theology* (London: Continuum, 2006)

Temple, William, *Christianity and Social Order* (Harmondsworth: Penguin, 1942)

—— *Religious Experience and Other Essays and Addresses* (London: James Clarke, 1958)

—— *The Nature of Personality* (London: Macmillan, 1911)

Turner, Denys, *The Darkness of God: Negativity in Christian Mysticism* (Cambridge: Cambridge University Press, 1995)

Van Ommen, Armand Léon, *Suffering in Worship: Anglican Liturgy in Relation to Stories of Suffering People* (London: Routledge, 2017)

Volpe, Medi Ann, *Rethinking Christian Identity: Doctrine and Discipleship* (Oxford: Wiley-Blackwell, 2013)

Walker, Alison Mary, 'A Place for Joining? The Theology of Willie James Jennings and the Anglican Parish' (PhD Thesis, University of Aberdeen, 2021)

Walker Grimes, Katie, *Christ Divided: Antiblackness as Corporate Vice* (Minneapolis, MN: Fortress Press, 2017)

Wannenwetsch, Bernd, *Political Worship: Ethics for Christian Citizens* (Oxford: Oxford University Press, 2009)

Ward, Graham, *Christ and Culture* (Oxford: Blackwell, 2005)

—— *Cities of God* (London: Routledge, 2000)

—— *How the Light Gets In: Ethical Life I* (Oxford: Oxford University Press, 2016)

—— 'Radical Orthodoxy: Its Ecumenical Vision', *Acta Theologica* 37, Suppl. 25 (2017), 29–42

—— *The Politics of Discipleship: Becoming Postmaterial Citizens* (London: SCM Press, 2009)

Watkins, Clare, 'Organising the People of God: Social-Science Theories of Organization in Ecclesiology', *Theological Studies* 52 (1991), 694–7

Welby, Justin, *Reimagining Britain: Foundations for Hope* (London: Bloomsbury, 2018)

Wells, Samuel, *A Nazareth Manifesto: Being with God* (Chichester: Wiley, 2015)

—— 'Bernd Wannenwetsch, Political Worship: Ethics for Christian Citizens, trans. Margaret Kohl (Oxford: Oxford University Press, 2004)', *Studies in Christian Ethics* 18, no. 2 (2005), 119–22

―――― 'God Is with Us', sermon presented at the Focus, Holy Trinity, Brompton, 6 August 2014, https://www.youtube.com/watch?v=Ru hx6Gm2l9w

―――― *God's Companions: Reimagining Christian Ethics* (Oxford: Blackwell, 2006)

―――― *Improvisation: The Drama of Christian Ethics* (London: SPCK, 2004)

―――― *Transforming Fate into Destiny: The Theological Ethics of Stanley Hauerwas* (Carlisle: Paternoster Press, 1998)

Wells, Samuel and Sarah Coakley, eds, *Praying for England: Priestly Presence in Contemporary Culture* (London: Continuum, 2008)

Williams, Raymond, *The Country and the City* (London: Chatto & Windus, 1973)

Williams, Rowan, *Anglican Identities* (London: Darton Longman & Todd, 2004)

―――― 'Augustine and the Psalms', *Interpretation: A Journal of Bible and Theology* 58, no. 1 (2004), 17–27

―――― *Being Disciples: Essentials of the Christian Life* (London: SPCK, 2016)

―――― 'Bonhoeffer's Ethics: Representing Humanity in Christ', Lecture given at Sewanee, University of the South, 2016, https://vimeo.com/185983143

―――― *Christ on Trial* (Grand Rapids, MI: Zondervan, 2002)

―――― *Christ the Heart of Creation* (London: Bloomsbury Continuum, 2018)

―――― 'Debate on a Covenant for the Anglican Communion', presented at the General Synod, 13 February 2008, http://rowanwilliams.archbishopofcanterbury.org/articles.php/1522/debate-on-a-covenant-for-the-anglican-communion.html

―――― 'Encountering the Other', presented at the Encounter, St Martin-in-the-Fields, Autumn 2018, https://www.stmartin-in-the-fields.org/rowan-williams-encountering-the-other/

―――― 'Epilogue' in *Praying for England: Priestly Presence in Contemporary Culture*, eds Samuel Wells and Sarah Coakley (London: Continuum, 2008), 171–82

―――― *Faith in the Public Square* (London: Bloomsbury, 2012)

―――― 'Good for Nothing? Augustine on Creation', *Augustinian Studies* 25 (1994), 9–24

―――― *Grace and Necessity: Reflections on Art and Love* (London: Continuum, 2005)

―――― Interview with Radio 4 'Today' programme ahead of G20 summit, 31 March 2009

―――― 'Liberalism and Capitalism Have Hollowed out Society – so

BIBLIOGRAPHY

Where Do We Turn Now?', *The New Statesman*, 18 October 2016, https://www.newstatesman.com/culture/books/2016/10/liberalism-and-capitalism-have-hollowed-out-society-so-where-do-we-turn-now

——— 'Liberation Theology and the Anglican Tradition' in *Politics and Theological Identity: Two Anglican Essays*, eds David Nicholls and Rowan Williams (London: The Jubilee Group, 1984), pp. 7–26

——— *Lost Icons: Reflections on Cultural Bereavement* (Edinburgh: T&T Clark, 2000)

——— 'Making Moral Decisions' in *The Cambridge Companion to Christian Ethics*, ed. Robin Gill (Cambridge: Cambridge University Press, 2001), pp. 3–15

——— *On Christian Theology* (Oxford: Blackwell, 2000)

——— *Open to Judgement* (London: Darton, Longman and Todd, 2002)

——— 'Poetic and Religious Imagination', *Theology* 80 (1977), 178–87

——— 'Politics and the Soul: A Reading of City of God', *Milltown Studies* 19/20 (1987), 55–72

——— *Resurrection: Interpreting the Easter Gospel* (London: Darton, Longman and Todd, 2002)

——— 'Rethinking the Church: Lesslie Newbigin and the Household of God', lecture presented at the Lesslie Newbigin Summer Institute 2017, Magdalene College, Cambridge University, https://newbiginhouse.org/rt-revd-dr-rowan-williams-lnsi-talk/

——— 'Saving Time: Thoughts on Practice, Patience and Vision', *New Blackfriars* 73 (June 1992), 319–26

——— 'Speech in Debate on the Windsor Report', 17 February 2005, http://rowanwilliams.archbishopofcanterbury.org/articles.php/1680/general-synod-speech-in-debate-on-the-windsor-report.html

——— 'The Church as Sacrament', *International Journal for the Study of the Christian Church* 10, no. 1 (2010), 6–12

——— *The Edge of Words: God and the Habits of Language* (London: Bloomsbury, 2014)

——— 'The Ethics of SDI' in *The Nuclear Weapons Debate: Theological and Ethical Issues*, eds Richard Bauckham and John Elford (London: SCM Press, 1989), pp. 162–74

——— *The Poems of Rowan Williams* (Manchester: Carcanet, 2014)

——— 'The Suspicion of Suspicion: Wittgenstein and Bonhoeffer' in *Wrestling with Angels: Conversations in Modern Theology* (London: SCM Press, 2007), 186–202

——— *The Tragic Imagination* (Oxford: Oxford University Press, 2016)

——— *The Truce of God* (London: Fount, 1983)

―――― *The Wound of Knowledge: Christian Spirituality from the New Testament to St John of the Cross* (London: Darton, Longman & Todd, 1979)
―――― 'Theological Integrity', *New Blackfriars* 72 (1991), 140–51
―――― *Wrestling with Angels: Conversations in Modern Theology* (London: SCM Press, 2007)
Williams, Rowan and James Atkinson, 'On Doing Theology' in *Stepping Stones: Joint Essays on Anglican Catholic and Evangelical Unity*, ed. Christina Baxter (London: Hodder & Stoughton, 1987), pp. 1–20
Williams, Rowan and Richard Bauckham, 'Jesus: God with Us' in *Stepping Stones: Joint Essays on Anglican Catholic and Evangelical Unity*, ed. Christina Baxter (London: Hodder & Stoughton, 1987), pp. 21–41
Williams, Rowan, Kenneth Stevenson and Geoffrey Rowell, eds, *Love's Redeeming Work* (Oxford: Oxford University Press, 2001)
Winner, Lauren, *The Dangers of Christian Practice: On Wayward Gifts, Characteristic Damage, and Sin* (New Haven, CT: Yale University Press, 2018)
Wolin, Sheldon, *Democracy Incorporated: Managed Democracy and the Specter of Inverted Totalitarianism* (Princeton, NJ: Princeton University Press, 2008)
―――― *The Presence of the Past: Essays on the State and the Constitution* (Baltimore, MD: Johns Hopkins University Press, 1989)
Wolterstorff, Nicholas, 'Liturgy, Justice, and Tears', *Worship* 62, no. 5 (1988), 386–403
Worthen, Jeremy, *Responding to God's Call: Christian Formation Today* (Norwich: Canterbury Press, 2012)

Reports, news articles and documentaries

Audickas, Lukas, Noel Dempsey and Philip Loft, 'Membership of Political Parties', Standard Note, House of Commons Library, August 2019, https://researchbriefings.files.parliament.uk/documents/SN05125/SN05125.pdf
BBC *Panorama*, 'Is the Church Racist?', BBC, 19 April 2021, https://www.bbc.co.uk/iplayer/episode/m000vc34/panorama-is-the-church-racist
Bingham, John, 'Expenses Scandal Helped Shatter Faith in "public service" – Rowan Williams', *The Telegraph*, 16 June 2012, https://www.telegraph.co.uk/news/newstopics/mps-expenses/9335001/Expenses-scandal-helped-shatter-faith-in-public-service-Rowan-Williams.html
Bowcott, Owen, 'Council of Europe Accepts UK Compromise on Prisoner Voting Rights', *The Guardian*, 7 December 2017, https://www.theguardian.com/politics/2017/dec/07/council-of-europe-accepts-uk-compromise-on-prisoner-voting-rights

BIBLIOGRAPHY

The British Social Attitudes, 'Key Findings', *British Social Attitudes Survey* 30, 2013, https://www.bsa.natcen.ac.uk/latest-report/british-social-attitudes-30/key-findings/trust-politics-and-institutions.aspx

'Church Attendance Dominated by Middle Class', *Premier Christian News*, 29 January 2015, https://premierchristian.news/en/news/article/church-attendance-dominated-by-middle-class

The Church of England Evangelical Council, *The Beautiful Story*, https://ceec.info/resources/the-beautiful-story

The Church of England, *From Lament to Action*, https://www.churchofengland.org/sites/default/files/2021-04/FromLamentTo Action-report.pdf

The Church of England, *Living in Love and Faith: Christian teaching and learning about identity, sexuality, relationships and marriage* (London: Church House Publishing, 2020)

The Church of England Archbishops' Council, 'Setting God's People Free', February 2017, https://www.churchofengland.org/sites/default/files/2017-11/GS%20Misc%202056%20Setting%20God%27s%20People%20Free.pdf

The Church of England Education Office, *Church of England Vision for Education: Deeply Christian, Serving the Common Good* (2016), https://www.churchofengland.org/sites/default/files/2017-10/2016%20Church%20of%20England%20Vision%20for%20Education%20WEB%20FINAL.pdf

The Church of England House of Bishops, 'Who is My Neighbour? A Letter from the House of Bishops to the People and Parishes of the Church of England for the General Election 2015' (2015), https://www.churchofengland.org/sites/default/files/2017-11/whoismy neighbour-pages.pdf

The Church of England Mission and Public Affairs Council, 'Mission-Shaped Church: Church Planting and Fresh Expressions of Church in a Changing Context' (London: Church House Publishing, 2004)

Commission on Race and Ethnic Disparities, 'Report' (March 2021), https://www.gov.uk/government/publications/the-report-of-the-commission-on-race-and-ethnic-disparities

Davies, Madeleine, 'Class Divide at Church Must Be Addressed, New Study Suggests', *The Church Times*, 4 August 2017, https://www.Churchtimes.co.uk/articles/2017/4-august/news/uk/class-divide-at-Church-must-be-addressed-suggests-new-study

—— 'Selection Procedures "Favour Middle Class"', *The Church Times*, 27 April 2018, https://www.Churchtimes.co.uk/articles/2018/27-april/news/uk/selection-procedures-favour-middle-class

'Extracts from the Will of Christopher Codrington', Bodleian Library, http://emlo-portal.bodleian.ox.ac.uk/exhibition/uspg/items/show/33.

Freedland, Jonathan, 'The Road to Somewhere by David Goodhart – a liberal's right wing turn on immigration', *The Guardian*, 22 March 2017, https://www.theguardian.com/books/2017/mar/22/the-road-to-somewhere-david-goodhart-populist-revolt-future-politics

Jay, Alexis, Malcolm Evans, Ivor Frank and Drusilla Sharpling, 'The Anglican Church. Case Studies: Chichester/Peter Ball Investigation Report', The Independent Inquiry into Child Sexual Abuse, May 2019, https://www.iicsa.org.uk/publications/investigation/anglican-chichester-peter-ball

Kelly, Jon, 'We, the Undersigned', BBC *News*, https://www.bbc.co.uk/news/extra/SZSozzeSOh/Petitions

Kirkup, James and Robert Winnett, 'Theresa May Interview: "We're Going to Give Illegal Migrants a Really Hostile Reception"', *The Telegraph*, 25 May 2012, https://www.telegraph.co.uk/news/uknews/immigration/9291483/Theresa-May-interview-Were-going-to-give-illegal-migrants-a-really-hostile-reception.html

Oliver, Mark, 'Archbishop urges church to consider slavery reparations', *The Guardian*, 26 March 2007, https://www.theguardian.com/world/2007/mar/26/religion.race

Talking Jesus: 2015 Research, https://talkingjesus.org/2015-research/

Turner, Carlton, 'Christopher Codrington's Will: A Personal Reflection on Anglican Theological Education in the Caribbean', https://glos.academia.edu/CarltonTurner

Rawlinson, Kevin, 'Windrush: 11 people wrongly deported from UK have died – Javid', *The Guardian*, 12 November 2018, https://www.theguardian.com/uk-news/2018/nov/12/windrush-11-people-wrongly-deported-from-uk-have-died-sajid-javid

'Shamima Begum: IS Teenager to Lose UK Citizenship', BBC *News*, 20 February 2019, https://www.bbc.co.uk/news/uk-47299907?int link_from_url=https://www.bbc.co.uk/news/topics/cd7klnzkyd3t/syria-schoolgirls-case&link_location=live-reporting-story

Sherwood, Harriet, 'Justin Welby prostrates himself in apology for British massacre at Amritsar', *The Guardian*, 10 September 2019, https://www.theguardian.com/world/2019/sep/10/justin-welby-apologises-in-name-of-christ-british-massacre-amritsar

Taylor, Russell, 'Impact of "Hostile Environment" Policy Debate on 14 June 2018', Library Briefing, House of Lords, 11 June 2018

Williams, Wendy, *Windrush Lessons Learned Review*, https://assets.publishing.service.gov.uk/government/uploads/system/uploads/attachment_data/file/876336/6.5577_HO_Windrush_Lessons_Learned_Review_LoResFinal.pdf

Wo Lakota, 'Faith Spotted Eagle pt 3 Trauma & Resiliency - Essential Understanding #2', *Youtube*, 4 September 2013, https://www.youtube.com/watch?v=bqd_gYAhBII&t=13s

Index of Names and Subjects

abundance 9, 25, 34, 36, 44, 48, 56, 126, 128, 131, 164, 166, 167, 215
abuse (of power) 1, 116, 118, 159
accountability 118, 179
acknowledgement of sin *see* sin – conviction (of sin)
agency 83, 113, 119, 172–3, 175
alienation *see* exclusion
Anglicanism 3, 5–7, 12, 18, 73–4, 78, 88–9, 91, 94, 96, 97, 100–1, 108n29, 118, 125, 136n48, 141, 145, 165, 189–91, 193–201, 203–6, 211, 212, 214, 219n37
  Anglican Communion: 13n8, 67n35, 84n2, 111n45, 118, 191, 195, 199, 202, 205, 218n29
  Anglican liturgy and worship: 63, 81, 88, 112n46
  Anglican polity: 6, 73, 78, 84n2, 89, 108, 116, 132n1, 190, 191, 193–205

Anglican social and political theology: 13n7, 14n10, 142–4, 170, 190, 160n54
apophaticism 49, 64
Appiah, Kwame Anthony 203
asceticism 150, 159n36, 162
asset-based community development 152, 163–7
attention 23, 28, 33–4, 36, 46–8, 50–6, 60–1, 64, 82–3, 87, 102, 115, 121, 124–7, 131, 144–5, 148–50, 154, 159, 164–6, 169, 181, 206, 212–14
  failure of attention and reception of gifts 25, 31, 49, 53, 66n17, 88, 95, 121, 131
  to sin 10, 87, 104, 115
Augustine 41n53, 174, 180
authority 72n2, 90, 143, 155n5, 172–5, 182n13, 183n14, 185n19, 186n31, 206

Backhouse, Stephen 181n3
Baker, Ella 152

baptism 21, 35, 39n21,
  40n21, 85n6, 96, 99,
  111–12
Barrett, Al 26, 42n73, 126,
  128, 135n36, 164, 166
Beckford, Robert 112n46
Bonhoeffer, Dietrich 170–7
boundaries 69n53, 85n24,
  184n14, 195–200
Bretherton, Luke 72n2,
  75, 85n7, 91, 93, 106n5,
  121–3, 131, 158n22,
  181n3, 182n15, 184n14,
  184n15
Brexit 192

capitalism 26–7, 30, 41, 151
catechesis *see* baptism
Chaplin, Jonathan 184n15
character 18, 20–2, 30
Church of England *see*
  Anglicanism
citizenship 4–5, 12, 19,
  74–5, 84n6, 93, 139, 142,
  147, 151, 156n7, 156n8,
  156n12, 157n12, 157n13,
  170, 184n14, 188n48,
  192, 196, 200–1, 204,
  206, 215, 216n6, 216n7
  deportation and
  statelessness: 192, 216n7
civil rights 152
civil society 12, 84, 139,
  140, 142, 154, 161, 162,
  163, 169, 170, 178–80,
  186, 201, 215
class 89, 90–2, 94–5, 100–1,
  104, 106n5–6, 107n17,
  117, 122–3, 125, 134n13,
  135n37, 186, 196
clergy 74, 85n24, 91–5,
  108n26, 108n29, 109n30,
  111, 113, 118, 125,
  134n13, 136, 160n54,
  165–9, 193, 196, 205,
  see also laity
  ministerial selection and
  training: 18, 38n8, 95
Coles, Romand 146–54,
  158n23, 159n35, 198
colonialism 13n8, 89,
  96–101, 106n6, 107n20,
  109–11, 118, 120, 126,
  132n2, 145, 166, 192,
  194–5, 197, 200, 202–3,
  216n7
community organizing
  146–7, 152, 163, 167–9,
  183n13
confidence 9, 10, 29, 35, 45,
  47, 61, 69, 73, 76–8, 82–3,
  94, 124, 133n2, 166, 169,
  207, *see also* humility
congregation (including
  gathered worship) 8, 10,
  12, 17, 22–3, 29, 33–4,
  60, 73, 79–83, 90–1, 93,
  95, 103, 115, 118–23,
  125–31, 134n13, 136,
  137n49, 139–40, 165–6,
  180, 181n3, 198
scattered 10–11, 73, 79–83,
  95, 115, 125, 127–30,
  136, 137n49

INDEX OF NAMES AND SUBJECTS

constitution *see* Anglicanism
– Anglican polity
contemplation 49–50, 52,
 129, *see also* attention

Daggers, Jenny 102, 113n52,
 117, 126
deliberation 22, 142–3, 157,
 190, 205, 210–11, 213–14,
 220n5
democracy 140, 161,
 169–70, 173–4, 176–9,
 181n3, 183, 184n14, 186,
 187n45, 211, 215
desire 5, 7, 9, 17, 22–3,
 25–8, 30–1, 33, 35, 41n44,
 44–6, 48–52, 72, 81, 129,
 136, 142, 208–9
disability 108n26, 126–7,
 136
disagreement 205–6, 209–
 12, 221n59
discomfort 7, 48, 58, 103,
 144, 149–50, 212
discovery 1, 21, 30–1, 34,
 36, 47, 51–2, 56, 61,
 68n39, 68n46, 72, 81–2,
 136, 147, 164, 166, 178,
 208–9, 211–12
doubt 9, 33, 36, 44–5, 50,
 52, 64, 71, 101, 207, 209,
 211

election *see* voting
empire *see* colonialism
England *see* nationhood
Eucharist 22–3, 34, 68n46,
 79–80, 85n24, 93, 112,
 128
exclusion 3, 84n6, 89–95,
 99, 101, 119, 123–6, 129–
 31, 133n13, 146, 165–6,
 191–8, 201, 205, 216n10,
 see also inclusion
extensity 10, 58–9, 61,
 67n35, 79, 82, *see also*
 intensity

Farneth, Molly 152, 158n31,
 160n51
France-Williams, Azariah
 94, 108n25, 217n14

Garrigan, Siobhán 93,
 106n6, 107n22–4, 117,
 118, 121, 123, 133n4–5,
 134n24–5, 135n33,
 217n17
Gittoes, Julie 68n35, 76–7,
 79, 82–3, 85n17
government 162, 167,
 169–71, 173–6, 186, 192,
 196, *see also* authority, the
 state and democracy

habits *see* practices
Hardy, Daniel 6, 14, 56–9,
 63–4, 79, 82, 103, 108n29,
 125, 144, 199–200
Hauerwas, Stanley 18, 20,
 154n1, 158n23
Higton, Mike 69, 86n27,
 130, 132, 206, 211, 212,
 213, 219n42

Holy Spirit 11, 59, 103, 117,
  144–5, 154, 166
  activity outside the church
  9, 12, 32, 57–8, 60, 81,
  125–6, 144, 147, 153–4,
  159n36, 161, 215
  convicting of sin 87–8,
  102–5, 116, 123, 150,
  166, 190
  disruption 11, 132
  finding and the Found 34,
  36, 58–64, 69n53, 80–1,
  87, 101–5, 113, 144–5,
  148–50, 154, 176, 181,
  193
  formation by 25, 28, 35,
  39n21, 44, 56, 58–9, 63,
  79, 104–5, 117, 124, 131,
  140, 144, 147, 153–4, 215
  giving and the Given
  57–62, 64, 80–2, 101–5,
  126, 130, 145, 148–9,
  154, 166, 181
  openness to work of 61–5,
  145, 159n35, 163, 165
  troubling gifts of 72,
  101–2, 104–5, 115, 117,
  120, 125–6, 129, 135n39,
  166
Hordern, Joshua 13n3, 142,
  156n9
humility 10, 33, 73, 76–8,
  82–3, 189, 116, 122,
  124, 219n42, *see also*
  confidence

imagination 24, 28, 30, 32,
  34, 36, 64, 100, 156n8,
  165, 195
immigration 216n6–7
improvisation 24–5, 33–5,
  40, 40n33–4, 42n76
inclusion 107, 165, 195,
  131, *see also* exclusion
intensity 10, 58–9, 63,
  67n35, 79–80, *see also*
  extensity
intercession 11, 81, 129,
  217n17, *see also* prayer
intermediate associations
  157n12, 170, 183,
  184n14, 186n26

Jagessar, Michael 112n46
Jenkins, Timothy 66n26, 80,
  132n1, 136n48, 190–1,
  193, 205
Jennings, Willie James 96,
  109n32, 112, 132n2,
  133n3, 197–8, 218n21
Jesson, Stuart 52–4, 120
joint attention 53–4, 131,
  136n44, *see also* attention

laity 40n31, 85n24, 93,
  109n30, 125, 128–9,
  165–6, 168, *see also* clergy
lament 95, 115, 119–20,
  134n20, *see also* prayer
legislation 156, 176
Leith, Pete 136n44
LGBTQ+ 119
Lloyd, Vincent 183n13

INDEX OF NAMES AND SUBJECTS

MacIntyre, Alasdair 18, 38n3–4, 132n2
marginalisation *see* exclusion
margins 115, 125–6
Mathewes, Charles 13n5, 68n49, 157n15, 159n36, 187n45
membership 3–4, 6–8, 10–12, 17, 20–3, 25, 27–9, 35, 37, 71–2, 74–5, 83, 85n6, 86n35, 90, 92, 95–6, 103–5, 106n9, 107n17, 112n46, 115–17, 120, 122–32, 142–3, 147, 154n1, 161–9, 171, 176, 180–1, 182n10, 183n14, 189, 191, 194, 197, 201–2, 204–5, 209, 210, 212
  gifts of each member 11, 21, 24, 33–5, 52, 81, 95, 103–4, 115, 117, 121, 124–5, 127–9, 131, 136n41, 136n44, 149–50, 159n35–6, 163–6, 169, 182n8–10, 198, 212
  hierarchy within 34, 80, 89–91, 93, 94, 99, 137, 155n7, 168, 191–2, 194–5, 204
  kinship relations within 74–6, 84
middle axioms 143
Milbank, John 114n56, 141, 154n2, 156n7, 156n11
Morris, Jeremy 201, 218n33
Mysticism 49, 51, 78, *see also* apophaticism and negative theology

narrative 20–1, 24–5, 29, 33–6, 40n33, 89, 95–6, 109n32, 145, 148, 175, 203
nationhood/national identity/nationalism 4–6, 12, 89, 100, 183, 190–206, 211, 218n30, 216n6
negative theology 45–7, 49–50, 52, 55, 215, *see also* apophaticism and mysticism
neighbour 161–4, 169, 181n3, 182n4, 214
neighbourhood 129, 159n38, 164–6, 182, 200–1
neighbourliness 162, 181, 182n4, 196, 203
Newheiser, David 65n1–2

O'Donovan, Oliver 79, 141, 143, 155n5, 156n10, 157n12
Ochs, Peter 204
offertory 11, 128–9
oikos 10, 73–4, 74, 83–4, 93, 112n46
Ommen, Léon van 119, 121, 133n5, 134n16
oppression 6–7, 10, 43n94, 52, 89–90, 92, 94–6, 100, 102–5, 106n3, 106n6, 107n19–20, 109n31, 115,

118, 120–3, 126, 130, 137n52, 166, 185, 220n51

Papanikolaou, Aristotle 150, 155n3, 157n15, 161–2, 187n45, 188n51
parish 85n24, 112, 128–9, 136, 162, 168, 193, 195–203, *see also* Anglicanism – Anglican polity
Parish Communion Movement 128–9, 136n47
participation 2–4, 7–9, 11–12, 17, 44, 63, 116–17, 119, 148, 151–4, 155n7, 156n12, 159n36, 184n15, 185n26, 186n31, 189, 201, 215
 in communities and polities 75, 79, 95, 106n7, 124–7, 131–2, 139–40, 142–3, 161–2, 172, 181, 192–3, 195–6, 211–13
 in practices 21–2, 25, 31, 36, 50, 81–2, 88, 90, 92–3, 122, 136n44, 167–70, 174–8
passing the peace *see* reconciliation
peace 25, 29, 91, 118, 121–4, 135n28, 174, 182n4, *see also* reconciliation
place 77, 80, 86n27, 86n35, 136, 163–4, 165, 182, 190–1, 193–4, 197–9, 201–5, 214
Plant, Stephen 173–5, 184n17
pneumatology *see* Holy Spirit
polis 10, 73–6, 83, 84n6, 93, 154n1, 188n49
power 7, 10, 52, 57, 72, 78, 84n3, 88–90, 92, 94, 96, 106, 108n29, 114n56, 116, 118, 120, 126, 129, 132n2, 151, 156n8, 157n12, 159, 167–9, 174, 180, 183n13, 184–6, 195, 198, 219n37
 negotiation of 7, 72, 75, 90, 123, 157n13, 183n13–14, 200
practices 9, 17, 19–22, 24–5, 27–37, 38n4, 40n34, 42, 44–6, 49–50, 62–5, 72, 88, 90–2, 96, 100, 112, 114n56, 116–18, 123, 128–32, 136n43, 140–1, 147–50, 165, 167, 176, 179, 191–6, 200, 204, 214
 liturgical 8, 11–12, 17–18, 20, 29, 36, 49, 57, 83, 88, 91, 93, 95, 100, 106n3, 106n6, 107n20, 109, 115, 119–20, 126–30, 136n44, 140, 152, 156n8, 164, 201
prayer 22–3, 34, 36, 40n31, 49–50, 80–1, 93, 129, 201
Providence 96–8, 110, 149, 193–5, 204, *see also* colonialism

INDEX OF NAMES AND SUBJECTS

provisionality 59, 77, 82, 85n17, 88, 116, 146, 148, 151, 162, 175–6, 177, 194, 210

Quash, Ben 6, 57–63, 68n40, 69, 101–3, 128, 144, 145, 176, 188n54, 204, 219n37

race and ethnicity 7, 89–90, 92, 94–6, 99, 100, 101, 104, 106n5–7, 106n9, 107n17, 108n26, 109, 111n44, 112, 113n46, 117, 120, 122–3, 125, 153, 192, 194–6, *see also* colonialism

white supremacy 1, 89–90, 94–6, 100, 104, 112–13, 137, 192

Radical Democracy 11, 141–2, 144–7, 150–1, 153–4, 158n23

Radner, Ephraim 178–80, 187n44, 187n46, 188n48–50

receptivity 1–2, 7, 9, 11–12, 31, 33–7, 44, 50–2, 56, 59, 61, 63, 65, 81, 102, 104, 115, 116–17, 120, 125–7, 129–31, 135n36, 136n44, 143–5, 149, 151, 153, 157n21, 159n35, 163, 163–5, 169, 198, 203–4

reconciliation 11, 20, 30, 115, 121–4, 134n26

Reddie, Anthony 111n45, 112, 120

Reed, Esther 184n16

refugees and asylum seekers 160n44, 192, 193, 202, 216n10

repentance *see* sin – confession of sin and penitence

Robinson-Brown, Jarel 217n14

Rowlands, Anna 157n15, 216n10

Rumsey, Andrew 182n4, 193, 195, 197, 200, 203

Saliers, Don 88

scepticism 190, 206–15

Scharen, Christian 38n2

Sedgwick, Peter 78, 108n29

self-deception 29, 35, 48–51, 101, 105, 129, 188n48, 206–9, 213, *see also* sin

sin

complicity in 6, 29–30, 45, 88–90, 100, 102, 104, 115–20, 171, 173, 176, 178, 187n46

confession of sin and penitence 10, 11, 29–30, 35, 46, 48, 77–8, 93, 115, 117–19, 122–3 133n5, 133n8, 134n20, 203, 215

conviction of sin 3, 11, 30, 31, 46, 62, 72, 87, 102–5, 115–17, 122, 124, 126, 145, 150, 166, 190, 203, 205, 206, 211

correction of 37, 44–5, 77, 104–5, 116, 180

243

distortion and malformation 3, 10, 22, 26–8, 30–3, 36–7, 41n50, 44–5, 48, 56, 64, 71–2, 87–8, 90, 93, 95–6, 100, 103–4, 111–12, 116–18, 129, 134n20, 162, 173, 192, 197

forgiveness of sin 11, 20, 78, 121–2, 133n5

slavery *see* empire

Smith, James K. A. 13n3, 18, 41n44, 106n3, 109n31, 113n47

Society for the Propagation of the Gospel 96–101, 109n33–4, 110n36–7, 111, 203

Soskice, Janet 48

Spencer, Nick 181

Spirit *see* Holy Spirit

state 12, 84, 140, 142, 151, 154, 161–2, 167, 169–74, 177–80, 183n14, 185n26, 186n31, 188n48, 196, 201–2, 204, 215, 216n10

parliament 170, 175–6, 201

story *see* narrative

strangers 11, 22, 34, 61, 145–7, 149, 150, 153, 154, 159n36, 159n38, 162, 169, 217n17

Strong, Rowan 96, 110n36, 111n44

Suggate, Alan 157n13

surprise 9, 11, 34, 44, 52, 55, 56, 58, 61–5, 77, 103, 124, 132, 144–9, 151, 161, 164, 166, 181

disruption 6, 11, 14n9, 44, 55–6, 71, 76, 112, 120–1, 130–2, 136, 147, 154, 170, 172, 175, 181n3, 214

unexpected 3, 11, 34, 36, 44, 52, 56, 60, 62, 65, 72, 115, 116, 129, 136, 159n35–6, 198, 215

unsettling 9, 47, 55, 126

suspicion 114, 208

Sykes, Stephen 92, 107n20, 108n29, 114n56, 122

Temple, William 110n37, 142–3, 155n6, 156n10, 157n13

tending 147–9, 151–4, 159n38

territory 76, 97, 100, 110, 190–1, 194–200, 204, 214

Turner, Denys 46, 66n18, 130,

USPG 195, *see also* Society for the Propagation of the Gospel

virtue 7, 18, 46, 52, 75, 142, 148, 150, 155, 156, 157n12, 159n35, 175, 178, 185n20, 187n37

virtue ethics 18, 38

Volpe, Medi 65n6, 187n38

voting 147, 169, 175–6, 192, 204

INDEX OF NAMES AND SUBJECTS

Walker, Alison 112
Walker Grimes, Katie 111
Wannenwetsch, Bernd 13n5,
  74, 84n3, 123, 157n13,
  182n4
Ward, Graham 9, 19, 22–33,
  36, 40n32, 41n44, 42n73,
  44, 47–8, 68n39, 142,
  155n2, 156n8
Weil, Simone 52–3, 66n17
Wells, Samuel 9, 19–31,
  33–6, 44, 47–8, 50, 59,
  128
Williams, Rowan 6, 13n7,
  46–7, 51, 59, 62, 69n53,
  75–8, 80, 152–3, 157n21,
  158n23, 159n36, 170,
  174–5, 177, 183n14,
  184n15, 198, 203, 210,
  212, 220n47
Winner, Lauren 38n4,
  41n65, 42n65, 112,
  114n57, 119, 132n2,
  133n8, 134n20
Wolin, Sheldon 146–8, 151,
  154, 158n28
Wolterstorff, Nicholas 119
worship 4–5, 17–18, 23,
  32, 39n8, 79, 83, 90, 103,
  112, 122–3, 126–8, 130–1,
  141, 166, *see also* practices
Worthen, Jeremy 18, 38n8

www.ingramcontent.com/pod-product-compliance
Lightning Source LLC
Chambersburg PA
CBHW022047290426
44109CB00014B/1019